Macromedia®
Flash™ MX 2004
fast&easy® web development

Macromedia® Flash™ MX 2004

fast&easy® web development

Lisa A. Bucki

Premier
Press™

SVP, Retail Strategic Market Group: Andy Shafran

Publisher: Stacy L. Hiquet

Senior Marketing Manager: Sarah O'Donnell

Marketing Manager: Heather Hurley

Manager of Editorial Services: Heather Talbot

Acquisitions Editor: Arlie Hartman

Associate Marketing Manager: Kristin Eisenzopf

Project Editor/Copy Editor: Justak Literary Services, Inc.

Technical Reviewer: Michelle Jones

Retail Market Coordinator: Sarah Dubois

Interior Layout: Jay Hilgenberg

Cover Designer: Mike Tanamachi

Indexer: Sharon Hilgenberg

Proofreader: Janette Lynn

Macromedia, Flash MX 2004, and Fireworks are trademarks or registered trademarks of Macromedia, Inc. in the United Sates and/or other countries.

Windows and Internet Explorer are registered trademarks of Microsoft Corporation in the United States and/or other countries.

All other trademarks are the property of their respective owners.

Important: Premier Press cannot provide software support. Please contact the appropriate software manufacturer's technical support line or Web site for assistance.

Premier Press and the author have attempted throughout this book to distinguish proprietary trademarks from descriptive terms by following the capitalization style used by the manufacturer.

Information contained in this book has been obtained by Premier Press from sources believed to be reliable. However, because of the possibility of human or mechanical error by our sources, Premier Press, or others, the Publisher does not guarantee the accuracy, adequacy, or completeness of any information and is not responsible for any errors or omissions or the results obtained from use of such information. Readers should be particularly aware of the fact that the Internet is an ever-changing entity. Some facts may have changed since this book went to press.

ISBN: 1-59200-119-X

Library of Congress Catalog Card Number: 2003094428

Printed in the United States of America

04 05 06 07 08 BH 10 9 8 7 6 5 4 3 2 1

Premier Press, a division of Course Technology

25 Thomson Place

Boston, MA 02210

To my sister, Jen, who is there when people need her.

Acknowledgments

IMHO, animation has been one of the coolest things to hit the Internet, even though some sites now sport far too many flashing geegaws. I've spent some time working with earlier Flash versions, and my experience has given me a great appreciation for the technical skills and artistry of Flash professionals. When Publisher Stacy Hiquet and Acquisitions Editor Arlie Hartman asked me to write this book about Flash, I jumped at the chance. Thanks to Stacy and Arlie for giving me another reason to spend time working with Flash. The real star of this production is Project Editor Marta Justak, who assembled the team that made this book. Thank you, Marta, for expertly guiding this title from manuscript to bound book. I extend thanks as well to Technical Reviewer Michelle Jones, who provided valuable feedback about the clarity and accuracy of the text and illustrations. Final thanks go to the unsung heroes: Page Layout guru Jay Hilgenberg, Indexer Sharon Hilgenberg, and other members of the production team.

About the Author

An author, a trainer, and a publishing consultant, **Lisa A. Bucki** has been involved in the computer book business for more than 12 years. She wrote *Fireworks MX 2004 Fast & Easy Web Development, Keynote Fast & Easy, iTunes 4 Fast & Easy, Mac OS X Version 10.2 Jaguar Fast & Easy, FileMaker Pro 6 for the Mac Fast & Easy, iPhoto 2 Fast & Easy, Adobe Photoshop 7 Fast & Easy, Adobe Photoshop 7 Digital Darkroom,* and *Managing with Microsoft Project 2002* for Premier Press. She also has written or contributed to dozens of additional books and multimedia tutorials, as well as spearheading or developing more than 100 computer and trade titles during her association with Macmillan. Bucki currently also serves as a consultant and trainer in western North Carolina.

Contents at a Glance

Introduction xv

PART I
FLASH MX 2004 BASICS. 1

Chapter 1   Getting Started with Flash MX 2004. 3
Chapter 2   Commanding the Flash Workspace 13
Chapter 3   Examining the Flash Workflow 53
Chapter 4   Using Layers to Build Movie Content 75
Chapter 5   Using Symbols and the Library 91

PART II
MOTION AND SOUND. 121

Chapter 6   Creating Basic Animation 123
Chapter 7   Animation with Motion Tweening 137
Chapter 8   Animation with Shape Tweening. 169
Chapter 9   Masking 193

PART III
FINISHING TOUCHES. 213

Chapter 10   Adding Sound and Embedded Video 215
Chapter 11   Publishing in Flash. 239
Chapter 12   Using Simple ActionScript. 275
Appendix A   Installing Flash MX 2004 305
Appendix B   Customizing Flash MX 2004 313
Appendix C   Quick Reference Glossary 327
Appendix D   What's Next? 331

Contents

Introduction xv

PART I
FLASH MX 2004 BASICS. 1

Chapter 1   **Getting Started with Flash MX 2004**. 3

What Flash Can Do 4

Looking at Macromedia Flash MX 2004 5

Organizing the Development Process 6

    Gather Requirements 8

    Design 9

    Develop 10

    Review 10

Chapter 2   **Commanding the Flash Workspace** 13

Touring the Flash MX 2004 Workspace 14

Using the Start Page 16

Moving, Hiding, Closing, and Opening Panels 17

The Property Inspector 19

The Tools Panel 20

    Selection Tools 20

    Drawing Tools 25

    The Text Tool 36

    Editing Tools 38

    View Tools 47

    Colors Tools 48

Moving and Deleting Objects 49
Using Undo and the History Panel 49
Refining Text 50

Chapter 3   Examining the Flash Workflow **53**
Creating and Saving a Movie 54
Creating a Blank Document 54
Creating a Document from a Template 55
Saving and Closing 56
Managing the Stage 58
Understanding the Timeline 59
Changing Movie Properties 65
Working with the Movie Explorer 68
Organizing Movies with Scenes 71

Chapter 4   Using Layers to Build Movie Content **75**
What Is a Layer? 76
How Do You Work with Layers? 77
Adding a Layer 77
Changing a Layer's Name 78
Selecting a Layer and Adding Objects 80
Deleting a Layer 81
Hiding a Layer 82
Locking a Layer 83
Viewing Layer Outlines 84
Changing Layer Properties 85
Organizing Layers in Folders 87
Adjusting Object Layering 89

Chapter 5   Using Symbols and the Library **91**
What Is a Symbol? 92
Graphics 94
Buttons 94
Movie Clips 95
Creating Symbols 96
Naming Symbols 97
Creating Symbols 99
Converting Existing Graphics to Symbols 105

Adding a Symbol to the Movie Stage 109
Previewing Movie Clip Symbols in a Movie 111
Editing Symbols and Instances 112
   Changing an Instance 112
   Editing the Symbol 114
Organizing Symbols with the Library 116
   Copying Symbols between Libraries 117
   Using a Common Library 117
   Working with a Shared Library 118

PART II
MOTION AND SOUND 121

Chapter 6 **Creating Basic Animation** 123
What Is an Animation? 124
What Is a Frame? 124
How Do You Create Simple Frame-by-Frame Animations? 128
   Creating the Movie 128
   Adding Content and Keyframes 129
   Using Frames and Keyframes to Control Motion Changes . . . 131
Previewing a Movie 134
Troubleshooting Simple Animation 135

Chapter 7 **Animation with Motion Tweening** 137
Understanding Motion Tweening 138
Creating a Motion Tween for a Layer 138
Applying Motion Tween Effects 143
   Resizing an Object in a Motion Tween 145
   Rotating an Object with a Motion Tween 147
   Applying Other Transform Settings with a Motion Tween . . . 149
Tweening with Color Settings 154
   Applying the Color Tween 154
   Examining the Color Property Settings 156
Animating an Object Along a Motion Guide 159
Applying What You've Learned 164

Chapter 8 **Animation with Shape Tweening** **169**

What Is Shape Tweening? 170

Making a Basic Shape Tween 170

Shape Tweening Complex Shapes 173

Tweening Text 177

Tweening Shapes to Characters 177

Tweening Words or Phrases 180

Working with Shape Hints 185

Using a Timeline Effect 189

Chapter 9 **Masking** **193**

What Is a Mask? 194

Adding a Mask to a Movie 194

Creating a Static Mask over Static Content 195

Creating a Moving Mask over Static Content 197

Creating a Static Mask over Moving Content 201

Adding a Second Layer under a Mask 205

Creating an Animated Mask over Animated Content 207

Using Movie Clip Symbols with Masks 212

PART III
FINISHING TOUCHES **213**

Chapter 10 **Adding Sound and Embedded Video** **215**

Understanding Sound Basics in Flash 216

Importing a Sound File 217

Adding Sound to the Movie 220

Using a Sound Event 220

Streaming Sound 223

Working with Sound and Buttons 225

Modifying and Customizing Sound 226

Applying Compression to a Sound 229

Troubleshooting Sound 233

Importing Embedded Video 234

Chapter 11   Publishing in Flash **239**

Understanding Publishing and Movie Formats 240

Specifying Publishing Options 241

    Formats 243

    Flash Options 244

    HTML Options 249

    GIF Options 253

    JPEG Options 256

    PNG Options 257

    QuickTime Options 261

Publishing a Movie 263

Looking at a Size Report 266

HTML Basics 268

    HTML Structure 269

    <HTML> 270

    <HEAD> 270

    <TITLE> 270

    <BODY> 270

    <H1>, <H2>, <H3>, <H4>, <H5>, and <H6> 271

    <P> 271

 271

    <A> 271

    <IMG> 272

HTML in Practice 272

Chapter 12   Using Simple ActionScript **275**

What Is ActionScript? 276

Basic Programming Concepts 279

ActionScript and the Actions Panel 282

Understanding Programming Building Blocks 285

    Constants and Variables 285

    Using Variables 287

    What Are Conditionals? 290

    Looping Constructs 294

Arrays 297

Applying What You've Learned 298

Appendix A **Installing Flash MX 2004** **305**

Identifying System Requirements 306

For Windows Users 306

For Mac Users 306

Installing Flash MX 2004 on a Windows Computer 307

Appendix B **Customizing Flash MX 2004** **313**

Setting Preferences 314

Setting General Preferences 315

Setting Editing Preferences 317

Clipboard Preferences 317

Setting Warnings Preferences 318

Setting ActionScript Preferences 319

Customizing the Tools Panel 320

Working with Keyboard Shortcuts 322

Choosing Another Shortcut Key Set 322

Changing a Keyboard Shortcut 323

Appendix C **Quick Reference Glossary** **327**

Knowing Your Workspace 328

Frequently Used Panels 328

Flash Functionality 329

Components 330

Appendix D **What's Next?** **331**

Helpful Resources 332

New Directions 334

Introduction

When programmers figured out how to add animation to Web pages, the Internet turned an important corner. It evolved from a fairly static medium to one that engaged the viewer and offered enhanced interaction.

Flash MX 2004 from Macromedia sets the standard for Web animation development packages. With its companion products—Fireworks and Dreamweaver—any user can develop robust and attractive Web graphics, animations, and pages. The latest version, Flash MX 2004, packs in even more tools that will appeal to beginners and experienced Web authors.

Macromedia Flash MX 2004 Fast & Easy Web Development equips you with all the skills necessary to create Web animations. The book's clean, visual format walks novice developers through key Flash MX 2004 operations. It covers how to create a movie project, how to add objects to the Stage, and how to create motion and interest. This book also explains how to publish finished animations for the Web.

PART I

Flash MX 2004 Basics

This section teaches you the Flash MX 2004 fundamentals you need to put components together into a production. Chapter 1 starts with an overview of the development process in Flash. From there, you will learn how to navigate the Flash workspace and how to use tools, layers, and symbols to create and organize movie content. This section also presents how to work with the Timeline, organize movie content into scenes, work with movie properties, and save movie project files.

1

Getting Started with Flash MX 2004

From its humble beginnings as a small computer network for academic researchers, the Internet evolved into an immense medium for commercial ventures, including entertainment, education, shopping, advertising, and just plain expressing yourself. Early Web sites offered only static text and basic text links. These pages were very simple and—to today's Web-savvy eye—incredibly boring.With the advent of the commercial Internet, Web developers looked for ways to make sites more interesting in an effort to draw more people to their sites and to make money. Graphics became commonplace for enhancing page design. Scripting and interactivity emerged, enabling Web sites to gather input directly from their viewers. Multimedia content soon followed, enabling video and audio playback on the Web.

In this chapter, you will learn the answers to these questions:

- What can Flash do?
- What are the new features in Flash MX 2004?
- How can the development process be organized?

What Flash Can Do

Macromedia Flash MX 2004 enables Web developers to create interactive, dynamic, eye-grabbing sites. Using Flash, developers can animate graphics, add sound, and create movies, just to name a few possibilities. From subtle image movement to complex movie clips, Flash can help you create the look you want. Flash also includes a powerful, native scripting language, named ActionScript (see Chapter 12, "Using Simple ActionScript"). ActionScript enables you to automate tasks and add data-driven functionality to your site.

You have seen flashing advertisements on Web pages. Many of these were created with Flash. However, you can use Flash to create even more useful movies for your Web pages.

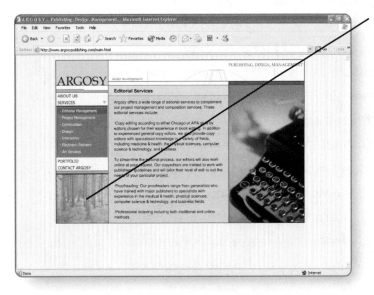

For example, this pane of the Web site for Argosy Publishing (which often provides services to Premier Press) displays different images as the viewer lingers on the page. The site also features a movie introduction.

If you go to www.nasa.gov, the main page presents a link to a Flash movie (click on Flash Feature). After you click the link, it may take a few moments for the movie to load, but waiting to view it will give you a good idea of the possibilities you can explore in Flash: animated text and images, navigation buttons, including music with a movie, and so on.

As you work through this book, you will gain hands-on experience with Flash's capabilities. You will create symbols and buttons, learn about animation and the Timeline, and produce a complete movie clip.

Looking at Macromedia Flash MX 2004

The latest version, Flash MX 2004, simplifies the process of creating Web sites that interact with visitors and includes a multimedia experience. Flash MX (also known as Flash 6) builds on the previous generation of tools by adding new features and improving existing features. These features include

- **Video**. Flash MX supports most common video formats, including QuickTime movies (.mov), MPEG movie (.mpg), Video for Windows, (.avi), and Digital Videos (.dvi).

- **Multiple languages**. Flash is available in 11 different languages.

- **Multiple platforms**. Flash is available in both Windows and Mac versions, so you can develop movies on either platform. Flash Players are available for major Web browsers on most popular computer operating systems. Flash movies can be created once and viewed on almost any computer.

- **Scripting**. Flash includes a full-featured scripting language, ActionScript, to aid in interactive design, to control navigation, and to enable user interaction. Flash and ActionScript have been used to create Web sites, greeting cards, and video games.

- **Built-in components**. Flash includes a number of components that simplify the design of user interfaces. Example components include text input fields, buttons, and check boxes; you can easily add any of these elements to a Flash movie.

Macromedia Flash MX 2004 is a standard platform for Web designers and Web developers because of the platform's flexibility and power. You can feel confident that the vast majority of Web users can view your Flash files with no download. And, when the Flash player does need to be downloaded, the process is quick and simple.

Organizing the Development Process

Before diving into the details of Flash, you need to consider a few basic steps in the development process. You're probably thinking, "Why do I need to know some *process*?" The answer is simple: Creating a Web site can quickly go from being a simple project to a horrible disaster if you don't have a plan.

Let's look at an example. Bob is a Web developer for a small but growing company. His boss tells him that the company Web site needs to be redesigned so that it looks better. Bob likes a challenge, so he dives in. A few weeks later, he emerges from his office after publishing the new site. His boss looks at it, and Bob now has a to-do list as long as his arm of changes to be made to the site. Bob makes the changes, publishes the updated site, and tells his boss. The boss is happy, so Bob tells him to check out the site. This process results in another list of changes that Bob needs to make. Of course, while Bob is working on this new list, people start talking about the site, and he ends up with instructions from several different high-level executives telling him how the site should work. Unfortunately, two of his instructions, from different vice presidents, are "Get rid of the graphics on the site" and "We need more graphics on the site." Bob is now in a no-win situation, but he works long hours and begins to burn out trying to keep everyone happy. In the end, he is fired not because he was a bad developer, but because his requirements were not identified at the beginning.

Bob's project didn't have to spiral out of control. Developers typically use one of a number of common development paths, and numerous books describe the available design models. For simplicity, I'll show you a simple, condensed design process. In this four-step design process, you will:

1. Gather requirements.

2. Design.

3. Develop.

4. Review.

Simple, right? Let's look at each step in detail from the perspective of developing a Web site. You can easily apply the same process to application development or moviemaking.

Gather Requirements

In this step, identify what needs to be done. Your company's or client's requirements can be as simple as creating a small, one-page site that lists a company name, address, and phone number; or it can be as complex as developing an e-commerce system for selling 10,000 products in 12 countries. Of course, you will need to gather these requirements from the decision-makers who have a stake in the project—the CEO of a company, a client, or maybe just you, depending on the site. From this list, make sure that you know the answer to the following questions.

- **Who is the intended audience**? Audience identification is crucial during the initial stages of a project. For example, a site designed for an association representing senior citizens looks very different from a site designed to sell products to teens.

- **What is the purpose of the site**? Is the site's primary purpose to convey information, complement a marketing strategy, or sell products? Again, the answer to this question will lead to significant differences in the design of a movie or Web site.

- **What are the decision-makers' expectations in terms of general look and feel**? Are they comfortable with blinking objects or is subtle movement preferred? Do they have a classic design in mind or something eye-catching?

  For example, a more formal site might follow a very rigid template or grid, like the one illustrated previously. A template not only creates formality in the site, but it also facilitates site updates for sites where the information changes frequently. With a formal design to follow, you always know what size graphics should be and how long articles should be. If a site has a less formal design, you could have to rearrange and resize page elements with every change in the content.

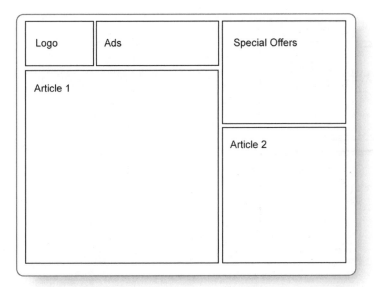

- **How should the navigation work**? What is the general organization of the site?

After you have some foundation knowledge in these areas, you're ready to move to the next step.

Design

Now that you know what needs to be done, you can figure out how to do it. The design process often includes sketches, prototypes, and storyboards. Each situation is different, and each designer prefers a different design medium. Find what works best for you. The important part of the design phase is figuring out how to accomplish each requirement. For most Web site design projects, the design usually ends with a storyboard that shows not only the different pages in the site but also the connections and links between pages. The design also shows the interface to any back-end databases, accounting systems, or other data the user may need. This is your opportunity to put those creative juices to work and illustrate how the entire site flows.

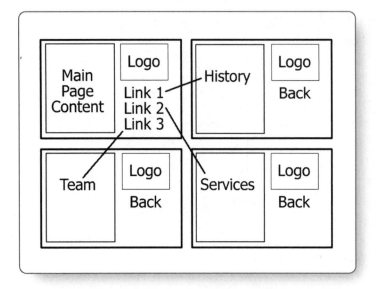

Develop

Now that you know *how* your project will be done, you have to actually *do* it. In this stage, you will build the site. This subject is what most of this book covers: the mechanics of building graphics, buttons, movie clips—whatever you want—in Flash. Often, you'll discover that you missed an important piece of the design of the project and must revise it before the project can be fully developed. Don't worry, because this situation is normal. The design of a big project is usually a living, breathing, changing document.

Review

In the review stage, you will compare the developed site with the design and its requirements. Test, and then test again. Create as many different environment variables as possible (for example, different browsers, different monitor resolutions, and Macintosh versus PC) so that you have a solid idea of which audiences can access your site and are prepared for those questions when they come your way. If you missed something, this stage is where mistakes are caught. Update the design as needed and fix any problems (usually called *bugs*) that appear in the developmental process. When everyone is satisfied that all the requirements are met, publish the site and congratulate yourself on a job well done.

This design process is a simple, but powerful tool. Now that you have some background information and organizational tools, take a look at Flash MX 2004.

2

Commanding the Flash Workspace

At first glance, all the different windows, panels, and tools on the Flash MX 2004 screen can seem a bit overwhelming. If you don't know where to start, stop and look at the screen in sections. Let's do that now, starting with a broad introduction and then dealing with specific tools. In this chapter, you will learn to do the following:

- Understand the different parts of the workspace.
- Hide, show, and move panels.
- Use each tool in the Tools panel.
- Work with the Property Inspector.
- Undo actions.
- Refine text.

Touring the Flash MX 2004 Workspace

Here is a quick tour of the default workspace in Flash MX:

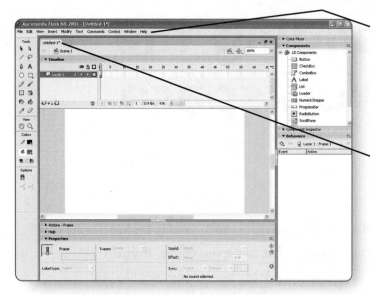

The *menu bar,* at the top of the workspace, contains 10 menus. Most menu options are duplicated in the various panels on the screen, and are covered throughout the book.

When you have multiple documents open, each document name appears here in a *file tab.* Click on a document name to switch to that document.

TIP

You also can choose Window, Toolbars, and then click on a toolbar name to display or hide a toolbar below the menu bar.

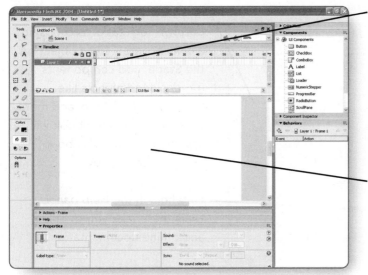

The *Timeline* controls the flow of your animated movie. *Animations* play many separate *frames*, in sequence, to create the appearance of motion. The Timeline allows you to add, delete, and move frames around in your movie.

The *Stage* appears at the center of the workspace. Create text and graphical content for the individual frames of your movie in this area.

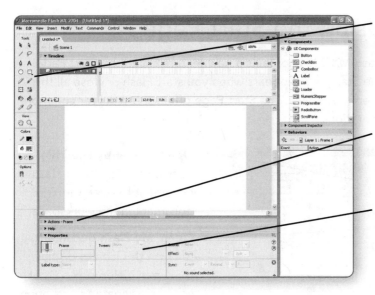

The *Tools panel* contains most of the tools for creating graphic content on the Stage. Drawing and text tools live there, where they are easily accessible.

The *Actions panel* controls the flow of your movie and the scripting within it.

The *Property Inspector* manipulates the characteristics of the selected object. When no object is selected, the panel contains the properties for the movie as a whole.

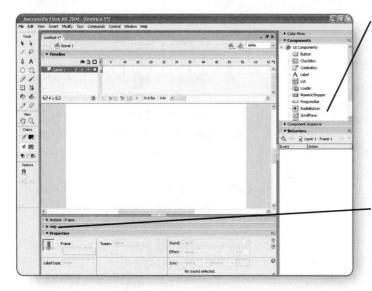

In the *other panels,* you can perform such tasks as choosing a color to apply to an object on the Stage, add *components* (predesigned objects like buttons) to the stage, and more. Later sections in the book will provide more details about using specific panels.

Find help in the *Help panel.* Links there take you to online and offline documentation.

Using the Start Page

Flash MX 2004 contains a new feature called the *Start Page.* The Start Page appears when you start Flash or close all the open movie files. The Start Page offers shortcuts for common operations:

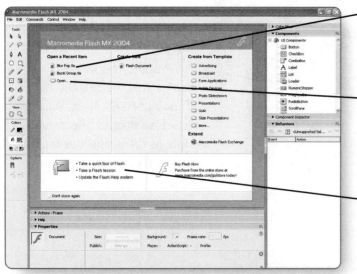

- **Open a recently used file.** Click on the icon for a Flash document to open the document in the workspace.

- **Open any Flash document.** Click on this icon to display the Open dialog box so that you can navigate to and open a file.

- **Get help with Flash.** Click on one of the choices at the bottom of the Start Page to learn more about using Flash.

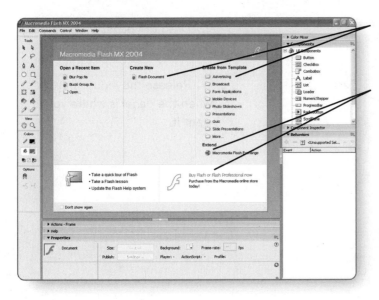

- **Create a new file**. Click on this icon to create a new, blank file in Flash.

- **Go to Macromedia's Web site to learn more**. Click here to launch your Web browser and connect with helpful resources online.

Moving, Hiding, Closing, and Opening Panels

All the panels—those visible by default and those hidden—dock with the workspace. Dockable panels or toolbars want to cling to the edges of the screen, but you can move them around. To move a panel, follow these steps.

1. Move the mouse pointer over the dotted handle to the left of the panel's name.

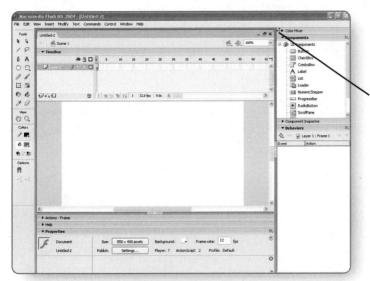

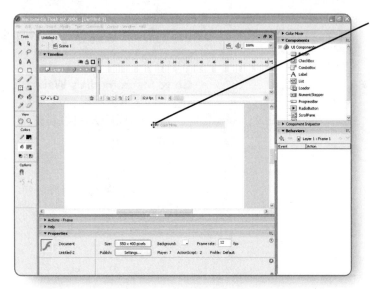

2. Drag the panel while holding down the mouse button.

3. Release the mouse button when the panel is where you want it.

To dock a panel again, drag the panel back toward the edge of the workspace. A darkened border appears, showing where the panel will be placed when you release the button.

Hiding a panel is simple: Just click on the panel's name to make it hide. To show the hidden panel, click on the panel name again.

To close a panel, right-click on the panel's name and choose Close Panel.

Not all panels are visible by design. Flash MX 2004 just has too many to show at one time. If you need a panel that is not visible on the screen, choose the name of the panel from the Window menu. The panel will appear in the workspace.

One problem with so many different panels being available is that the workspace can quickly get too cluttered to work in. If this happens, you can restore the workspace to the default configuration by selecting Window, Panel Sets, Default Layout.

NOTE

The screen shots for this book will show additional panels when necessary. Also note that the screen shots for this chapter show a new movie file. Refer to "Creating and Saving a Movie" in Chapter 3 to learn how to create a new movie file.

The Property Inspector

The Property Inspector, as the name suggests, enables you to control the properties of the currently active tool, the selected object, or the movie. The options in the panel change based on the current selection, as described here:

- If you select a tool in the Tools panel, the Property Inspector displays settings available for the selected tool, such as stroke (outline) and fill settings.

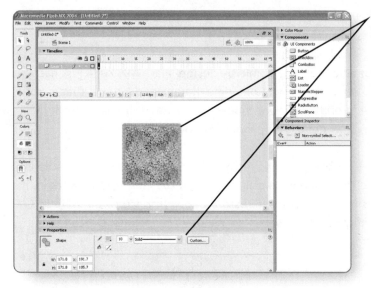

- If you select an object in the Document window, the Property Inspector displays the properties assigned to the selected object. For example, if a text object is selected, the Property Inspector displays text properties, such as the font, size, and color.

- If no object or tool is selected, the Property Inspector displays the document properties, which include canvas color, canvas size, image size, and default export options.

The Tools Panel

The Tools panel contains many tools that you can use to create and change content in any frame in your movie. This section presents tools by function or group: Selection tools, Drawing tools, Editing tools, View tools, and Color tools.

Selection Tools

Flash has three selection tools: the Selection tool, the Subselection tool, and the Lasso tool.

The Selection Tool

The Selection tool, which has an arrow on it, enables you to select one or more objects to edit. You can use the Selection tool in one of two modes. To select objects by clicking:

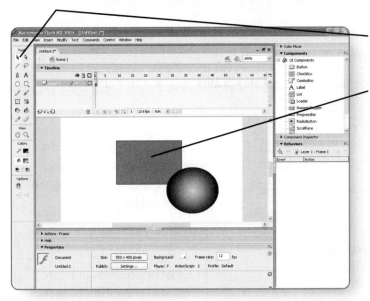

1. Click on the Selection tool in the Tools panel.

2. Click on the object to select.

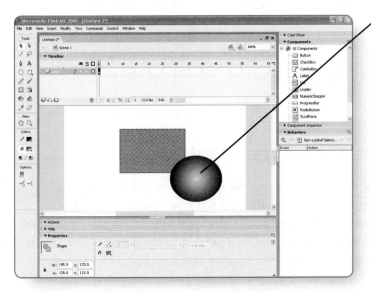

3. Shift+click on additional objects to select them.

TIP
Press Ctrl+A (⌘+A on the Mac) to select all objects on the Stage.

You also can drag with the Selection tool to select multiple objects, as follows:

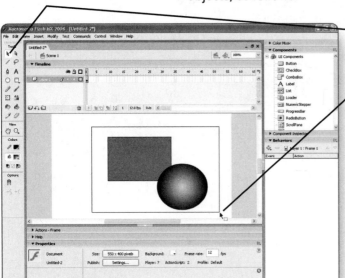

1. Click on the Selection tool in the Tools panel.

2. Drag diagonally over the objects to select. When you release the mouse button, the objects will be selected.

> **NOTE**
>
> Selected objects in Flash look a little different than in some other graphics applications. Rather than handles appearing, shading or hatching appears in the selected object(s). Click outside a selection to deselect the object(s).

The Subselection Tool

The Subselection tool enables you to manipulate an object's shape and position. The tool has two modes. In the first mode, a small filled square appears beside the mouse pointer; when you see this mouse pointer, use the Subselection tool to move objects. Use the second mode, indicated by a small hollow square next to the mouse pointer, to manipulate the points that define the shape of the selected object.

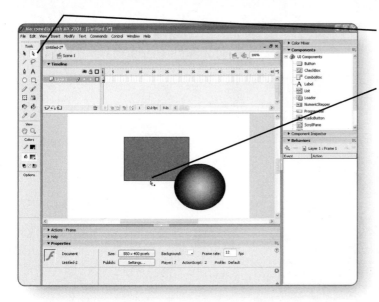

1. Click on the Subselection tool in the Tools panel.

2. Point to the border of an object. The filled square appears beside the mouse pointer.

3. Click on the object outline. Green selection borders and the points that define the object will appear.

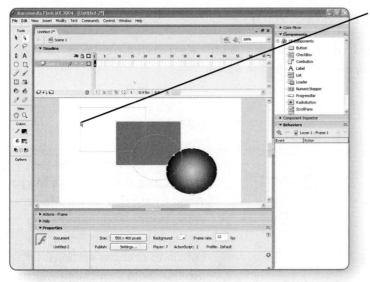

4. Point to a green selection border and then drag the object(s) to a new location.

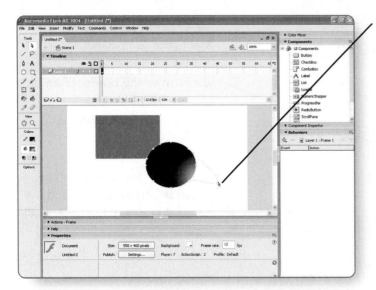

5. Drag a point to change the object's shape.

The Lasso Tool

The Lasso tool enables you to select irregular areas or parts of multiple objects on the Stage.

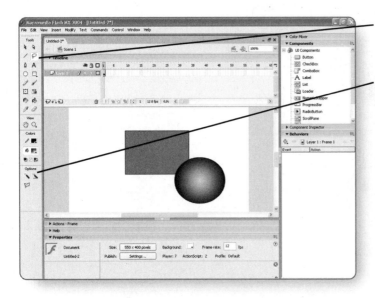

1. Click on the Lasso tool in the Tools panel.

2. Select Options for the tool. You can use the Lasso as a Magic Wand by clicking on the Magic Wand button and then clicking on the Magic Wand Properties button to changes settings. Or use the Lasso to make polygonal selections by clicking on the Polygon Mode button. (In this mode, click on points to determine the selection shape.) Click on either button again to toggle its mode off.

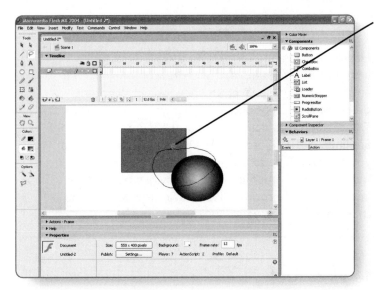

3. Drag with the mouse to make the selection. When you release the mouse button, the specified area will be selected. (When using the Polygon Mode, double-click to finish the selection.)

TIP

Press Esc to remove the selection.

Drawing Tools

The Tools panel includes a number of tools for creating drawn objects on the Stage, including the Line, Pen, Oval, Rectangle, Pencil, and Brush tools.

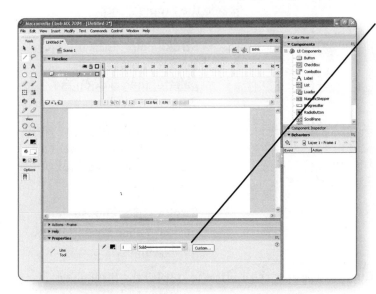

After you click on the desired tool in the Tools panel, specify tools settings in the Property Inspector and additional options at the bottom of the Tools panel, in the Options section.

This section introduces you to each of the drawing tools.

> **NOTE**
>
> Flash's drawing and formatting tools have some limitations. For example, if you draw one object over another on a single layer, the new object's content deletes the content underneath it from the first object. The gradients you can add from the Paint Bucket tool are limited. There aren't many predefined shapes that you can add. Due to these limitations, if you want a more complex graphic for your movie, create it in an image creation program like Fireworks MX 2004 and then import it into your movie.

The Line Tool

Use the Line tool to draw straight-line segments. The following steps show you how to use this tool.

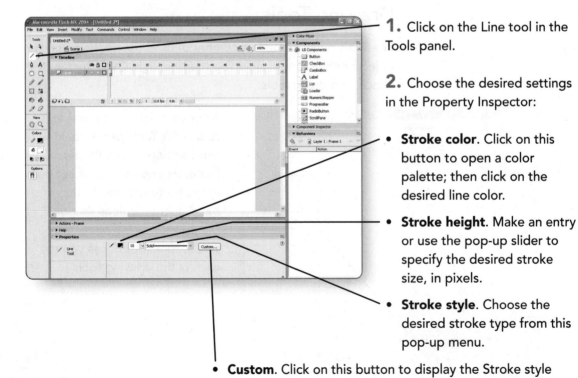

1. Click on the Line tool in the Tools panel.

2. Choose the desired settings in the Property Inspector:

- **Stroke color**. Click on this button to open a color palette; then click on the desired line color.

- **Stroke height**. Make an entry or use the pop-up slider to specify the desired stroke size, in pixels.

- **Stroke style**. Choose the desired stroke type from this pop-up menu.

- **Custom**. Click on this button to display the Stroke style dialog box, so you can choose custom stroke settings.

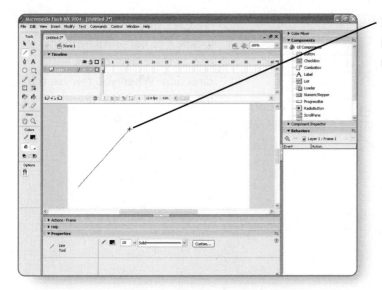

3. Drag on the Stage to draw a line. When you release the mouse button, a line will appear.

The Pen

The primary use for the Pen tool is to create curved lines called *Bézier curves*.

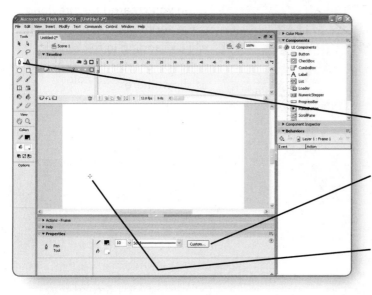

This technique is a little tricky and takes a bit of practice, but it enables you to draw beautiful curved lines.

1. Click on the Pen tool in the Tools panel.

2. Choose line formatting settings in the Property Inspector.

3. Click on the point where the curve should start on the Stage.

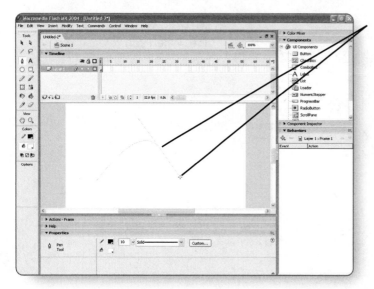

4. Click and drag in another location to establish both the end of the curve and its direction. When you release the mouse button, the curved segment will appear.

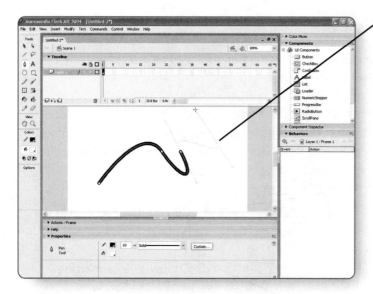

5. Repeat Step 4 to add additional curve segments, as desired. Note that dragging in the opposite direction (such as when you created the previous curve segment) creates an arch, while dragging in the same direction creates a wave shape, as shown here.

> **NOTE**
>
> You also can use the Pen tool to draw a straight line: click to establish the first end and then double-click to establish the other end. You also can use the Pen tool to create a zig-zag line or shape. Simply click to create the various line segments, and double-click to finish the last segment.

The Oval Tool

Flash has a special tool in the Tools panel for drawing ovals and circles: the Oval tool. An *oval* in Flash is composed of several curves defined by a bounding rectangle. These curves are drawn from the center of one side of the rectangle to the center of the adjacent side, hitting each side at a tangent. (It sounds more confusing than it really is.)

> **NOTE**
>
> In Flash, shapes are composed of two elements: an outline and a fill. The *outline* is the line around the outside of the shape, and the *fill* is the inside part of the shape. You can choose separately the colors for solid outline and fill.

Use the following steps to draw an oval or circle.

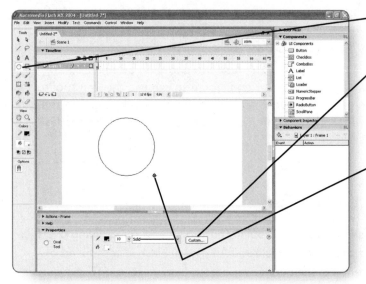

1. Click on the Oval tool in the Tools panel.

2. Choose Stroke color, height, and style settings—as well as a Fill color—in the Property Inspector.

3. Drag diagonally on the stage to define the oval. If you press and hold Shift as you drag, you will create a perfect circle, and the crosshair pointer will include a dark circle, as shown here.

The Rectangle Tool

You can use the Rectangle tool to draw rectangles and squares on the Stage. The smaller triangle in the lower-right corner of the Rectangle tool indicates that you can use the Rectangle tool to access another tool—the PolyStar tool, used to draw polygons.

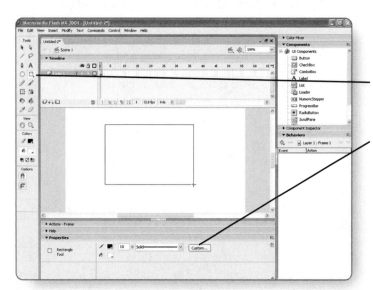

Drawing a rectangle or square is simple—just follow these steps.

1. Click on the Rectangle tool in the Tools panel.

2. Choose Stroke color, height, and style settings—as well as a Fill color—in the Property Inspector.

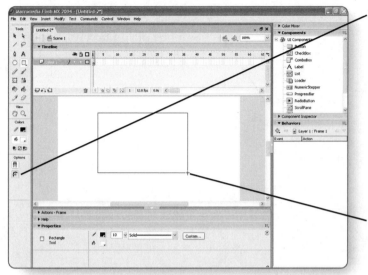

3. If you want the rectangle to have rounded corners, click on the Round Rectangle Radius button in the Options section of the Tools panel. The Rectangle Settings dialog box will appear. Type a new Corner radius value to specify the amount of curve applied to each corner of the rectangle and then click on OK.

4. Drag diagonally on the Stage to define the rectangle. Press and hold Shift while dragging to create a perfect square. When you release the mouse button, the rectangle will appear.

If you need to create a polygon instead, here's how to access and use the PolyStar tool:

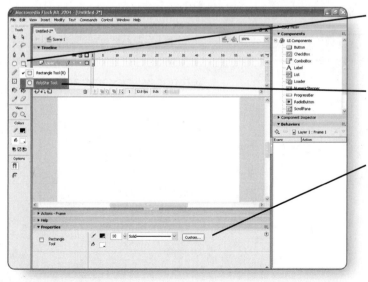

1. Click and hold on the Rectangle tool in the Tools panel to display a shortcut menu.

2. Click on PolyStar Tool. The PolyStar tool will become the active tool.

3. Choose Stroke color, height, and style settings—as well as a Fill color—in the Property Inspector.

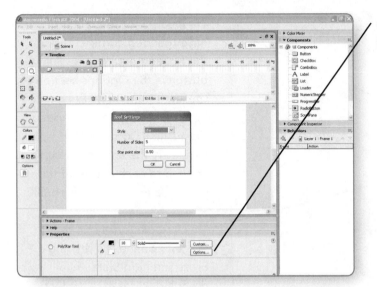

4. Click on Options. The Tools Settings dialog box will appear.

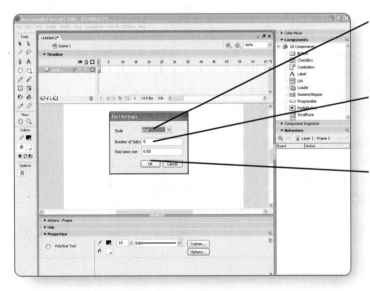

5. Choose shape style—polygon or star—from the Style list.

6. Specify the Number of Sides for the shape, as well as a star point size.

7. Click on OK. The dialog box will close, and the specified tool settings will become active.

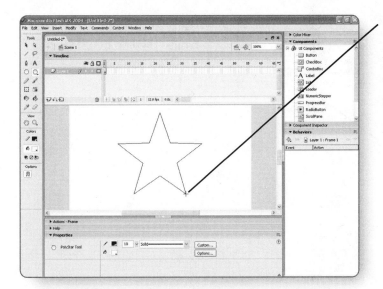

8. Drag diagonally from the center point out on the Stage to define the polygon or star. When you release the mouse button, the shape will appear.

The Pencil

The Pencil tool enables you to draw freehand lines in any shape on the Stage. Follow these steps to use the Pencil tool:

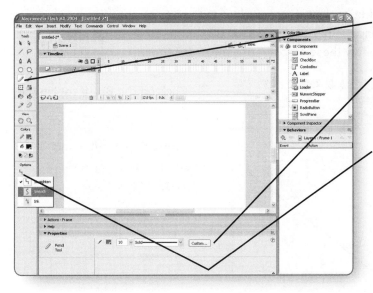

1. Click on the Pencil tool in the Tools panel.

2. Choose Stroke color, height, and style settings in the Property Inspector.

3. Click on the drawing mode button in the Options section in the Tools panel and then click on the mode to use:

- **Straighten**. Evaluates what you draw and straightens all the lines and shapes.

- **Smooth**. Softens the lines.

- **Ink**. Leaves the lines as you draw them.

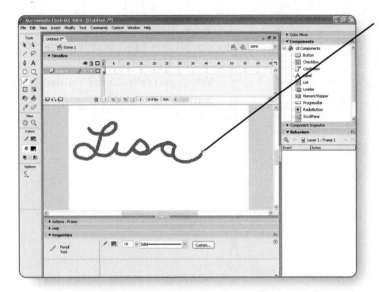

4. Click and drag on the Stage to create the line by using the designated settings.

The Brush

Like the Pencil tool, the Brush tool enables you to draw freeform lines on the Stage. However, the Brush tool includes additional settings—such as the ability to choose a brush shape—that enable you to create more numerous effects. Follow these steps to use the Brush tool:

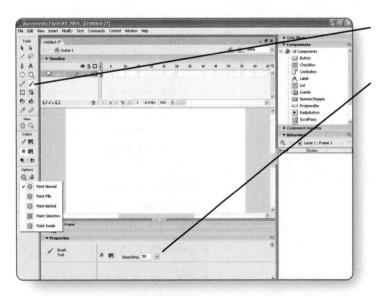

1. Click on the Brush tool in the Tools panel.

2. Choose a Fill color and Smoothing settings in the Property Inspector.

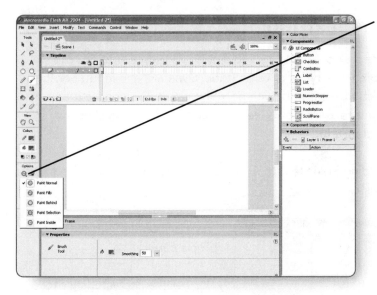

3. Choose a brush mode from the Options section of the Tools panel. The brush mode determines what happens when you paint on the Stage with the Brush tool, as follows:

- **Paint Normal**. Paints wherever you move the mouse while the button is pressed.

- **Paint Fill**. Covers the fill part of objects, but leaves the outlines alone.

- **Paint Behind**. Paints behind objects on the Stage.

- **Paint Selection**. Paints the selected object or objects.

- **Paint Inside**. Paints inside and only inside whatever object you start painting in.

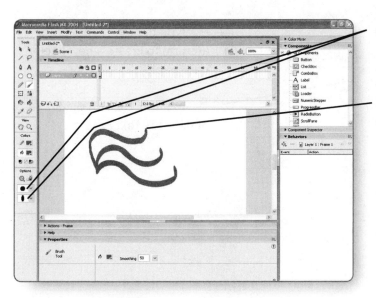

4. Choose a Brush Size and Brush Shape from the Options area of the Tools panel.

5. Click and drag the mouse on the Stage to draw as desired.

The Text Tool

The task of adding text to a movie is simple. You can choose from three types of text: Static, Dynamic, and Input. For this section, we'll work with only Static text. Dynamic text and Input text are introduced in Chapter 12, "Using Simple ActionScript."

Adding Static text to a movie is simple, as the following steps illustrate.

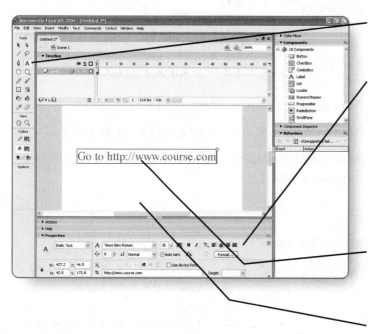

1. Click on the Text tool in the Tools panel.

2. Set the characteristics for the text in the Properties panel. All the properties are described in the bulleted list following these instructions.

3. Click on the Stage to specify the text position.

4. Type the text. Press Enter (Return) to create a new line or paragraph.

5. To finish, click on the Stage outside the text box.

The Property Inspector offers a number of settings for formatting text, as described here:

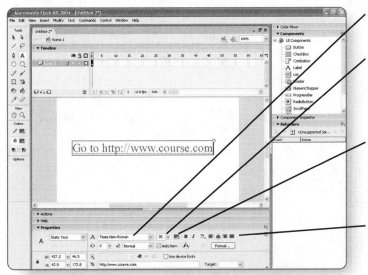

- Choose which Font the text will use.

- Specify a Font Size by either typing a number in the box or selecting a size from the drop-down list.

- Click on the Text (fill) color box to display a palette so that you can choose a text color.

- Apply bold or italics; orient text vertically or horizontally; or specify text alignment.

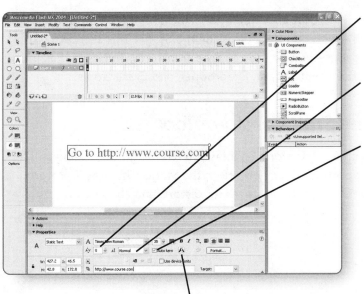

- Set Character Spacing, the amount of space that appears between characters.

- Alter Character position to create subscripted or superscripted text.

- Decide whether Flash should use a font's built-in kerning. *Kerning* determines how much space a specific character will occupy when it is next to another specific character. Flash uses the font's kerning settings when Auto Kern is checked.

- Use the Alias text button, new in Flash MX 2004, to turn on the alias feature, which smoothes text outlines.

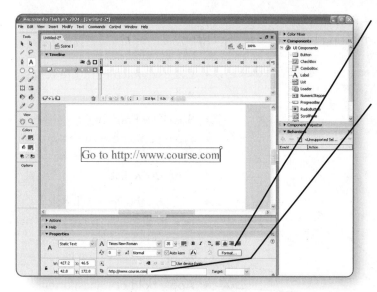

- Select the Format button to set paragraph properties, including indent spacing, line spacing, and margins.

- Create a hyperlink by typing a URL (Uniform Resource Locator) into the URL Link box. (First, drag over the link text to select it in the text box.)

Editing Tools

The Flash MX 2004 Tools panel includes a number of tools you can use to edit the objects on the Stage. This section describes how to use the Free Transform, Transform Fill, Ink Bottle, Paint Bucket, Eyedropper, and Eraser tools.

The Free Transform Tool

The Free Transform enables you to change the scaling and proportions of any object on the Stage. The Free Transform tool can resize, rotate, skew, distort, and shape.

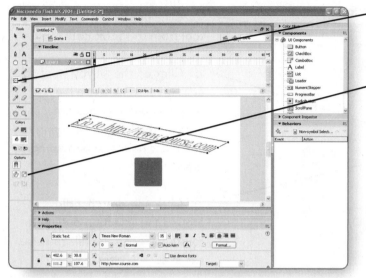

To use the Free Transform tool, click on it and then click on the object to change.

The Free Transform tool's effect depends on which mode you select for it (either Rotate and Skew or Scale) in the Options area of the Tools panel and whether you drag a handle or bounding side for the selected object, as follows:

- **Move**. Move an object by dragging from its center, in either mode.

- **Resize**. Click on the Scale button on the Tools panel, and then drag a corner or side handle.

- **Rotate**. Rotate objects by clicking on the Rotate and Skew button and dragging a corner. The object rotates around the center dot. You can move this dot by clicking and dragging it. The text shown here is both rotated and skewed.

- **Skew**. You skew an object by clicking on the Rotate and Skew button and dragging a side between the handles.

NOTE

You also can resize a selected object by editing the W and H values in the Property Inspector. Enter the desired dimensions in pixels.

The Transform Fill Tool

When an object has a gradient or a bitmap as its fill, the Transform Fill tool manipulates the fill.

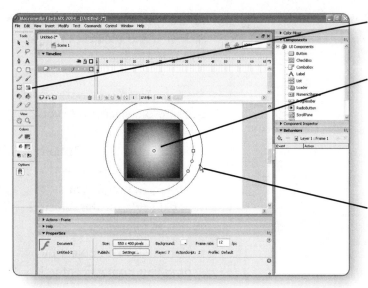

1. Click on the Transform Fill tool from the Tools panel.

2. Click on the fill you want to edit. If you click and a black selection outline does not appear, the fill you are trying to change is neither a bitmap nor a gradient.

3. Click and drag handles around the selection outline to rotate or resize the fill. You also can skew the bitmap fill.

Gradient Fills

Gradient fills transition from one solid color to another, with shades of the two colors mixed in-between. You can use two types of gradients: linear and radial. *Linear* gradients change from the first color to the second color along a line, and *radial* gradients change from a point outward in a circle. This explanation is a little tricky, but seeing a gradient helps.

To change an existing fill to a gradient, follow these steps.

1. Use the Selection tool to select the object with the fill to change.

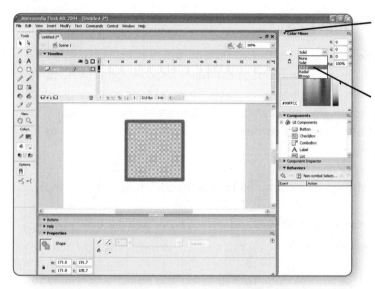

2. Choose Window, Design Panels, Color Mixer to open the Color Mixer panel.

3. Select the type of gradient, either Linear or Radial, from the Fill style drop-down list in the Color Mixer panel.

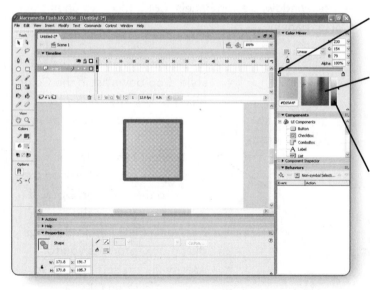

4. Click on the left color stop on the Gradient Definition bar.

5. Choose a color for the left side of a linear gradient or the center of a radial gradient from the Color selection area.

6. Choose an intensity level for this color from the Brightness Control bar.

7. Click on the right color stop, and repeat Steps 4 through 6 to set the second gradient color.

Bitmap fills

When you apply a bitmap fill, you select a bitmap graphic file to fill in a shape. Bitmaps can be created in Paint (Microsoft's simple graphics creation tool), Fireworks, or another graphics program. You also can use File, Export Movie and select Bitmap to export content from a Flash movie and use it as a bitmap fill.

To change an existing fill to a bitmap fill, follow these steps:

1. Create the bitmap and save it by using whatever program you want to use.

2. Use the Selection tool to select the object with the fill to change.

3. Choose Window, Design Panels, Color Mixer to open the Color Mixer panel.

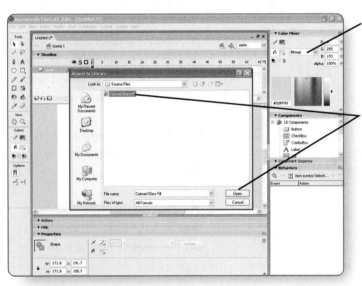

4. Select Bitmap from the Fill style drop-down list in the Color Mixer panel. The Import to Library dialog box will appear.

5. Navigate to the folder holding the bitmap, click on the File, and then click on Open. If a dialog box, such as the Fireworks PNG Import Settings dialog box, prompts you to specify import settings, do so and then click on OK.

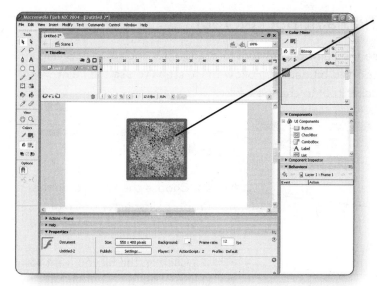

The fill will appear on the selected object, as in the example shown here. If it does not appear, you can use the Paint Bucket tool, described shortly, to apply the fill.

The Ink Bottle Tool

Use the Ink Bottle tool to change the color of lines, outlines, and pen strokes.

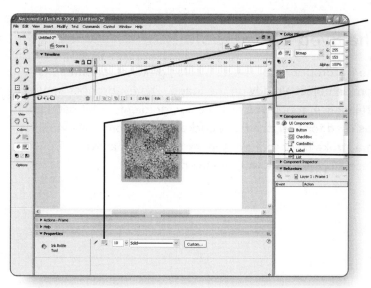

1. Click on the Ink Bottle tool in the Tools panel.

2. Choose the desired Stroke color tool in the Property Inspector.

3. Click on any object to change the outline color.

The Paint Bucket Tool

Use the Paint Bucket tool to change fills, including applying an imported bitmap fill. Follow these steps to use the Paint Bucket tool to change a fill.

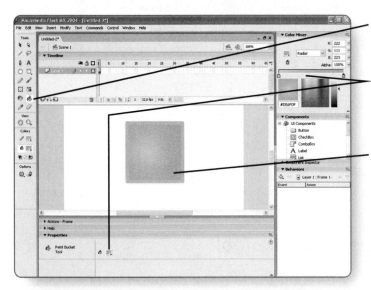

1. Click on the Paint Bucket tool in the Tools panel.

2. Choose the Fill color in the Property Inspector or Color Mixer.

3. Click on the fill you want to change. The fill color changes to the specified color, gradient, or bitmap.

The Eyedropper Tool

The Eyedropper tool selects a color, gradient, or bitmap fill from an object already on the Stage. The Eyedropper applies intelligence, too. If you pick a color, gradient, or bitmap that was used for a fill, the Paint Bucket tool becomes active. Click on a stroke color to make the Ink Bottle tool active. Follow these steps to work with the Eyedropper:

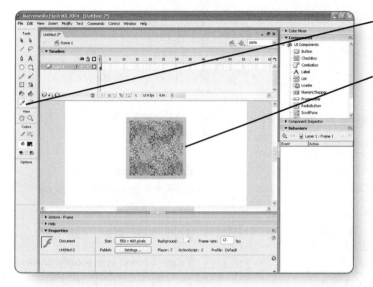

1. Click on the Eyedropper tool in the Tools panel.

2. Click on the color or fill you want to use. The Eyedropper determines from the location you clicked on whether to load a stroke or fill, and whether to activate the Ink Bottle or Paint Bucket tool.

3. Use the new color by using the automatically selected tool.

The Eraser Tool

Not surprisingly, the Eraser erases. When the Eraser is activated, you use it by dragging it over items on the Stage. You can set a few options to determine exactly what gets erased when you use the eraser.

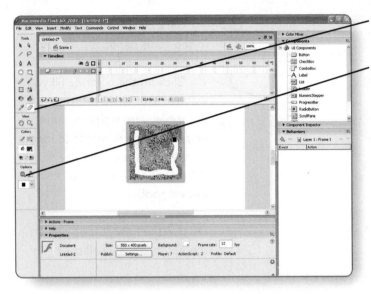

1. Click on the Eraser tool in the Tools panel.

2. Choose a mode for the Eraser from the drop-down list. The different modes for erasing include:

- **Erase Normal**. Erase everything that the mouse pointer passes over.

- **Erase Fills**. Erase only fills.

- **Erase Lines**. Erase only lines.

- **Erase Selected Fills**. Erase only those fills that were previously selected with the Arrow tool.

- **Erase Inside**. Erase only items that are inside the object you first clicked in.

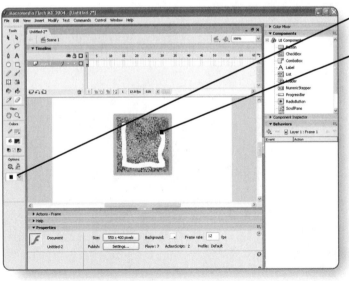

3. Choose an Eraser Shape.

4. Click and drag over anything you want to erase.

TIP

To erase entire objects, outlines, or fills, click on the Faucet button. The mouse pointer becomes a faucet, and Flash erases any object on which you click.

View Tools

The Tools panel includes two tools in a small section labeled View. You use these tools to change your view of the Stage in Flash.

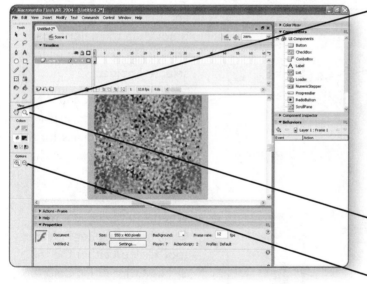

When the Stage is zoomed to a size that's larger than can appear at once in the workspace, use the Hand tool to scroll the Stage contents. (This technique is much faster than using the scroll bars.) Click on the Hand tool in the Tools panel, and then drag the Stage to move it.

The Zoom tool zooms in and out on the Stage.

After you click on the Zoom tool, click on the Enlarge or Reduce button on the Tools panel to determine whether to zoom in or out, and then click on the Stage.

Colors Tools

The Colors tools enable you to specify stroke and fill colors. These tools often correspond with settings in the Property Inspector. You can pick from the default range of colors or create your own custom color, as follows:

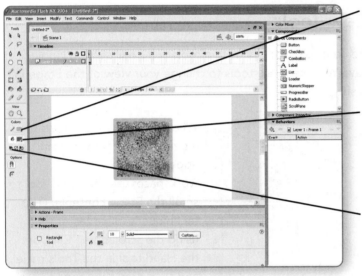

- Click on the Stroke Color box and then click on a color in the palette that appears to choose a color for outlines, lines, and the pencil.

- Click on the Fill Color box and then click on a color or gradient in the palette that appears to apply the fill to a selected object.

- Click on the Black and White button to reset the stroke and fill defaults: black for the stroke and white for the fill.

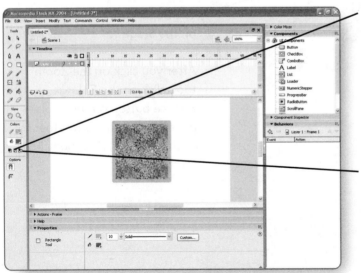

- When you've chosen the Oval, Rectangle, or PolyStar tool, click on either the the Stroke Color or Fill Color box, and then click on the No Color button. This will enable you to draw an object without a stroke or fill color.

- The Swap Color button switches the selected stroke and fill colors.

Moving and Deleting Objects

Once you've selected an object with the Selection tool, you can manipulate it in a variety of ways, including moving and deleting the object.

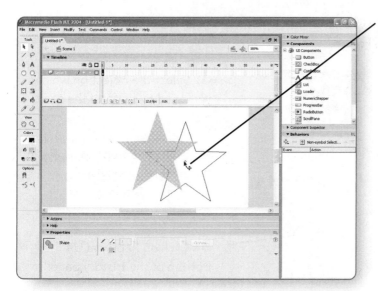

- To move the selected object, drag it from within the selected area.

- To delete the selected object, press the Backspace or Delete key.

Using Undo and the History Panel

Because each Flash movie may require hundreds or thousands of actions and changes, you're bound to make a mistake now and then. To fix a mistake in Flash, choose Edit, Undo (action name) or press Ctrl-Z (⌘-Z on the Mac). This command undoes the last action you did. If you need to undo more than just one action, you can select Edit, Undo more than once. By default, Flash enables you to undo up to 100 prior actions.

Let's say that you want to redo actions instead of undoing them. The History panel records all the steps that you perform while working on a movie. You can replay all or some of these steps to reproduce the same result. To replay steps, follow these steps:

1. Perform the steps required for a task, such as applying the desired formatting or effects.

2. Choose Window, Other Panels, History. The History panel will open.

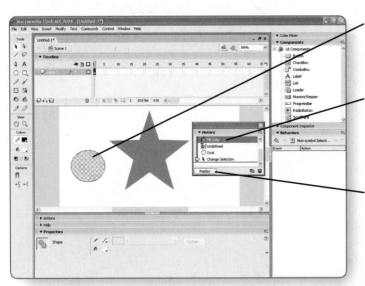

3. Select the object on which you need to perform the same task.

4. Select the steps to replay in the History panel. (Use Shift+click to select multiple steps.)

5. Click on Replay at the bottom of the History panel.

Refining Text

A spelling error undermines all the formatting work that you do to make text appealing and readable. Flash offers a Check Spelling command you can use to check spelling in a selected text block. To spell check the text in the current document, follow these steps:

1. Use the Selection tool to select the text block.

2. Click on the Text menu. The Text menu will appear.

3. Click on Check Spelling. The Check Spelling dialog box will open. It will identify any word not recognized by the active dictionaries by highlighting the word in the Word not found area at the top of the dialog box.

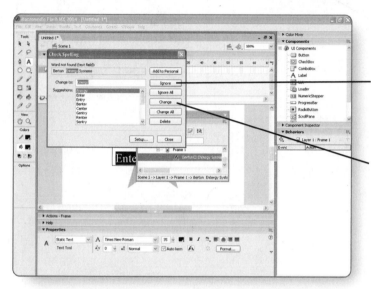

4. Specify whether or not to change the word, as follows:

- **Ignore**. Skips the word without changing it. (Ignore All ignores all instances of the found word.)

- **Change**. Changes the word to the spelling shown in the Change to text box. To choose an alternate correction, click on the desired spelling in the Suggestions list before clicking on Change. Change All changes all instances of the found word.

5. Repeat Step 4 for each spelling error identified in the Check Spelling dialog box. When the spell checker finds no more incorrect words in the current selection, it will display a message box telling you that the spell check is complete.

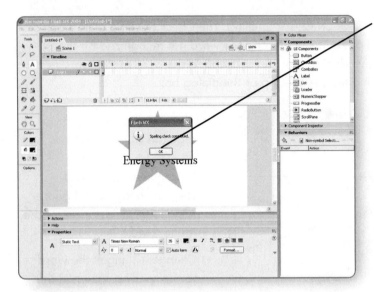

6. Click on OK. The spell checker will close.

NOTE

You can use the Edit, Find and Replace command to replace a word or phrase in your movie file.

3

Examining the Flash Workflow

Now that you've explored some of the tools in Flash MX 2004, move on to create your first movie and see how the separate components of Flash movies fit together. To build a movie, you need to understand how to work with the Stage, the Timeline, the Movie Explorer, and other key aspects of Flash. In this chapter, you will learn how to do the following:

- Create and save movie files.
- Adjust your view of the Stage.
- Understand the Timeline.
- Change the properties for a movie.
- Use the Movie Explorer.
- Use scenes.

Creating and Saving a Movie

You start each new Flash movie in a separate document file. If you create a new movie from scratch, you specify the size for the Stage (and therefore the movie itself). You also have the option of using a template that provides a standardized movie size. After you create the elements of the movie on the Stage, you will need to save the working movie file. This section covers these key aspects of creating a movie.

Creating a Blank Document

When you create a new blank movie document, Flash MX 2004 assigns a default movie size (550 x 400 pixels), background color (white), and frame rate (12 fps—*frames per second*). These settings work well for a basic movie, but you can change them at any time as described in the later section "Changing Movie Properties."

To create a new working document, follow these steps:

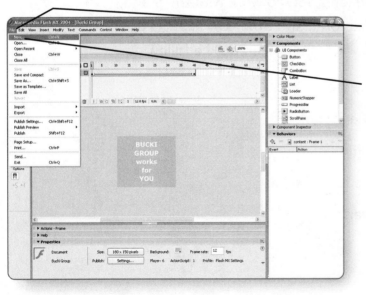

1. Click on File. The File menu will appear.

2. Click on New. The New Document dialog box will open.

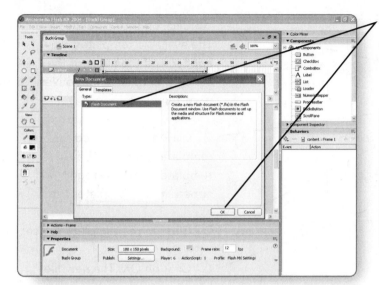

3. Leave Flash Document selected on the General tab and then click on OK. The new, blank movie will appear.

> ### NOTE
> You also can create a new movie from the Start Page, as described in "Using the Start Page" in Chapter 2.

Creating a Document from a Template

Flash includes a number of templates designed for particular purposes from advertising to interactive quiz applications. Some templates apply minimal settings to a file, such as a Stage size and background color, while others supply interactive features to save you time in building a movie. For example, the templates in the Advertising category supply standard sizes used for Web advertisements.

Follow these steps when you want to use a template to create a new movie document:

1. Click on File. The File menu will appear.

2. Click on New. The New Document dialog box will open.

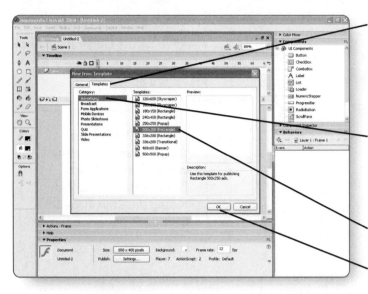

3. Click on the Templates tab. The available templates will appear, and the name of the dialog box will change to New from Template.

4. Click on the desired template category. The templates in that category will appear in the Templates list.

5. Click on the template to use.

6. Click on OK. The new file based on the template will open.

Saving and Closing

You save the working file for each movie project as an .fla file. As you make changes to the .fla file, you need to resave it to preserve your work. However, the .fla file is not the finished movie file. You must later *publish* the .fla file as a finished movie file in the .swf format. Chapter 11, "Publishing in Flash," will explain that process.

Follow these steps when you need to save and close your working .fla document:

1. Click on File. The File menu will appear.

2. Click on Save. The Save As dialog box will open.

TIP
Use the File, Open command to open an existing Flash document.

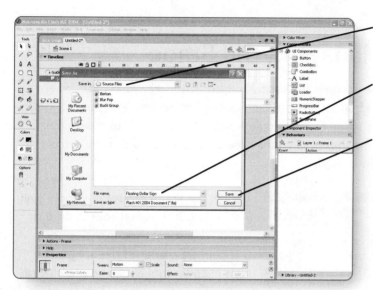

3. Choose the folder in which you want to save the document.

4. Type the desired document name in the File Name text box.

5. Click on Save. The document will be saved in the specified location.

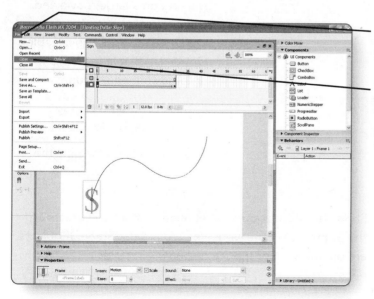

6. Click on File. The File menu will appear.

7. Click on Close. The document will be closed. (You also can right-click on the file's tab and then click on Close.)

> **TIP**
>
> After you save and name a Flash file, you can press Ctrl+S (⌘+S on a Mac) to save changes to the file.

Managing the Stage

The Stage is the central part of the Flash workspace, where the bulk of the work in creating animations is done. Think of the stage as your scratch pad. You will use it to create the components of your movie as well as to lay out the actual movie itself.

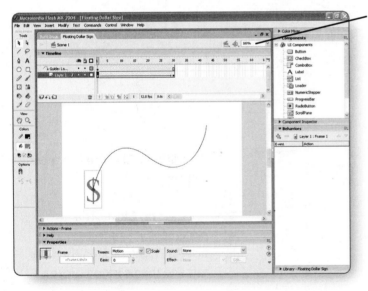

The Stage has several tools built into it. The first tool to note is the Zoom tool, in the upper-right corner of the Stage. The Zoom tool allows you to change the view of the stage. If you are working on a large movie and only part of it fits on the screen at a time, this tool is invaluable. Options available from this drop-down menu include:

- Preset zoom percentages, where 100 percent is full size.

- Show Frame, which fits the movie into the available space.

- Show All, which zooms out enough to show all objects on the Stage and in the work area around the Stage. If objects are on only part of the Stage, Show All zooms in, if necessary.

- Custom percentages, where you type a number into the combo box instead of choosing any of the options to view the Stage at a percentage of its actual size. Allowed percentages are between 8 percent and 2000 percent of actual size.

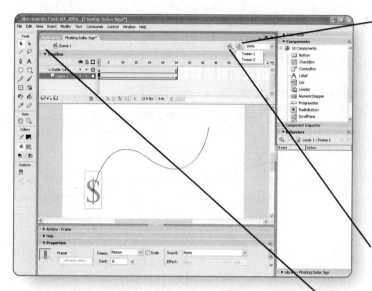

The Edit Symbols button enables you to change and manipulate symbols in the Library. When you've created symbols in a movie, clicking on this button shows a list of symbols you can edit. I discuss symbols in Chapter 5, "Using Symbols and the Library," and the Library in Chapter 6, "Creating Basic Animation."

The Edit Scene button allows you to choose from a list of scenes in your movie. I discuss scenes later in this chapter.

When you are editing a symbol, the Back to Stage button becomes enabled. Click on the Back to Stage button to return to the main Stage from the Symbol Editor.

Understanding the Timeline

The Timeline Panel, usually located at the top of the Flash workspace, shows vital information about your movie. It displays each frame in your movie and identifies key movie features such as motion.

You build Flash animations by adding a series of pictures. When viewed rapidly in order, the pictures blend to form the movie action. Each frame holds one of those pictures; several frames display every second when you play back the movie. Chapter 7, "Animation with Motion Tweening," explains how to use automated tools to create the frames and motion in your movie.

You'll work with these key features when you use the Timeline:

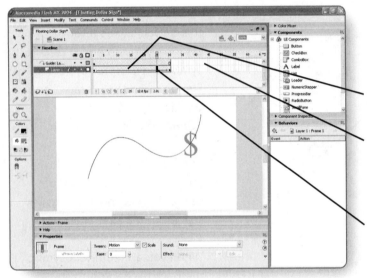

- The right area of the timeline shows the frames that compose the movie in order from left to right.

- Frames with content have a black border and shading.

- Unused frames retain their default white fill; every fifth unused frame has a light gray/tan fill.

- Click on a frame to select it. The selected frame has a black fill and a red vertical line; the frame number is also highlighted in red.

The bottom border of the Timeline lists several pieces of important information:

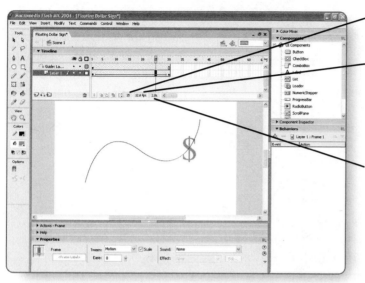

- **Current Frame**. The frame number of the selected frame

- **Frame Rate**. The rate at which the frames are displayed in the movie, in frames per second (fps). The default setting is 12 fps.

- **Elapsed Time**. The time from the beginning of the movie to the selected frame

Buttons at the bottom of the Timeline enable you to edit the movie as follows:

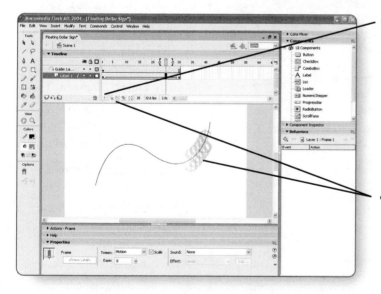

- **Center Frame**. When you are working with a long movie with a large number of frames, the Timeline can show only a portion of the frames onscreen at any time. This button scrolls the Timeline to center it on the selected frame.

- **Onion Skin**. This button shows several frames of the movie superimposed on one another so that you can see the movement of an animation. Markers appear on the Timeline and bracket the frames to which the onion skinning applies.

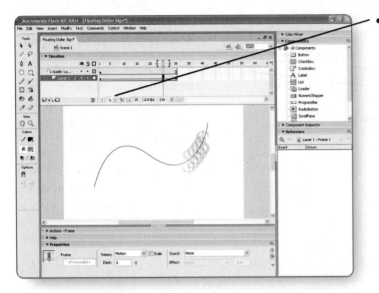

- **Onion Skin Outlines**. This button shows the outlines of the moving objects in a group of frames, all superimposed on the Stage.

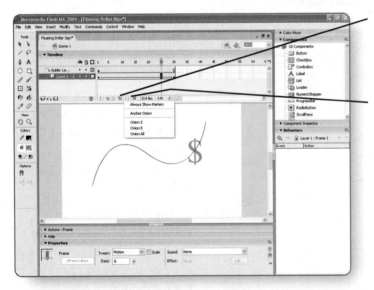

- **Edit Multiple Frames**. This button enables you to edit more than one frame at one time.

- **Modify Onion Markers**. The last button in this group allows several different options to be set, including:

  - **Always Show Markers**. This option shows the markers that bracket the frames shown in Onion Skin mode, whether or not the mode is turned on.

- **Anchor Onion**. The onion skin markers usually move in relation to the selected frame or frames. This option sets the markers and keeps them from moving.

- **Onion 2**. Two frames on either side of the selected frame are shown in Onion Skin mode.

- **Onion 5**. Five frames on either side of the selected frame are shown in Onion Skin mode.

- **Onion All**. Every frame in the animation is shown when Onion Skinning is turned on.

The area at the left side of the Timeline contains controls for editing and displaying layers. Each new layer you add to the movie is inserted above the existing layer. When using the default settings, Flash will read movie layers from bottom to top. Chapter 4, "Using Layers to Build Movie Content," will cover layers in more detail, but for now you can think of them as a way to organize the objects in a movie.

Use these Timeline buttons to manage layers:

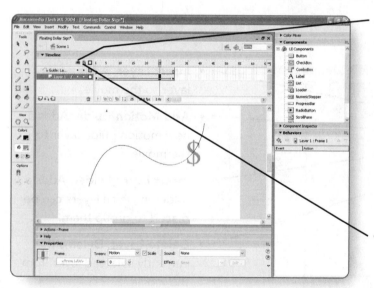

- **Show/Hide All Layers**. Layers are visible by default, but this button toggles the visibility of all layers. To toggle the visibility of a single layer, click on the dot beneath this button on the layer's row. A red X will indicate that the layer's content has been hidden on the Stage.

- **Lock/Unlock All Layers**. This button locks or unlocks all the layers in a scene so that they cannot be changed. To lock a single layer, click on the dot beneath this button on the layer's row. A lock icon will indicate that the layer's content has been locked to prevent editing.

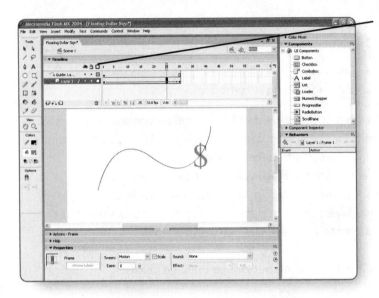

- **Show All Layers as Outlines**. Sometimes, a scene can get cluttered with too many objects that blend together. In such a case, viewing the outlines of the objects may help. This button switches between regular and outline views of all objects on all layers.

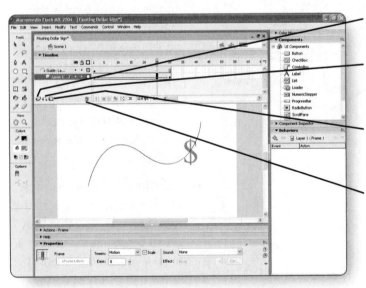

- **Insert Layer**. Adds a new layer to the movie.

- **Add Motion Guide**. Adds a new motion guide layer to the movie.

- **Insert Layer Folder**. Adds a folder in which layers can be placed to group them.

- **Delete Layer**. Deletes the currently selected layer from the movie.

Changing Movie Properties

You can determine overall properties for each Flash movie or animation, such as its movie size. When the Property Inspector is visible and no objects are selected on the Stage, the Property Inspector shows information about the entire movie or document.

You can view and change some of the movie properties by using the Property Inspector. Movie properties include:

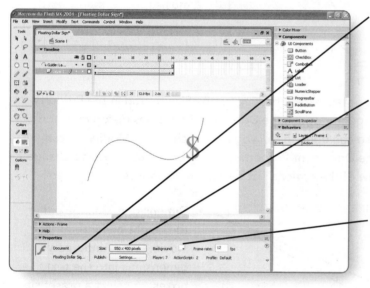

- The file name for the movie document. (You can only change this property by using File, Save As.)

- The Stage or movie size. Click on this button to open the Document Properties dialog box. Type new width and height values (in pixels) and then click on OK.

- The Background color for the movie. Click on this box to open a color palette and then click on the desired background color in the palette.

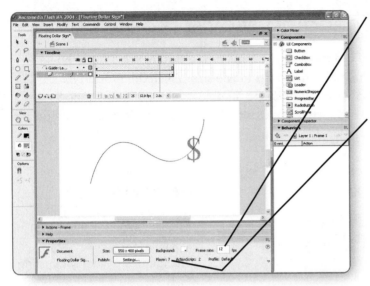

- The Frame rate, in frames per second (fps). Type a new value into this text box and press Enter to change the frame rate for the movie.

- The Flash Player version for which the movie will be published. Chapter 11, "Publishing in Flash," will cover publishing Flash movies.

As noted earlier, clicking on the Size button in the Property Inspector opens the Document Properties dialog box. You also can open this dialog box by choosing Modify, Document. The Document Properties dialog box enables you to change a few of the options just described, as well as some others:

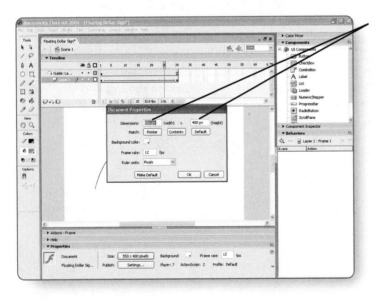

- **Dimensions**. Change either the height or width of the movie. Either enter new dimensions into the text boxes, or select a preset size by clicking on one of the Match buttons. The movie size must be greater than 1 by 1 pixel and smaller than 2880 pixels by 2880 pixels.

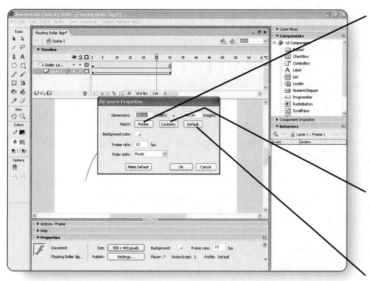

- **Printer**. Clicking on this button sets the size of the movie to the maximum size that will fit on a printed page. This option uses in its calculations the options set in the Page Setup dialog box that appears when you choose File, Page Setup.

- **Contents**. Clicking on the Contents button fits the entire contents of the Stage into the movie.

- **Default**. Sets the movie to the default size, 550 pixels wide by 400 pixels tall.

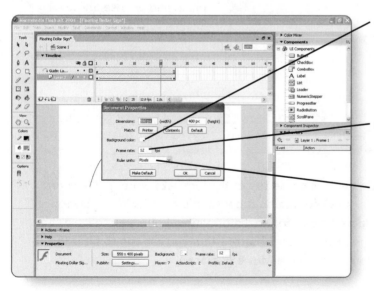

- **Background color**. Click on this box to open a color palette and then click on the desired background color in the palette.

- **Frame rate**. Type a new value into this text box to change the frame rate for the movie.

- **Ruler units**. Choose a measurement unit from this drop-down menu to set the type used for measurements in the movie. The default is pixels, but you can instead choose inches, points, centimeters, or millimeters.

Working with the Movie Explorer

The Movie Explorer panel shows the different elements of your movie, including scenes, objects, sounds, and ActionScripts. That may not seem important now, but for big projects this feature is very helpful because you can get an overview of the project.

To open the Movie Explorer panel, choose Window, Other Panels, Movie Explorer.

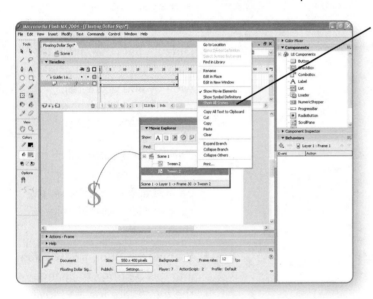

By default, the Movie Explorer shows only information about the current scene. To show the component parts for all scenes, right-click on white area at the bottom of the Movie Explorer panel and choose Show All Scenes.

The buttons at the top of the Movie Explorer panel control or filter the information shown in the panel. When a button is selected (pressed), the information it filters appears in the panel. Here are the buttons that you can use to filter the information in the Movie Explorer:

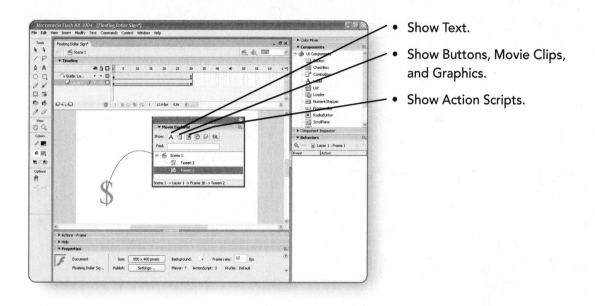

- Show Text.

- Show Buttons, Movie Clips, and Graphics.

- Show Action Scripts.

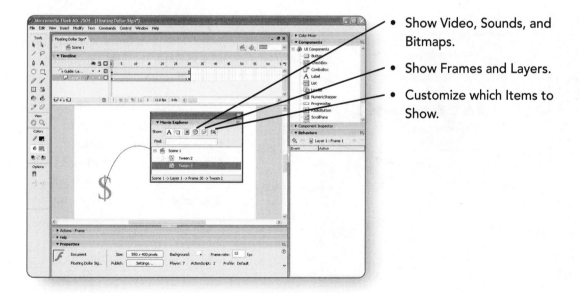

- Show Video, Sounds, and Bitmaps.

- Show Frames and Layers.

- Customize which Items to Show.

I recommend keeping the Show Frames and Layers button selected, as this option displays which objects are where in the movie.

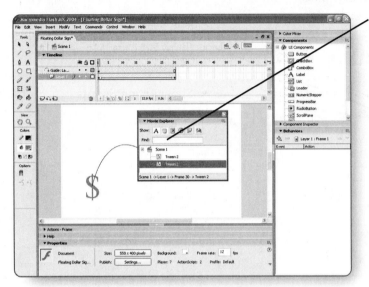

The Find box enables you to search the movie for specific items. Type a frame number, the name of an object or a layer, or a font name, and press Enter to display any occurrences of the matching item in the Movie Explorer panel.

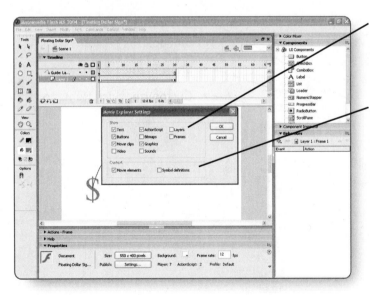

If you click on the Customize which Items to Show button, the Movie Explorer Settings dialog box will open.

Use the options in the Show area to choose the items to show in the Movie Explorer. Checking an options means that the specified type of item will appear in the Movie Explorer.

The Context area contains two options: Movie elements and Symbol definitions. When one of these options is checked, the designated information will appear in the Movie Explorer window. Movie elements are the actual components or objects in the movie. You can think of Symbol definitions as templates for objects in the movie. Chapter 5, "Using Symbols and the Library," covers symbols in more detail.

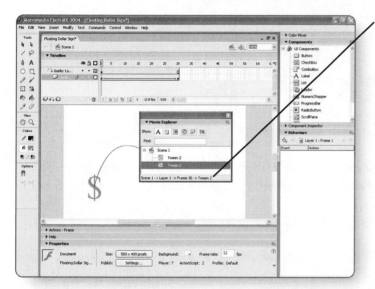

Finally, when you select an object in the Movie Explorer, the path to that item appears at the bottom of the panel. The path contains the scene name, the layer name, the frame number, and the type of object so that you can easily find objects.

Organizing Movies with Scenes

Flash movies, like Hollywood movies, organize content in scenes. Each scene usually has a coherent theme or contains one discrete part of a movie. For interactive movies, one scene often contains the response to one type of user action. For example, if a user clicks on one button, the movie plays a certain scene; if the user clicks on a different button, a different scene plays. When you work through the movie planning stage, the design you build should map out the movie scenes.

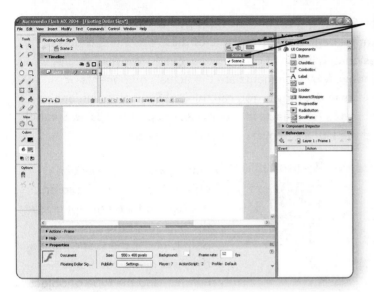

To switch between scenes in a movie, click on the Edit Scene button on the Timeline and then click on the desired scene.

You also can work with scenes by using the Scene panel. To show the Scene panel, choose Window, Design Panels, Scene.

Using the Scene panel, you can:

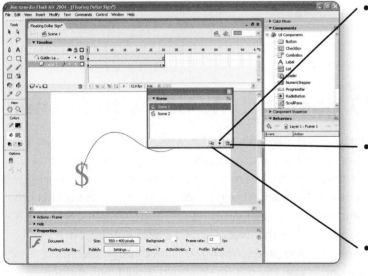

- Add a scene by clicking on the Add scene button. You also can choose Insert, Scene to add a new scene. When you add a new scene to a movie, it by default contains one layer and one frame.

- Delete a scene by clicking on the Delete scene button. Click on OK in the message box that appears to confirm the deletion.

- Copy a scene by clicking on the Duplicate scene button.

- Rename a scene by double-clicking on the scene name, typing a new name, and pressing Enter.
- Change the order of scenes in the movie by dragging a scene to the desired position in the list of scenes.

4

Using Layers to Build Movie Content

Chapter 3 briefly introduced the concept of layers as a way to organize the objects in your Flash MX 2004 movie. Each layer holds its own objects, but allows the objects on other layers to show through, as well. When you stack all the layers, the objects combine to form the finished image. As you may have guessed from this brief description, layers increase your speed and flexibility as you produce a new movie. In this chapter, you will learn the answers to these questions, and more:

- What is a layer?
- How do you work with layers?
- What are the properties of a layer?
- How can you organize layers?

What Is a Layer?

You can think of layers as transparent sheets, like transparencies for overhead projectors. Each transparent sheet can contain text and illustrations. The sheets can be stacked one on top of another so that you can see the contents of each, but more importantly so you can see how the contents of all the sheets combine to form the finished picture.

In Flash, use layers to organize and separate different pieces of a movie. For example, you can create a background image on one layer, foreground objects on another, a moving object on a third, and text on a fourth.

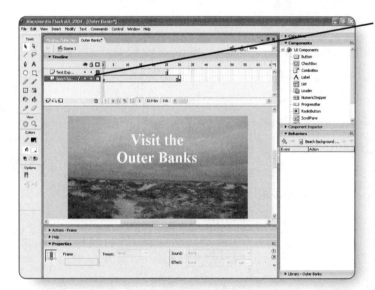

This example shows two layers, each holding a different object. The top layer, named Text Expand, holds the text. The bottom layer, Beach Background, holds the background image of the beach dune. Separating your objects onto layers makes the editing process much easier, because you can move and change the object on one layer without any impact on objects in other layers. As you will learn in this chapter, you can hide layers you are not working on so you can see only the one you want to edit.

> **TIP**
>
> If you add actions to your movie, it is a good idea to create a separate layer just for the actions to keep them together in one place.

How Do You Work with Layers?

You may spend a significant part of your movie development time working with layers, as it's such an integral part of the Flash process. You can add, delete, and hide layers; select a layer and add objects to it; or change layer names and view layer outlines. This section introduces you to these key layer operations.

Adding a Layer

Because you'll add layers so often in Flash, it takes only a moment. To add a new layer to a movie:

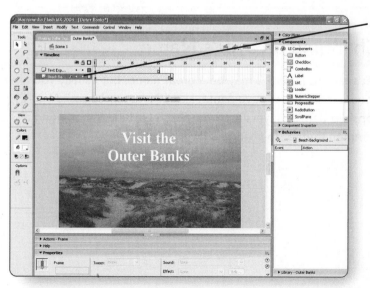

1. Click on the layer above which you want to insert the new layer in the Timeline.

2a. Click on the Insert Layer button.

OR

2b. Choose Insert, Layer.

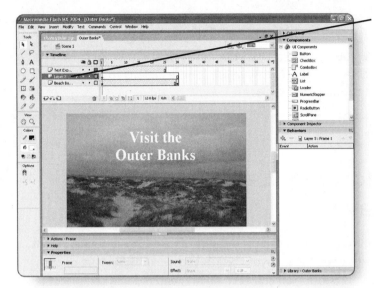

The new layer will appear in the list of layers in the Timeline, above the layer that you selected in Step 1.

NOTE

Each and every moving object in your movie should reside on its own layer. This gives you the most control when animating the objects, ensuring that you can apply the animation you want without interfering with another object or creating an error in the movie. There is no limit to the number of layers you can add.

Changing a Layer's Name

Let's face it: Layer 12 may be a great name, but usually you need a more descriptive name, like "Company Logo." Also consider naming layers according to their function or along a common theme. To change a layer's name:

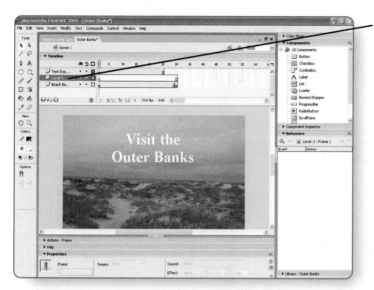

1. Double-click on the name of the layer you want to change. The layer's name will be highlighted for editing.

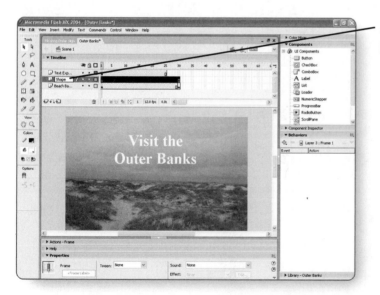

2. Type a new name for the layer and then press Enter.

Selecting a Layer and Adding Objects

After you add a layer in your movie, you need to place an object on the layer. To add an object to a specific layer, you must select the layer first, as described next:

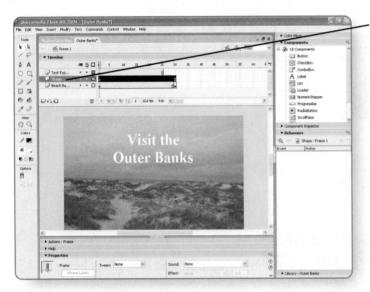

1. Click on the layer on which you want to add the object. This will select the layer. The selected layer and its frames will be highlighted, and a pencil icon will appear to the right of the layer's name.

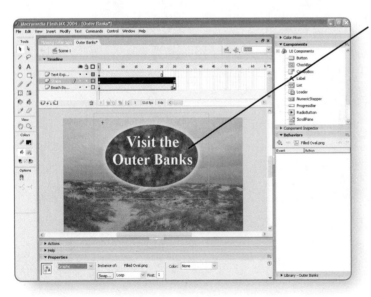

2. Add the object to the layer by drawing on the Stage or by importing a symbol as described in Chapter 5, "Using Symbols and the Library."

Deleting a Layer

As a movie project progresses, you may discover a need to organize the movie differently. In this case, you may need to delete a layer. To delete a layer:

CAUTION

Fireworks does not warn you before deleting the layer. It also lets you delete a layer that's locked. If you mistakenly delete a layer, be sure to choose Edit, Undo Delete Layer immediately to recover the layer and its contents.

1. Click on the layer you want to delete in the Timeline. The layer will be selected

2a. Click on the Delete Layer button.

OR

2b. You can right-click on the layer's name and choose Delete Layer from the context menu.

The layer will be deleted.

A movie must have at least one layer, so if only one layer exists, you will not be able to delete it.

Hiding a Layer

When a movie contains more than one layer, the objects on all layers appear on the Stage, by default. This feature makes it simple to position objects relative to one another, but the Stage can get cluttered. Flash enables you to hide individual layers, reducing Stage clutter. Hide layers that you are not currently editing to create more space on the stage.

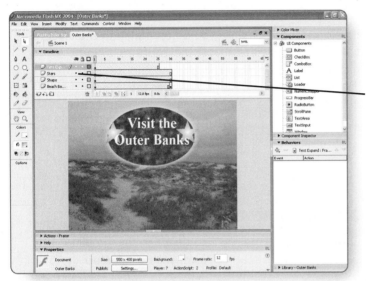

To hide a layer, click on the dot for that layer under the Show/Hide All Layers (eye) button.

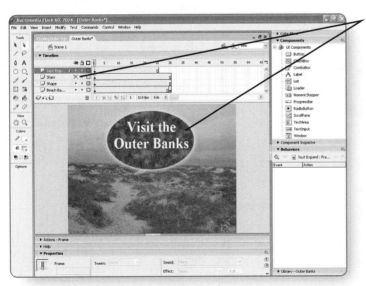

The layer contents will disappear from the Stage, and an X will appear through the dot. If the layer were selected first, a slash would also appear through the pencil icon, indicating that the hidden layer may not be edited.

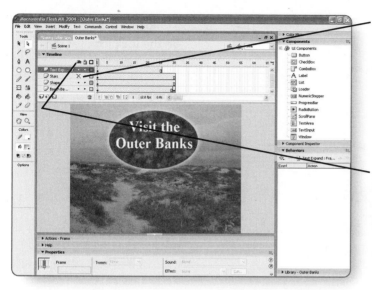

To show the layer again, click on the X (where the dot previously appeared). The layer will reappear. If the layer is selected, the pencil icon also returns to normal, indicating the layer can now be edited.

To hide all the layers, click on the Show/Hide All Layers button itself. Click on the button again to redisplay all the layers.

Locking a Layer

When you have a movie with more than one layer in it, which is usually the case, you can inadvertently make changes to a layer you have finished. To avoid this situation, lock each layer that you complete. A locked layer cannot be changed unless it is intentionally unlocked. (However, a locked layer can be deleted, so continue to use caution when you delete layers.) To lock and unlock a layer, follow these steps:

1. Click on the dot for the layer you want to lock in the Lock/Unlock All Layers column (below that button). A lock icon will appear in the layer's row in the Timeline.

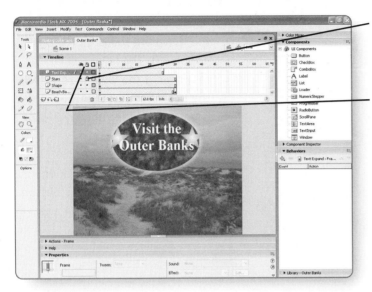

2. To unlock a locked layer, click on the lock icon for the layer in the Timeline.

3. To lock or unlock all layers, click on the Lock/Unlock All Layers button.

Viewing Layer Outlines

Things can quickly get cluttered with numerous objects on the Stage. In some situations, however, completely hiding the layers doesn't work because you need to be able to see, for

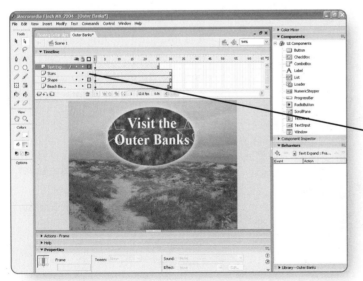

reference, where objects reside in the context of the stage. To deal with situations like this one, you can instruct Flash to show only the outlines of the objects on a layer.

The final button in each layer's row in the Timeline is a square below the Show All Layers as Outlines button. Click on the button for any layer to toggle the layer between normal view and outline view, allowing you to see the location of the object.

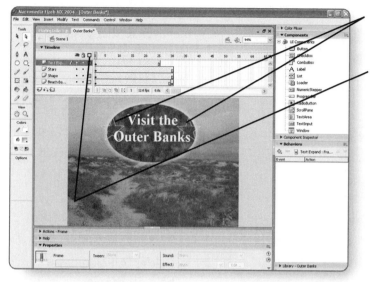

For example, these stars appear as an outline only.

Click on the Show All Layers as Outlines button to toggle the outline view on and off for all of the layers in the movie file.

Changing Layer Properties

You also can use the Layer Properties dialog box to work with and customize a layer. To open the Layer Properties dialog box to set properties for the selected layer, either choose Modify, Layer or right-click on the selected layer in the Timeline list and choose Properties in the shortcut menu. In the Layer Properties dialog box, you can change these elements:

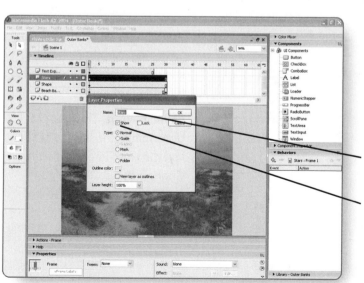

• **Name**. Type a new layer name here.

• **Show**. When this check box is checked, the layer contents appear on the Stage. Unchecking this check box hides the layer contents.

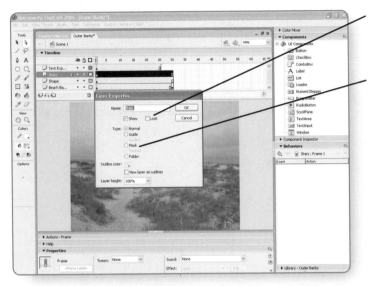

- **Lock**. Check this box to lock the layer so that its contents cannot be changed.

- **Type**. Flash has several types of layers, including Normal, Guide, Guided, Mask, Masked, and Folder. For the moment, concern yourself with only two types:

  - **Normal**. A Normal Layer contains objects that are part of your movie.

  - **Folder**. A Folder layer can hold other layers in it, just like a file folder in a filing cabinet.

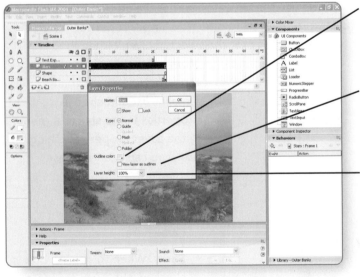

- **Outline Color**. Click on this color box and then click on the color to use when you display the layer outline.

- **View Layer as Outlines**. Checking this check box shows only object outlines for the selected layer.

- **Layer Height**. This feature determines the height of the layer in the Timeline display. Change this setting if you prefer the layer rows to be taller.

Organizing Layers in Folders

As was noted earlier in this chapter, the number of layers included in a Flash movie can start to add up. The simplest way to organize layers is to group layers with a similar theme or contents together in a folder. Use these steps to create a folder and add layers to it:

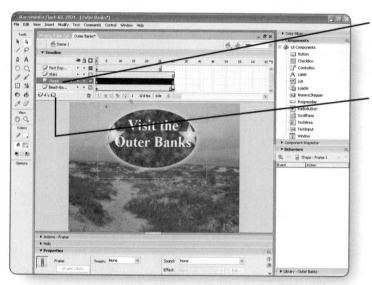

1. Click on the layer above which you want to create a folder.

2. Click on the Insert Layer Folder button. The new folder will appear.

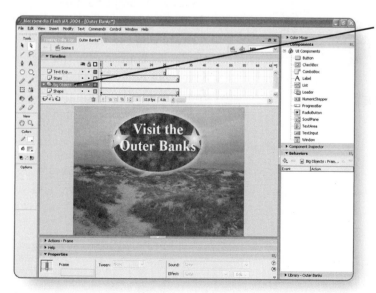

3. Rename the folder name by double-clicking on the folder name, typing a new name, and pressing Enter.

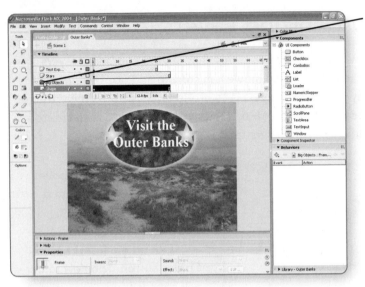

4. To move a layer into the folder, drag the layer's page icon and drop it onto the folder icon.

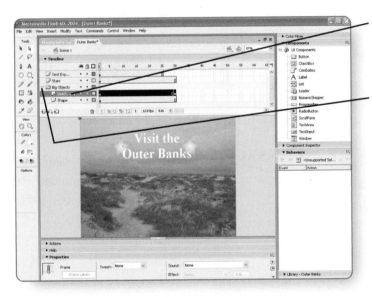

The layers in the folder will appear indented under the folder name, as shown here.

To collapse (hide) the layers in a folder on the Timeline, click on the down triangle to the left of the folder name. The triangle turns to point to the right, and the layers contained in the folder are no longer visible on the Timeline (although the layers' contents do remain visible on the Stage). To redisplay the layers in the timeline, click on the triangle again. It will rotate down, and the layers will reappear.

Adjusting Object Layering

In addition to helping you keep objects separate to facilitate object positioning, layers help you control how objects overlap on the Stage. The objects on the topmost layer listed in the Timeline appear in front of objects on all other layers, the objects on the second layer overlap objects on the third layer and lower, and so on.

To change the overlapping of objects on a layer, you can move the layer in the Timeline. Follow these steps to do so:

1. Click on the layer you want to move. The layer will be selected

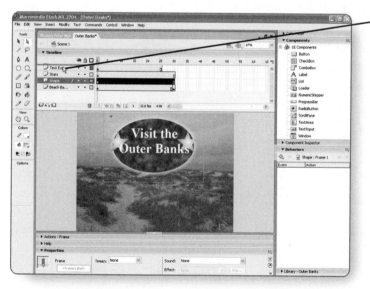

2. Drag the layer to the desired position in the Timeline list. A hatched gray bar will indicate where the layer will move when you release the mouse button.

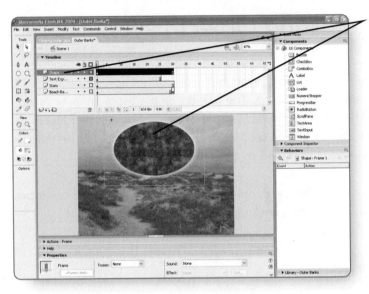

When you release the mouse button, the layer moves to a new position in the list, and its contents overlap (or move behind) other objects on the stage accordingly. In this example, the oval on the Shape layer now hides text on the Text Expand layer because the Shape layer appears higher in the list.

5

Using Symbols and the Library

Flash MX 2004 enables you to take advantage of *symbols*, reusable objects that streamline building animations and movies. When you create a symbol, Flash stores it in the Library. In this chapter, you will learn to do the following:

- What a symbol is.
- What kinds of symbols you can use.
- How to create symbols.
- How to edit symbols and instances.
- What the Library is.
- How to work with a shared library.

What Is a Symbol?

A symbol is a graphic object (in the simplest sense of the word, not in the programming sense) created for use throughout a Flash movie; more specifically, a *symbol* in Flash can be a graphic, button, or movie clip.

Consider the many Web sites you've recently browsed. These sites include, in part, graphic objects. Sometimes, these graphic objects are static, and at other times they have added behaviors—they *do* something when you move the mouse pointer over them or click on them. A symbol can be static or include a behavior.

You can create symbols from scratch by using the drawing tools in Flash. Or you can import a graphic created in a program like Fireworks and convert that graphic to a symbol. Flash stores each symbol you create or import in the Library.

Creating a symbol saves time, because you can reuse a single symbol as many times as you want in the movie. Each time you place the symbol in the movie, you create an *instance* of the symbol. If you edit the symbol, the changes you make affect every instance of the symbol in your movie. You also can edit an individual instance of a symbol without affecting the original symbol or other instances.

Using symbols reduces the movie file size while increasing the playback speed, important considerations for Web content. Each symbol downloads to the Flash player only once, no matter how many instances of the symbol appear in your movie. For these reasons and others covered later in this chapter, you should learn to use symbols as often as possible in your Flash movies.

You use the Library to work with symbols. To open the Library panel, choose Window, Library. As I mentioned, Flash enables you to use three basic types of symbols. Each type has different uses, as follows:

- **Graphics**. Can be created in Flash or another application such as Fireworks. For example, you might create your company logo as a symbol to be used over and over in the movie.

- **Buttons**. You can add functionality to a button.

- **Movie clips**. They include multiple frames of information. These movies can play back once or loop in the background.

NOTE

Movie clip symbols, for which you create animation and motion, are different from imported video that you captured with a video camera. See the section called "Importing Embedded Video" in Chapter 10 to learn more about importing video such as a QuickTime movie into Flash.

NOTE

You also can create a font symbol. However, font symbols are used primarily for exporting font information rather than enhancing the movie.

Let's take a closer look at each type of symbol.

Graphics

Graphic symbols have no interactivity. These static symbols simply add image content to the movie. You can use any of the tools in the Tools panel to create a graphic symbol.

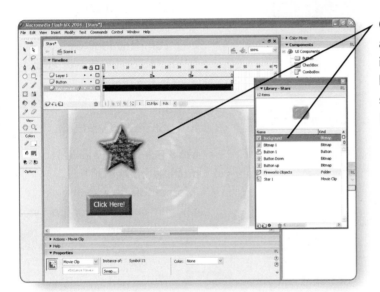

Or you can create a graphic in another application and import it into Flash. For example, the background graphic symbol shown here was created in Fireworks.

Buttons

When you think about *pointing and clicking* on something other than on a text link, the object you have in mind is usually a button. If you complete a form on the Web, you typically have to click on the Submit button to send in the form, for example. Buttons have states that respond to the user's mouse actions. A button can have a different state (or look different) when the user moves the mouse pointer over it or clicks on it. After you have created the look of the button's various states, you can assign an action for each state.

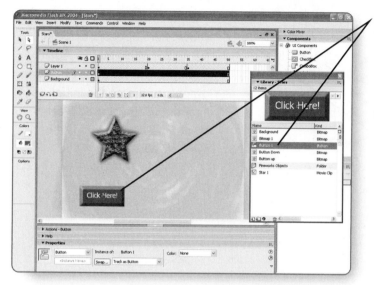

In this example, I created the button backgrounds in Fireworks, copying each background for the desired state as I created the button symbol in Flash.

Movie Clips

A movie clip is really a mini Flash movie within your main movie. Each movie clip symbol you create contains its own Timeline, complete with layers and frames. The Timeline of a movie clip, nested within the greater Timeline of the movie, plays when the layer containing the movie clip plays. This feature assists you in creating more complex animation.

NOTE

You see the movie clip symbol's Timeline only when you edit the symbol. Also, when you preview the main movie within Flash, the movie clip symbols do not play. See the later section called "Previewing Movie Clip Symbols in a Movie" to learn how to preview the movie clips.

The Star 1 movie clip symbol shown here appears twice in frame 26 of this movie. Again, I copied content from a Fireworks graphic to create the initial star image, but then I used Flash to create the animation for the symbol.

I recommend creating symbols as movie clips unless you are absolutely certain that you will never want to animate a particular symbol. Animation is mentioned in this chapter, but Chapters 6, 7, and 8 cover that topic more comprehensively.

> **NOTE**
>
> You also can add behaviors to the different images in a movie clip symbol, as you would with buttons. Chapter 12, "Using Simple ActionScript," offers more information about working with behaviors.

Creating Symbols

Flash by default stores each symbol you create in the Library for the current movie file only. (See "Copying Symbols between Libraries" later in the chapter to learn how to work with symbols from another file.) To create a new symbol in Flash, select Insert, New Symbol or press Ctrl+F8 (⌘+F8 on a Mac). You also can click on the New Symbol button in the lower-left corner of the Library panel.

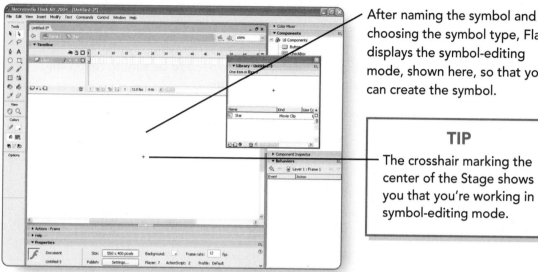

After naming the symbol and choosing the symbol type, Flash displays the symbol-editing mode, shown here, so that you can create the symbol.

TIP

The crosshair marking the center of the Stage shows you that you're working in symbol-editing mode.

As you become more familiar with the Library, you may prefer to create new symbols by clicking on the New Symbol button in the lower-left corner of the Library panel.

Naming Symbols

As noted previously, one of the first activities in creating a symbol is to specify the symbol name. Naming symbols is important.

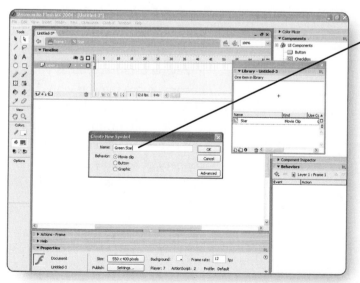

The Create New Symbol dialog box that appears will prompt you for the symbol Name, among other settings. Enter a name that's descriptive, not something like Symbol1 or Symbol2. Your goal is to be able to look at the Library panel and quickly identify each symbol when you need it. Symbol names are not limited to eight digits, so you can be a little more liberal with the name of your symbol.

NOTE

If you plan to use ActionScript with a symbol (more on that in Chapter 12), you need to be sure to follow the Flash naming convention:

- Button names should end with _btn; for example, SubmitButton_btn.

- Movie clips should end with _mc; for example, Earth_mc.

- Text files, which come into use with ActionScript, should end with _txt; for example, MylistofNames_txt.

Based on the ending letters of the symbol's name (_btn, _mc, or _txt), ActionScript provides a list of available programming options. Although you may or may not be using ActionScript right away, you should use these naming conventions. Using them also assists you in identifying your symbols.

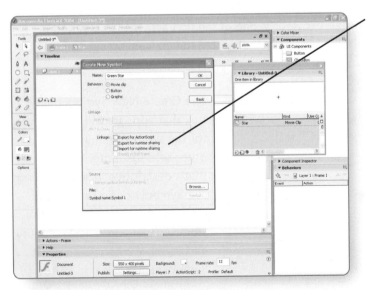

If you click on the Advanced button in the Create New Symbol dialog box, the Linkage options for ActionScript appear. Although you may not need to work with these choices initially, it may be useful to you as you become more familiar with Flash. The Linkage check boxes provide more options for import and export functionality. The concept of runtime sharing is discussed later in this chapter.

Creating Symbols

Now that you understand some of the important concepts behind symbols and why they should be named as such, you can explore the basic steps for creating each type of symbol: graphic, movie clip, and button.

Creating a Graphic Symbol

You can often create a graphic symbol in a matter of moments. The following steps provide the general process for creating a graphic symbol in a Flash document:

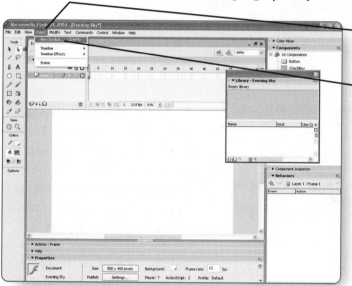

1. Click on Insert. The Insert menu will appear.

2. Click on New Symbol. The Create New Symbol dialog box will open.

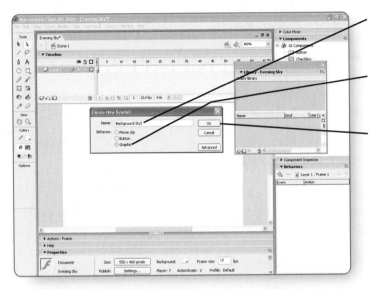

3. Enter a name for the symbol in the Name text box.

4. Click on the Graphic option button in the Behavior area.

5. Click on OK. The symbol-editing mode will appear.

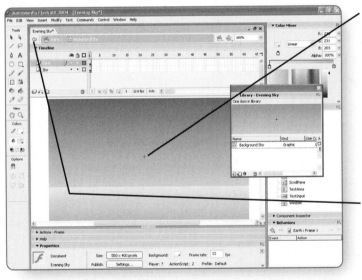

6. Draw or import the symbol on the Stage as needed. The later section called "Converting Existing Graphics to Symbols" will explain the import process. If you want to create multiple objects and layers for the symbol, use Tools panel tools and the Timeline as desired.

7. Click on the Back to Stage button to return to the main movie Timeline. This finishes and saves the symbol.

Creating a Movie Clip Symbol

A movie clip symbol has multiple frames that run when you view the publishing preview or the exported movie. You work in the symbol-editing mode to create a movie clip symbol, as follows:

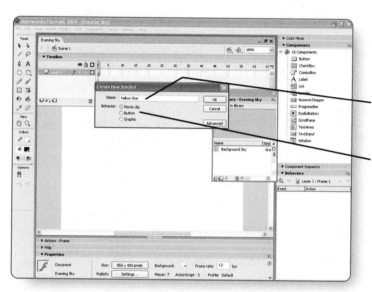

1. Click on Insert, New Symbol. The Create New Symbol dialog box will open.

2. Enter a name for the symbol in the Name text box.

3. Click on the Movie clip option button in the Behavior area.

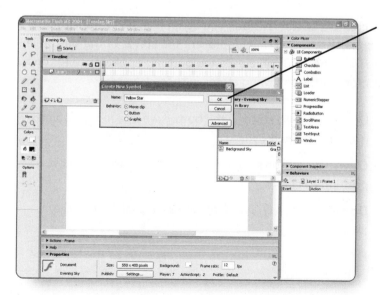

4. Click on OK. The symbol-editing mode will appear.

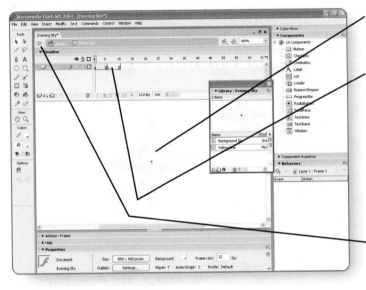

5. Draw or import the symbol on the Stage as needed.

6. Add frames and animation as needed. Chapters 6, 7, and 8 will provide details about creating animation in a movie. In this case, the movie clip symbol has a four-pointed star that will appear for five frames and then disappear for five frames.

7. Click on the Back to Stage button to return to the main movie Timeline. This finishes and saves the symbol.

Creating a Button Symbol

Buttons enable you to add user interactivity to a Flash movie. They can be used for navigation, changing the screen as in a rollover, or submitting information.

To create a button symbol, you again work in symbol editing mode. Also, four frames represent the states of the button in the Timeline. You can create the button's appearance for one or more of the following states in those frames:

- **Up.** The resting state of the button when a mouse pointer is *not* positioned over it.

- **Over.** The button's appearance when mouse pointer *is* positioned over it.

- **Down.** The button's appearance as it is *clicked* by the mouse.

- **Hit.** The area of the button that *responds* to the behavior of the mouse.

Use these steps to create a new button symbol:

1. Click on Insert, New Symbol. The Create New Symbol dialog box will open.

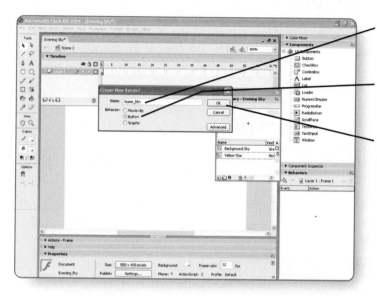

2. Enter a name for the symbol in the Name text box.

3. Click on the Button option button in the Behavior area.

4. Click on OK. The symbol-editing mode will appear.

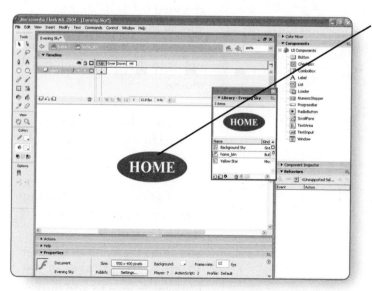

5. Draw or import the button symbol on the Stage as needed.

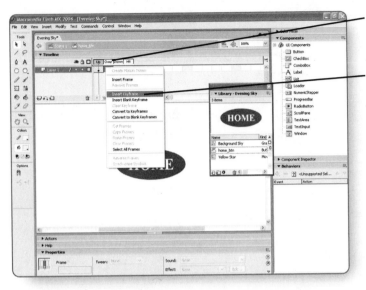

6. Right-click on the Over frame in the Timeline.

7. Click on Insert Keyframe. You can now modify the button on the Stage to specify how it will appear for the next state.

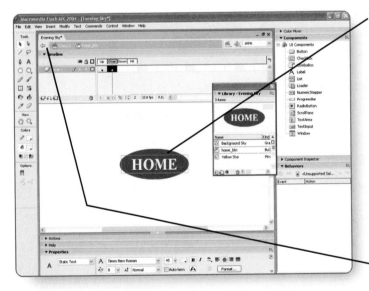

8. Edit the button's appearance as desired. You can see that in this case, I've changed the text color to specify that the button text color will change when the user points to the button with the mouse.

9. Add additional states as desired by repeating Steps 7 through 9.

10. Click on the Back to Stage button to return to the main movie Timeline. This finishes and saves the symbol. Chapter 12, "Using Simple ActionScript," will explain how to add the user interactivity to the button symbol.

Converting Existing Graphics to Symbols

There will likely be times when you want to use a graphic file already created outside of Flash. Flash enables you to import that artwork easily and give it the functionality of a symbol. Flash provides many methods for the conversion process, enabling you to convert objects created in Flash to symbols, as well as groups of objects on the Stage.

NOTE

Flash MX 2004 now supports all PostScript formats, including .PDF and .EPS, enabling you to import more types of graphic files for use as symbols in a Flash movie.

Importing an Existing Graphic as a Symbol

As mentioned, you can import an existing graphic (such as a JPEG or GIF file, or a graphic created in Fireworks) into your movie as a symbol. When you consider the role of Flash movies on the Web, however, large files do not make sense. Although the option of importing sophisticated graphics may be useful, do so sparingly.

Use the following steps to import a graphic, either when creating the movie or when working in symbol-editing mode:

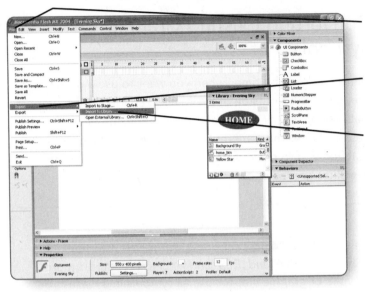

1. Click on File. The File menu will appear.

2. Point to Import. The Import submenu will appear.

3. Click on Import to Library (or Import to Stage if you're working in symbol-editing mode). The Import to Library dialog box will appear.

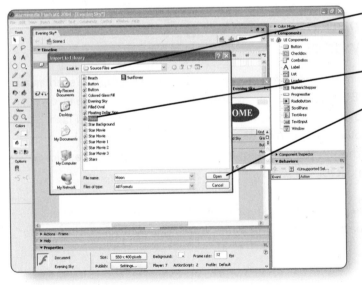

4. Navigate to the folder that holds the file to import.

5. Click on the file.

6. Click on Open. An Import Settings dialog box may appear, depending on the file format of the file being imported.

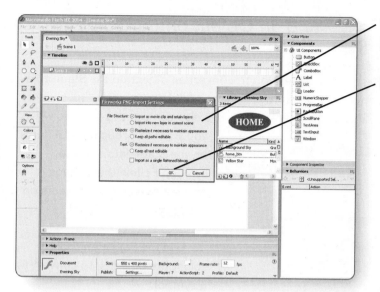

7. Choose import settings as desired.

8. Click on OK.

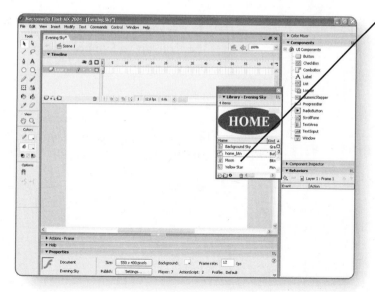

The newly-imported symbol will appear in the Library panel.

Converting an Object on the Stage to a Symbol

Flash also enables you to convert an object on the Stage to a symbol. This feature can be helpful if you miss the initial step of inserting a new symbol. You also can use this process when you want to group several items on the Stage into a single symbol. Follow these steps to convert one or more objects on the Stage into a symbol.

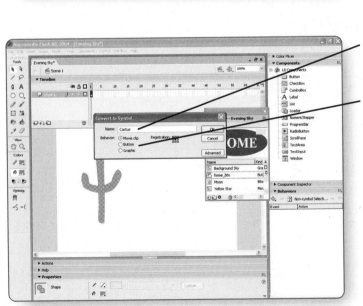

1. Use the Selection tool to select the object(s) to convert to a symbol.

2. Right-click on the selection.

3. Click on Convert to Symbol. The Convert to Symbol dialog box will open.

4. Type a name for the symbol into the Name text box.

5. Click on the desired Behavior option.

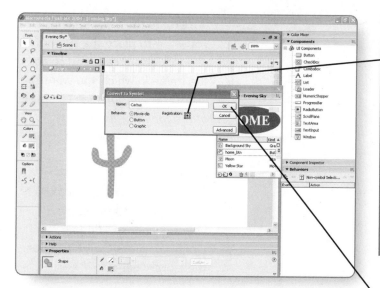

NOTE

If you wish, you also can click on an alternate Registration point, or *anchor*. When you drag the symbol, it moves from its registration point. The Free Transform tool also uses the registration point for rotation. Motion guides use it to lock on the desired path.

6. Click on OK. The new symbol will be added to the Library. The original object will remain in place on the Stage.

Adding a Symbol to the Movie Stage

After you've added a symbol to the Library by using your preferred method, you can then use the symbol in your movie. Each time you add a symbol from the Library panel to the Stage, you are creating an *instance* of the symbol. You can create as many instances of a symbol as desired in a movie.

Adding a symbol to the Stage is a simple matter of dragging the symbol from the Library panel to the desired location, as illustrated in the following steps:

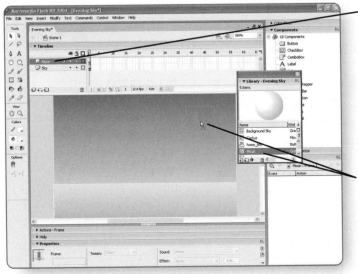

1. Create the layer on which you want to place the symbol. If needed, also create and select the frame in which you want to insert the symbol. (See Chapters 6 through 8 for more on working with frames and animation.)

2. Drag the symbol from the Library panel to the stage. (If needed, choose Window, Library or press Ctrl+L to open the Library panel.)

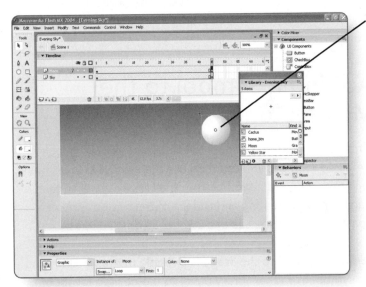

3. Position the symbol instance as desired. You also can use the Free Transform tool to resize and reshape the instance. These types of changes do not affect the size and shape of the original symbol.

NOTE

A movie clip symbol will loop (playback) repeatedly for the number of frames you include in the main movie Timeline. Therefore, if you want the clip to play back only once, place it on its own layer. Insert it on a frame, and then add only the number of frames contained in the symbol itself on the Timeline. The movie clip symbol will then run once and stop playing when it runs out of frames on its layer in the main movie.

Previewing Movie Clip Symbols in a Movie

To preview the movie that you're building within Flash, you can press Enter. The playback head will start from the currently selected frame and play back the movie. If you use this method, however, you will see that the movie clip symbols you've inserted on the Stage do not play back. That's because they have their own Timeline, independent of that for the Stage. To preview how movie clip symbols will play back, you must preview the finished, published movie by using the following steps:

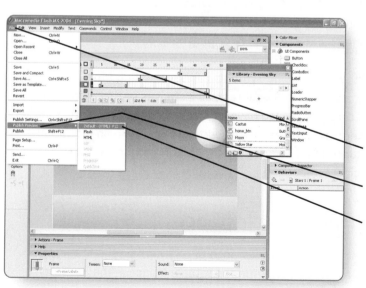

1. Click on File.

2. Point to Publish Preview.

3. Click on Default.

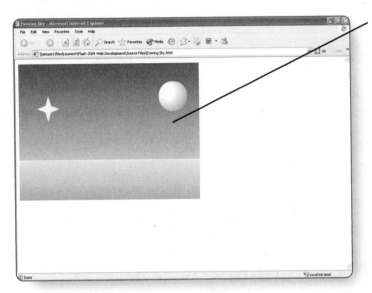

The movie will play back in your system's Web browser, previewing the movie clip symbol playback.

Editing Symbols and Instances

When you drag a symbol from the Library and place it on the Stage, you have created an instance of that symbol. Using instances helps to reduce movie file size because Flash downloads the entire symbol only once and uses smaller bits of information to display or play back each instance.

Furthermore, using symbols can save editing time. After you edit a symbol in the Library, all instances of that symbol reflect the changes, so you have to make changes only once. On the other hand, you can make certain changes to an individual instance of a symbol without affecting other instances or the original symbol.

Changing an Instance

When you select an instance of a symbol on the Stage, you can change some settings for the instance in the Property Inspector:

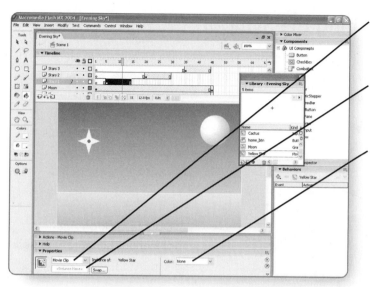

- **Behavior**. Select a new behavior (symbol type) from this pop-up menu.

- **Name**. Enter a name for the individual instance of the symbol in this text box.

- **Color Blending**. Choose a blending mode from this pop-up menu.

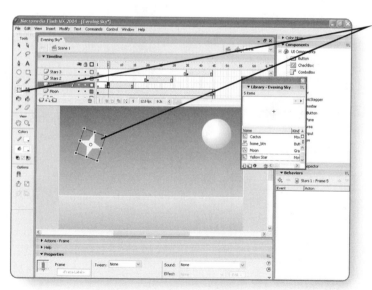

You also can use the Free Transform tool to skew, rotate, or scale an instance without affecting the original symbol or other instances.

Editing the Symbol

Editing a symbol itself causes changes to appear in all instances of the symbol throughout the movie. Follow these steps to edit a symbol:

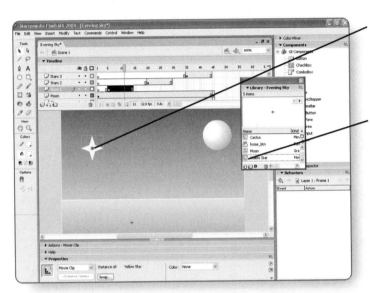

1a. Double-click on a symbol instance on the Stage.

OR

1b. Double-click on the symbol icon in the Library panel.

OR

1c. Click on the Edit Symbols button, and then click on the symbol to edit.

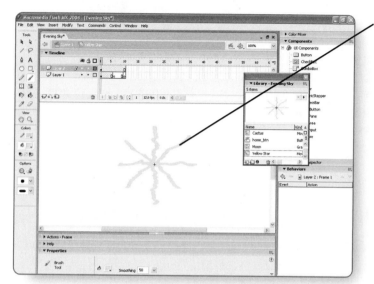

2. Make the desired changes to the symbol in the symbol-editing mode.

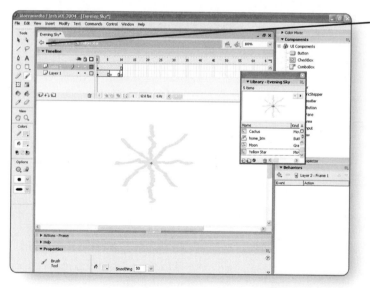

3. Click on the Back to Stage button. The symbol changes will appear throughout the main movie.

> **NOTE**
>
> If you right-click on a symbol, the shortcut menu presents three editing choices. Edit opens symbol-editing mode as usual. Edit in Place enables you to edit the symbol on the main stage. Edit in New Window opens a separate window for editing the symbol.

Organizing Symbols with the Library

The Library serves primarily to store all your symbols and let you check out instances of them. It can also store other objects, such as embedded sound or video, which you'll learn about in later chapters. Essentially, the Library enables you to view all the movie assets at a glance.

You can create folders in the Library to organize symbols and other objects, just as you create folders on your computer to organize files, as follows:

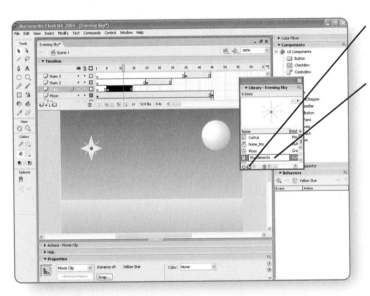

1. Click on the New Folder button on the Library panel.

2. Type a new folder name and press Enter.

3. Drag the desired symbols in the list in the Library panel onto the new folder.

Copying Symbols between Libraries

You may also copy or share library assets between movies. To do so:

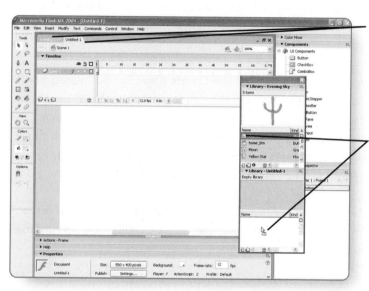

1. Open both movie files and the Library panel. If needed, resize the Library panel so that you can see the assets for both movies.

2. Drag a symbol or other asset from one file's Library to the other. When you release the mouse button, the asset will be copied to the second library.

Using a Common Library

For your convenience, Flash also includes some *common libraries* that offer predefined buttons, sounds, and other elements.

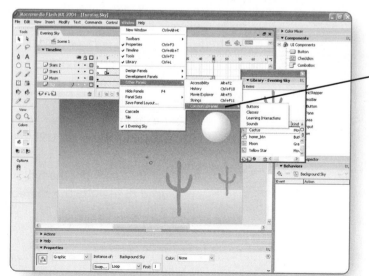

To access the symbols and other elements in a common library, choose Window, Other Panels, Common Libraries; then click on the library to open.

Working with a Shared Library

Using a shared library enables you to use items from one library in several different movies, cutting down on development time and improving efficiency. You can share items from the Library in two ways: runtime and author-time sharing.

If you click Advanced on the Create New Symbol dialog box (or click on a symbol and then click on the Symbol Properties button in the Library panel and then click on the Advanced button in the Symbol Properties dialog box), two of the check boxes that appear are Export for runtime sharing and Import for runtime sharing. In runtime sharing, the item has an absolute location and can be accessed outside the local network. If you are working on a project with a remote team member in Alaska, for example, you can still share via runtime sharing.

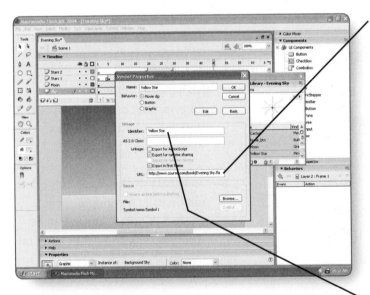

When you check either the Export for runtime sharing or Import for runtime sharing check box to enable runtime sharing, the URL text box becomes active. Enter the address (location) where the file holding the shared symbol will be stored. You can enter a relative (\\servername\ foldername\filename) or absolute (as in http://www. fast&easy.com/filename) URL.

Also edit the Identifier (name) entry used to identify the shared symbol as desired.

When you are sharing assets, note that Flash has a feature that resolves library conflicts. If a library item is being copied to a Flash file that already has an item designated by that name, you can choose whether you want to replace the current item with the new item.

NOTE

Flash does enable you to create a common library for the assets used in your movie. To do so, place the Flash file holding the assets \First Run\Libraries folder of the folder in which you installed the Flash application. The next time you start Flash, you can choose Window, Other Panels, Common Libraries and then click on the name of the copied file to access the new common library.

PART II

Motion and Sound

This section shows you how to add animation (movement) in Flash MX 2004 movies. After you learn to create animation on a frame-by-frame basis, you will see how to save time and add sophistication by using motion tweening, shape tweening, and masking. Finally, you will add sound to enhance a Flash movie and learn the information you need to make educated decisions about when and how to use sound.

6

Creating Basic Animation

The chapters up to this point in the book have focused primarily on creating static content—placing and arranging objects on the Stage and on layers. This chapter introduces you to the concepts that will get your movie moving—the basics of frames and animation. This chapter teaches you to to the following:

- How animation is created in Flash MX 2004.
- What a frame is.
- How to add a frame to a movie.
- How to create simple frame-by-frame animations.

What Is an Animation?

An animation shows a series of pictures in rapid sequence, creating the appearance of live movement. Both cartoon and traditional movies consist of thousands and thousands of pictures shown for a fraction of a second each. Because the human mind holds an afterimage of each picture for the fraction of a second until the next picture appears, your mind thinks the series of images form a continuous whole, with motion. Once this scientific concept was understood in the late 1880s, simple movies became possible.

Before the advent of computers, creating animation was a tedious process involving large numbers of cartoonists and artists. A picture, or animation cell, was created, and then a second cell, almost identical to the first, was created. The differences between the two cells were subtle. Another cell was drawn and then another and another. Because most animated cartoons and movies are shown at a rate of 12 to 45 pictures per second (if not faster), a single half-hour cartoon contained at least 21,600 separate pictures. The completed cells were transferred to film, the film was then placed in a projector, and the tireless efforts of the animation staff were finally shown on the screen.

Thankfully, computers and software have simplified this process a great deal. Flash MX 2004 helps you create movies in a number of ways. However, to fully appreciate the tools Flash offers, you should create a movie the "old-fashioned way" first.

What Is a Frame?

You can think of a frame as an individual picture, or animation cell, in an animation. Treat each frame in Flash almost like its real-world counterpart. All the objects in your movie reside in frames. You can add two types of frames in a Flash movie: keyframes and frames. Flash uses a keyframe as a marker in an animation; a keyframe indicates a change in the animation, such as an object jumping from one location to another on the Stage. Keyframes hold most of the items in an animation. Frames, which fill the areas between keyframes, either hold content identical to the keyframe that precedes them in the Timeline or display subtle content changes created by the built-in animation tools.

You can identify both frames and keyframes on the Timeline:

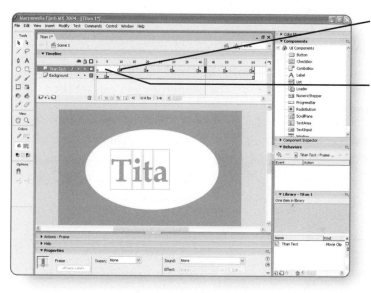

- Each keyframes in the Timeline has a black circle in it.

- Empty frames are white with a black border on the top and bottom.

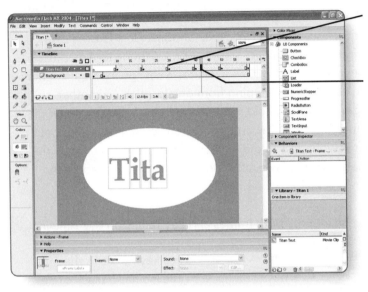

• The last frame in the group defined by the prior keyframe has a white rectangle in it.

• A black highlight appears around the selected frame.

When you select a frame in the Timeline, its properties appear in the Property Inspector. The properties you can set for a frame there include:

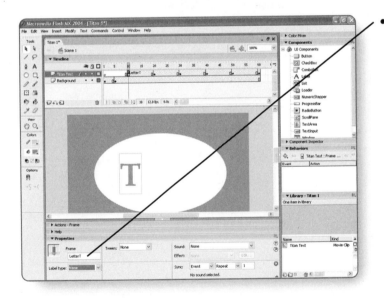

• The Frame Label text box enables you to enter a frame label that can be referenced from ActionScript. (See Chapter 12, "Using Simple ActionScript," to learn about scripting.) Labels also help with organizing movies by showing breakpoints or even things that need to be done. When you've added a label for a frame, a red flag appears in the frame in the Timeline. If enough space appears between a labeled keyframe and the next keyframe, the label appears in the Timeline. If not, point to the flag with the mouse to display a pop-up tip with the label.

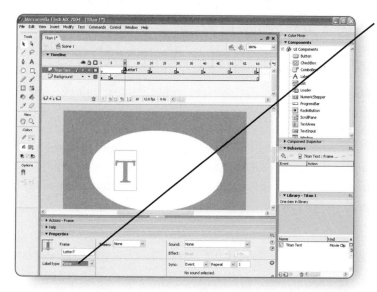

- Once you've entered a frame label, choose a Label Type here. (Choose Anchor if you need to reference the frame via a URL call.)

NOTE

If you don't see al the frame properties at first, click on the Expand/collapse the information area (arrow) button in the lower-right corner of the Property Inspector.

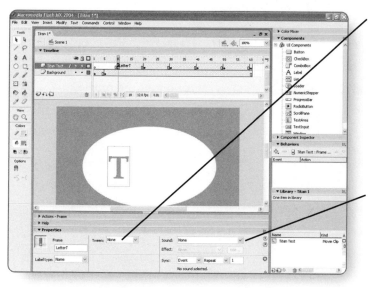

- The Tween list shows the type of animation that is filled in between keyframes by Flash. Chapter 7, "Animation with Motion Tweening," and Chapter 8, "Animation with Shape Tweening" cover the types of tweening you can apply.

- Properties for adding a sound for the frame appear at the right of the Properties panel. See Chapter 10, "Adding Sound and Embedded Video," for information on sounds in Flash.

How Do You Create Simple Frame-by-Frame Animations?

You build a simple animation by creating frames, objects, and keyframes to indicate changes in an object's position or formatting. Creating a simple animation will help familiarize you with manipulating the Timeline and also show the tedious nature of old-fashioned animation. The rest of this section breaks out the key aspects of creating a basic animation using manual techniques.

Creating the Movie

The animation process begins with a single movie, frame, and layer. In the example I show throughout this section, I'll be creating a simple animation that flashes the letter O and then the letter K.

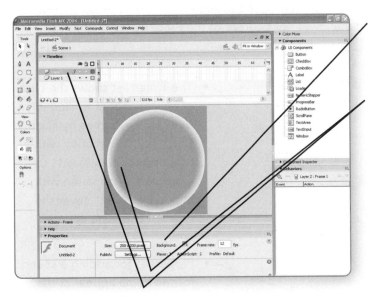

1. Create a new movie file by using the dimensions and background color you want.

2. Create a layer and add any background objects that you want. These objects will appear throughout the movie.

Adding Content and Keyframes

Once you've established the background contents for your movie, you can add the object(s) to animate. For greatest control, create each object on its own layer in the movie file. This will enable you to animate each object separately as needed.

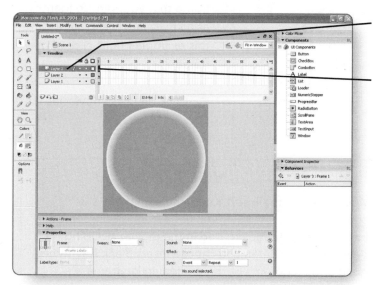

1. Add a layer for the object to animate.

2. Click on frame 1 in the Timeline.

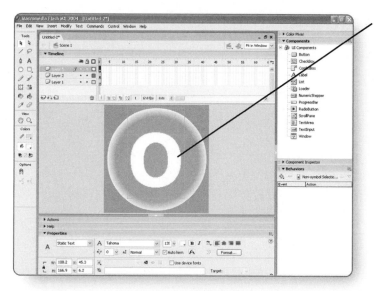

3. Use Tools from the Tools panel to add the desired content on frame 1. In this case, I used the Text tool to add the letter O.

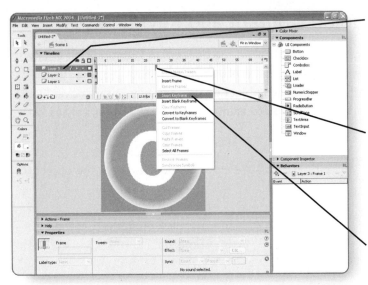

4. Leave the layer to animate selected in the Timeline. (Otherwise, you could click on another layer to which you wanted to add a keyframe.)

5. Right-click on the later frame that you want to identify as a keyframe. For example, in this example I right-clicked on frame 24.

6. Click on Insert Keyframe.

NOTE

When you use the Insert Keyframe command, the contents of the last keyframe are automatically copied into each new frame created in the movie, including the new keyframe. When you choose Insert Blank Keyframe, none of the contents of the preceding keyframe are copied into the new keyframe, but they are copied into the frames between keyframes.

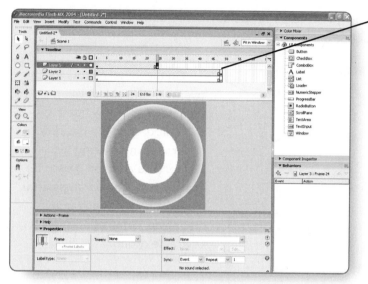

7. Select other layers as needed, and repeat Steps 5 and 6 to add keyframes for them, as well, so that their content will extend for the desired number of frames. In this case, I've added keyframes for Layers 2 and 3 at frame 48 to make the movie longer. Next, I'll go back and change the content on Layer 3 for frames 25 through 48.

Using Frames and Keyframes to Control Motion Changes

As noted earlier, the primary purpose of a keyframe is to enable you to introduce a change in the content on a layer. That is, the layer's contents remain the same in every frame until the next keyframe. Starting with that keyframe, the layer's contents change to something different: different formatting, a different size, a different position, or even a different object altogether.

In contrast, you typically insert one or more regular frames between keyframes or to define the end of the layer's action (by inserting regular frames after the final keyframe on a layer). Doing so increases the number of frames between the keyframes, thus extending the length of time the movie shows the particular content defined between the keyframes.

Follow these steps to use keyframes and frames to control action in a movie:

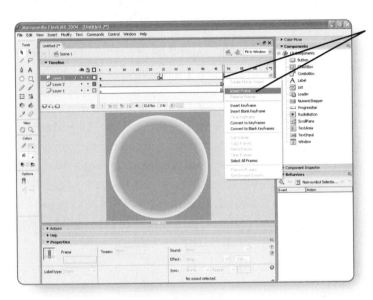

1. On the Timeline row for the layer with the object to animate, add a new frame by right-clicking on the desired end frame and clicking Insert Frame. (You also can press F5.) This will insert new frames after the existing final keyframe in the movie, completing the keyframe group.

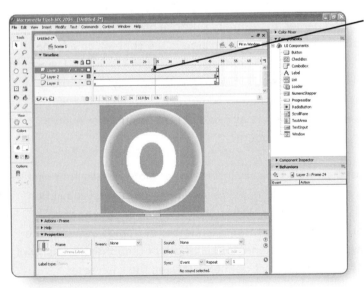

2. Click on the keyframe to the left of the frames you just inserted in the Timeline. Remember, a keyframe has a black circle in it, to help you click on the proper frame.

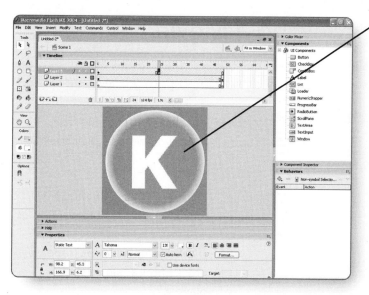

3. Use Tools from the Tools panel to change the content in the frame as desired. In this case, I used the Text tool to change the letter O to K. The change will be applied to all the frames from that keyframe through the next keyframe in the movie (or the end of the movie, in this case). You could move the object on the layer, reformat the object, or delete the object and insert another. Any of these changes will create the appearance of movement in the movie.

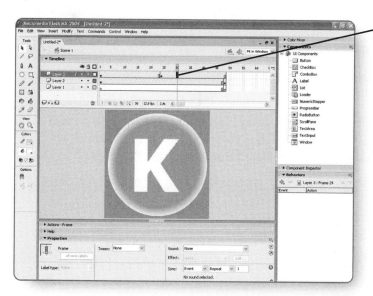

4. To verify that the change has been applied to the keyframe group, click on another frame to the right of the keyframe.

NOTE

To insert more frames within a keyframe group, select one or more frames and then press F5.

NOTE

If basic animations like this seem too simple for you, relax. Chapters 7 and 8 get into more sophisticated techniques like motion and shape tweening.

Previewing a Movie

Flash enables you to perform a simple preview of your movie right on the Stage. Follow these steps to preview your movie:

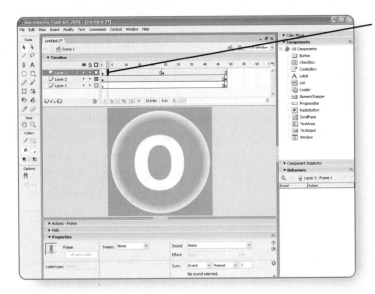

1. Click on the frame from which you want to play back the movie.

2. Press Enter. The movie will play back on the Stage.

3. If the movie loops (repeats), press Enter again to stop playback.

TIP

Choose Control, Loop Playback to turn looping on and off. If playback doesn't work at all, choose Control, Enable Live Preview to turn it back on.

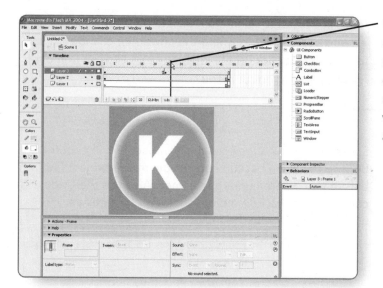

If you want a more slowly controlled playback, drag the red playback head along the top of the Timeline (where the numbers are). A heavy black line will appear on the current frame as you drag.

Troubleshooting Simple Animation

Now that you've previewed the movie, you should have a pretty good idea of what's working and what's not. Here are some troubleshooting tips to help you correct issues in your movie:

- *A movie clip symbol didn't play.* Movie clip symbols require a different preview method. See "Previewing Movie Clip Symbols in a Movie" in Chapter 5.

- *The last frame on a layer didn't play.* This might be because you inserted a blank keyframe rather than a regular frame or keyframe. Right-click on the frame and choose Convert to Keyframe. This will likely correct the problem.

- *The background image disappears.* This probably means you didn't add enough frames to the layer holding the background image. Add frames through the same frame number as the final frame on other layers in the movie.

- *There is unwanted animation.* Delete the keyframe at the left end of the section where the unwanted change occurs. To do so, right-click on the keyframe and click on Remove Frames in the shortcut menu.

CAUTION

Some of these changes can really impact movie content. Be sure to save a backup copy of the movie project file before you delete numerous frames. Also use the Undo command on the Edit menu if a deletion creates an unwanted change in the movie.

7

Animation with Motion Tweening

In the last chapter, you learned how to create animation manually by adding keyframes and moving or editing the stage content in them. In this chapter, you will learn how to use motion tweening and other techniques to add more sophisticated animation in a Flash MX 2004 movie. In this chapter, you will learn how to do the following:

- Understand the motion tweening feature.
- Apply different types of motion tweens.
- Tween from one color setting to another.
- Animate an object along a custom path.

Understanding Motion Tweening

The term *tweening* is short for "in be*tween*." When Flash MX 2004 tweens an object between two keyframes, it calculates how the content on the tweened layer should change for each frame between the two keyframes. This saves work and results in a more smooth and realistic animation.

When you apply a *motion tween*, Flash calculates how an object on the Stage (for the selected layer) should move from one location to another between keyframes. Basically, you can create the first keyframe, add the object to tween, create another keyframe on the same layer, move the object to the desired end location, and apply the motion tween. Flash will calculate the object's positioning for each frame in between the two keyframes.

Creating a Motion Tween for a Layer

You work on a single layer in your movie project file to create a motion tween. You should include only a single object or symbol on each layer you plan to tween. This object will become the *tweened object*. If you create a motion tween by using an objects that is not a symbol, Flash creates a symbol in the library for you; and from that point, you are editing only instances of that symbol (also know as the tweened object in this case) when you work with the tween.

By adding a single object to each tweened layer, you retain greater control over each tween in the movie file. The following steps show you how to create a motion tween for a symbol on a layer.

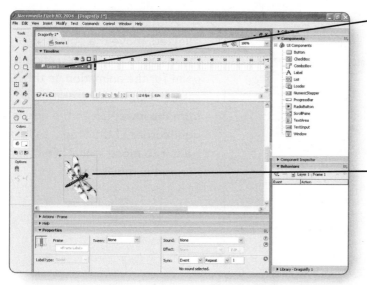

1. Create a new layer to hold the object to animate, if desired. If you want the animation to start at a frame other than frame 1, create a keyframe at the desired starting point and leave that keyframe selected.

2. Add or create an object on the Stage in the keyframe (frame 1 in this case). Position the object in the desired starting point for the animation on the Stage.

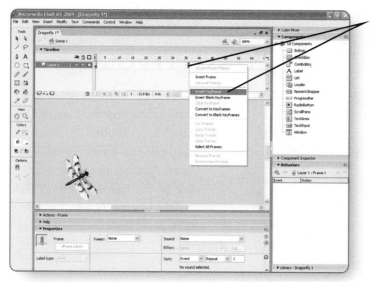

3. Insert a new keyframe for the layer at the frame where you want the animation to end. This example shows a keyframe being inserted at frame 36.

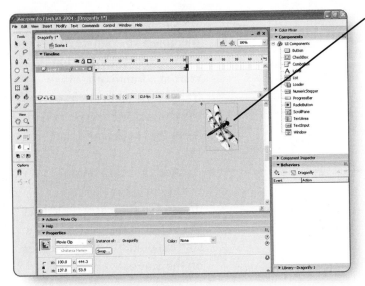

4. With the new keyframe still selected, move the object on the Stage to the desired ending point for the animation. In this case, I've moved the dragonfly from the lower-left to the upper-right corner of the Stage, as I want it to move in that direction during the movie.

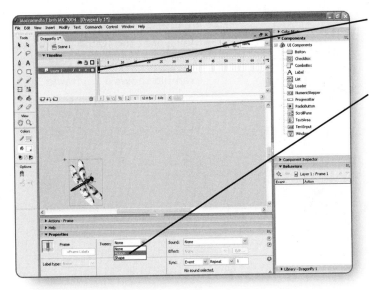

5. Click on the previous keyframe in the Timeline (in this case, frame 1).

6. Open the Tween drop-down menu in the Property Inspector and click on Motion. You also could choose Insert, Timeline, Create Motion Tween or right-click on the frame and then click on Add Motion Tween.

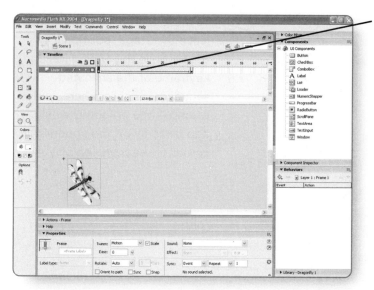

The frames between the two keyframes will turn blue and will include a long arrow. These changes indicate that the motion tween has been created.

7. Press Enter to watch your new animation.

NOTE

You can use motion tweening to make an object appear to enter and/or leave the Stage. To do so, zoom out on the Stage so that you can see the gray working area around it. To make an object enter the Stage, position it off the Stage in the starting (first) keyframe of the animated sequence.

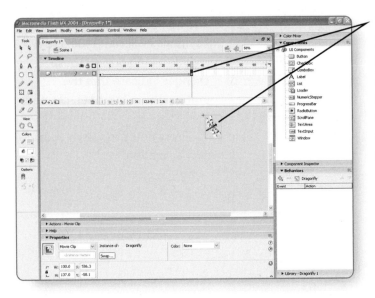

To make the object appear to leave the Stage, position it off the Stage in the ending (second) keyframe of the animated sequence, as shown here. In this example, the dragonfly would appear to fly off the upper-right corner of the Stage on playback.

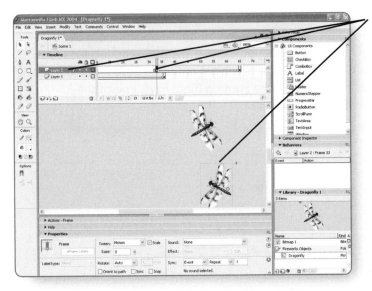

Repeat the previous steps to animate additional individual objects in your movie. Here, I've added a second layer. I inserted a keyframe at frame 33 of the new layer and added a second dragonfly to appear in the lower-right of that frame. I then inserted a second keyframe at frame 65 and moved the dragonfly to the upper-left corner of that frame. I then reselected the frame 33 keyframe, and selected Motion from the Tween drop-down menu.

TIP

Remember, you can click on the first frame in a movie in the Timeline and then press Enter to preview the movie at any time.

Applying Motion Tween Effects

You used the Property Inspector to apply a motion tween to a frame group between two keyframes. The Property Inspector offers additional settings you can apply when you establish the tween. You also can click on a frame in the tween (either the starting keyframe or one of the later frames) to change the tween effect settings at a later time. These settings apply additional effects to the motion tween, including the following:

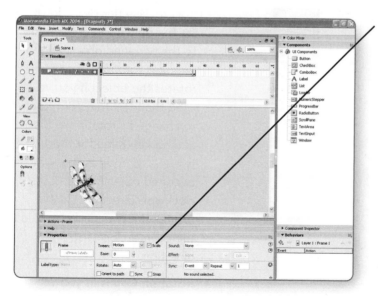

- **Scale**. When the Scale check box is checked, the tween will resize the layer object from the starting keyframe to the ending keyframe. Use the Free Transform tool to size the object to the desired initial size in the tween's starting keyframe and the desired final size in the tween's ending keyframe. The object will transition from the initial size to the starting size when you play back the tweened frames.

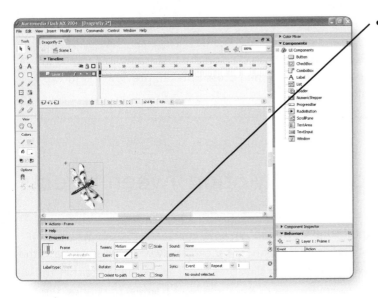

- **Ease**. The Ease value you enter determines the rate of change for the tween. All tweens use the available frames and proceed at a steady rate by default. Enter 0 in the Ease text box for this constant rate of change. To have the tween begin slowly and accelerate, enter a value from -100 to -1. To have the tween begin quickly and slow toward the end, enter a value between 1 and 100.

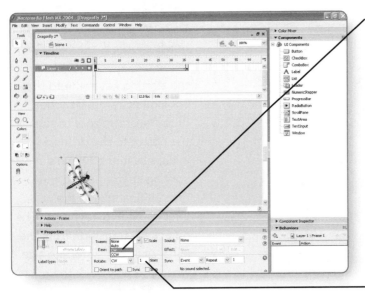

- **Rotate**. Use this drop-down list to apply a rotation setting to the tweened object. None removes rotation. Auto rotates the object if you've used the Free Transform tool to change its rotation in the ending keyframe for the tween. CW rotates the tweened object in the clockwise direction. CCW rotates the tweened object in the counterclockwise direction.

- **Rotation Count**. If you've applied the CW or CCW Rotate choice, enter the number of full (360-degree) rotations the object should make during the tween into this text box.

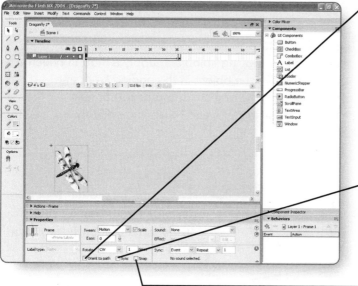

- **Orient to Path**. Check this option, which is used with motion guides, to tell Flash to orient which direction is up relative to the motion guide. See the later section called "Animating an Object along a Motion Guide" to learn more about this option.

- **Sync**. If you've inserted a movie clip symbol in the tween, check this option to synchronize its frame rate to the Timeline.

- **Snap**. When this option is checked, the tweened object will attach itself to the motion guide after you drag the object close enough to the guide.

Now that you've reviewed the available tween effects, take time to review how to use each one in greater detail.

Resizing an Object in a Motion Tween

Adjusting a motion tween to resize the tweened object only adds a few steps to the overall process of creating a tween. You can specify that the tweened object will become larger or smaller over the course of the tween and control the size of the tweened object. The following steps illustrate how to resize an object during a motion tween.

TIP

To resize or rotate an object during a sequence of frames without moving an object, apply a motion tween but do not move the object in the ending keyframe. Instead, change the object's sizing or rotation as described in these steps and those immediately following.

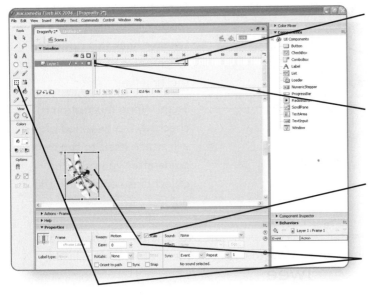

1. Create the motion tween as described in the earlier section "Creating a Motion Tween for a Layer."

2. Click on the starting keyframe (in this example, frame 1) for the tween in the Timeline.

3. Make sure that the Scale check box is checked in the Property Inspector.

4. Use the Free Transform tool to size the object as desired. The size you specify will be the object's initial size for the tweened sequence.

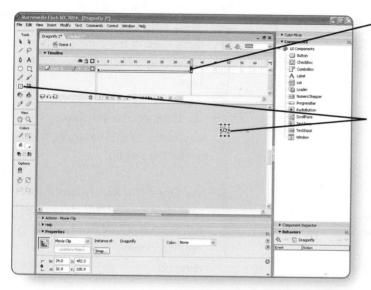

5. Click on the ending keyframe (in this example, frame 36) for the tween in the Timeline.

6. Use the Free Transform tool to size the object as desired. The size you specify will be the object's final size for the tweened sequence. In this example, I've resized the dragonfly to a much smaller size. When the tweened sequence plays back, the dragonfly will get smaller and thus appear to be moving away.

TIP

You could also skew the object if desired.

Rotating an Object with a Motion Tween

When you create or work with a motion tween, you can apply rotation to the object in addition to motion and/or scaling. Follow these steps to enhance a motion tween by rotating the tweened object:

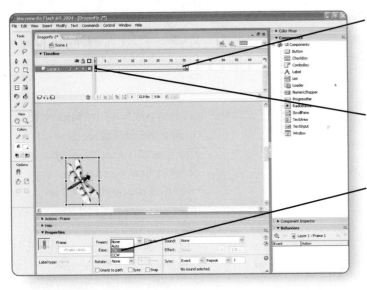

1. Create the motion tween as described in the earlier section "Creating a Motion Tween for a Layer."

2. Click on the starting keyframe (in this example, frame 1) for the tween.

3. Open the Rotate drop-down and click on CW (for clockwise rotation) or CCW (for counterclockwise rotation) as desired.

NOTE

If you select the Auto choice from the Rotate drop-down list, skip step 4. Instead, click on the ending keyframe and use the Free Transform tool to rotate the object to the desired ending position.

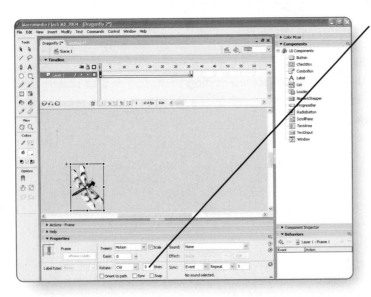

4. Select the value in the Rotation Count text box in the Property Inspector and type a whole number to specify the number of times the object should rotate during playback.

TIP

Don't forget that you can use the Ease setting along with movement, size, and rotation changes to further control the appearance of a motion tween.

Applying Other Transform Settings with a Motion Tween

In addition to using the Free Transform tool to apply a size or skew transform to a tweened object, you can use the Transform panel to apply additional transform settings or to apply a transform with greater precision.

Open the Transform panel by choosing Window, Design Panels, Transform or pressing Ctrl+T (⌘+T on the Mac). This panel contains eight settings you can apply to transform a selected object (whether it's part of a tween or not):

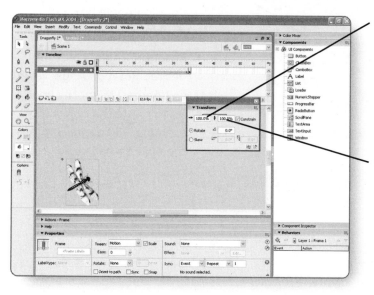

- **Width**. Enter a new width for the object as a percentage of the original width. Values greater than 100 percent expand the object, and values smaller than 100 percent shrink it.

- **Height**. Enter a new height for the object as a percentage of the original height.

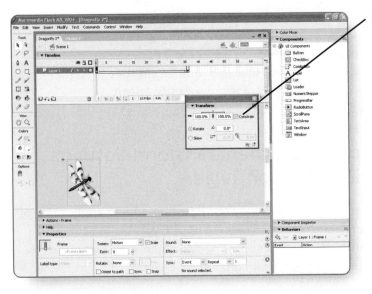

- **Constrain**. When the Constrain check box is checked, the Height and Width values must be the same value, to prevent distorting the object's proportions. When this option is not checked, you may enter different values in the Width and Height text boxes.

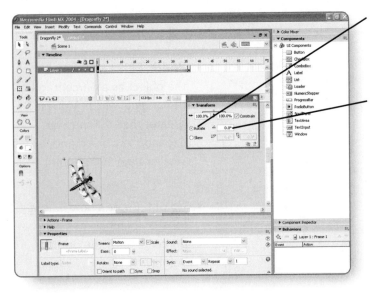

- **Rotate**. Clicking on this option button enables the Rotation Angle box and disables the skew options.

- **Rotation Angle**. Enter the desired Rotation Angle value (in degrees) to specify how far to rotate the object. For example, 180 degrees rotates the object a half-circle.

CAUTION

Applying rotation in this way rotates the object only in the final frame of the tween. If you want to rotate the object more slowly throughout the tween, use the Property inspector to apply the rotation, instead.

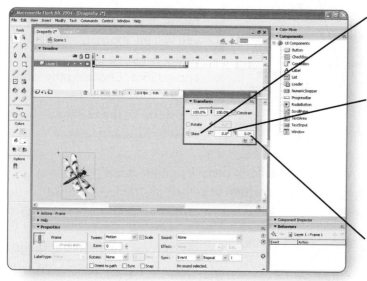

- **Skew.** Clicking on this option button enables the Skew Angle boxes and disables the rotation options.

- **Skew horizontally.** Enter an angle value (in degrees) in this text box to skew the object horizontally. Negative values lean the object to the left, and positive values tilt it to the right.

- **Skew Vertically.** Enter an angle value (in degrees) in this text box to skew the object vertically. Negative values bump the object up, and positive values tilt it down.

Now, see how to use the Transform panel with a tweened object. The following steps provide an example.

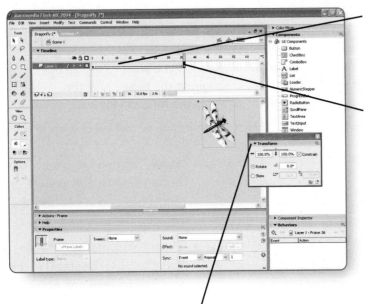

1. Create the motion tween as described in the earlier section "Creating a Motion Tween for a Layer."

2. Click on either the starting or ending keyframe (in this example, frame 36) for the tween. If you select the former, you will be applying a transform to the tweened object's initial appearance. Choosing the latter means you'll apply the transform to the tweened object's final appearance.

3. Open the Transform panel by either choosing Window, Design Panels, Transform or pressing Ctrl+T or (⌘+T on the Mac).

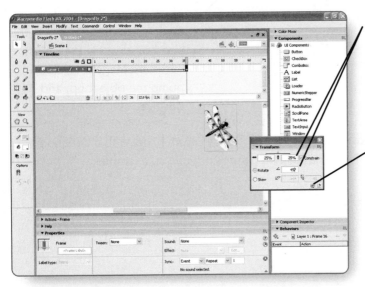

4. Specify the desired settings in the Transform panel. The settings in this example will make the dragonfly 25% of its original height and width and will rotate it by 45°.

5. Click on the Copy and apply transform button in the lower-right corner of the Transform panel. The tweened object will be copied, and the transform will be applied to the copy.

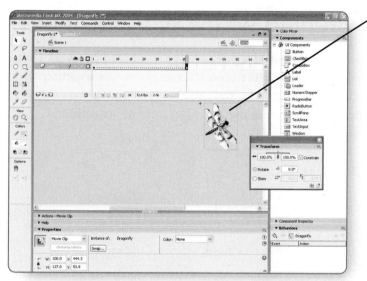

6. Use the Selection tool to select the original copy of the object.

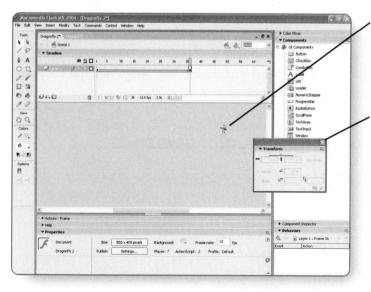

7. Press Delete. The original copy of the object will be deleted from the keyframe, leaving the transformed copy.

8. Click on the Transform panel window's close button. The Transform panel will close.

Tweening with Color Settings

After you've created a motion tween, you also can work with a symbol instance on the Stage to tween the Color setting in the Property Inspector. You can change the instance's Color property from one of the available settings, listed below, to another:

- Brightness

- Tint

- Alpha

- Any or all of these options, via the Custom option

Changing colors in motion tweens is somewhat limited because motion tweens can deal with only symbols and instances. However, you can tween the Color setting to achieve realistic effects. For example, you can change the instance's Alpha value to make the instance fade during movie playback. Couple that with making the object smaller, and the object will really appear to be moving away from the viewing and eventually disappearing in the distance.

Applying the Color Tween

The steps for applying a color tween are basically the same, no matter what type of color tween you want to apply, as follows:

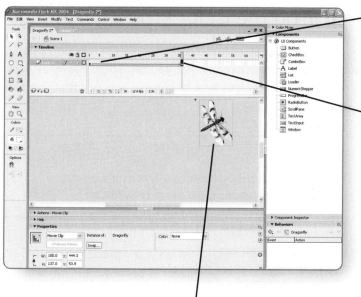

1. Create the motion tween as described in the earlier section "Creating a Motion Tween for a Layer."

2. Click on either the starting or ending keyframe (in this example, frame 36) for the tween. If you select the former, you will be applying a color change to the tweened symbol's initial appearance. Choosing the latter means you'll apply the transform to the tweened symbol's final appearance.

3. Use the Selection tool to select the instance on the Stage. The Property Inspector will display settings for that instance of the symbol.

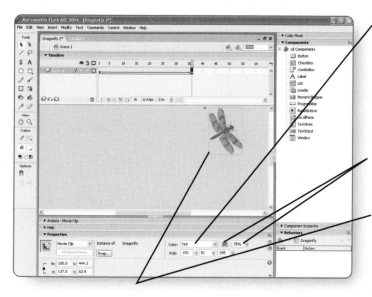

4. Open the Color drop-down list in the Property Inspector and click on the color property that you'd like to change during the tween. The specific settings for that property will appear.

5. Change color property settings as desired.

In this instance, I've used the Tint color property to add a strong purple tint to the dragonfly that will gradually gain strength until the end of the tweened sequence.

Examining the Color Property Settings

The previous steps illustrated tweening a symbol's tint. But, there are other color tweens that you can apply. Now review each of the Color choices and its specific settings that you can apply during a tween.

TIP

The settings described here also work for objects, symbols, and instances that aren't tweened.

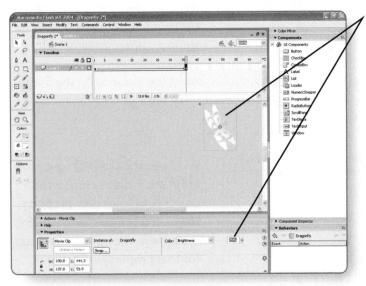

When you choose Tint from the Color drop-down list, several additional settings appear:

- **Tint Selector**. Click on this box and then click on the color to apply as the tint in the palette that appears. Flash will add the object's existing color and the color you select together. Point to a color swatch in the palette for a preview of what the resulting color will look like.

- **Tint Amount**. Enter a percentage value to specify how strong a tint to apply. A value of 0 leaves the instance unchanged, and a value of 100 percent completely covers the instance with the newly selected color.

- **RGB**. Rather than choose the color in the Tint selector, you can enter the red, green, and blue values directly to mix a custom tint color.

NOTE

RGB values include three numbers, each between 0 and 255. The first number represents how much red is in the color; the second, how much green; and the last, how much blue. The values (0,0,0) create the color black, white is represented by (255,255,255), and gray is (128, 128, 128). Other numeric values result in different colors in the spectrum.

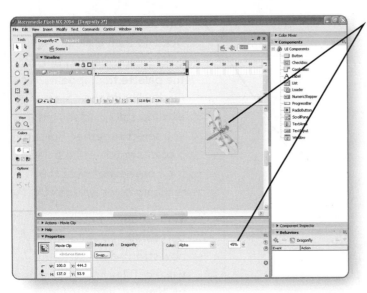

The alpha setting is not only fun to play with, but also useful. Think of the alpha setting as the object's transparency or visibility—for example, an object set to 100 percent alpha is completely opaque, and one set to 0 percent alpha is completely invisible or transparent. Using alpha settings, you can make objects fade in and out, which can be great for pop-up menus, special effects, and transitions. After you choose Alpha from the color drop-down list in the Property Inspector, specify the desired transparency setting in the Alpha Amount text box.

Changing one Color setting reverts to a previously applied setting. For example, changing the tint removes any previously applied brightness settings. Changing the alpha removes any previously applied tint, and so on. Use the Advanced color property to change both the tint and the alpha setting for an instance.

After you choose Advanced from the Color drop-down list in the Property Inspector, the Settings button will appear. Click on that button to open the Advanced Effect dialog box.

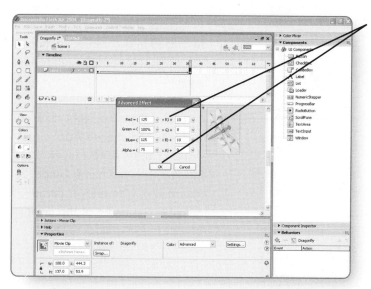

Specify changes in the Advanced Effect dialog box as desired (you can enter negative values for Red, Green, and Blue) and then click on OK. For each setting (Red, Green, Blue, and Alpha), you can enter two values: a percentage of the original value to use and a constant amount to add to that—or, more simply:

The new value = (the original value * percentage) + new number (0 ± 255)

Animating an Object Along a Motion Guide

In all the previous techniques presented in this chapter, the tweened object moved in a straight line only. However, for your movie to be more realistic, you need to be able to have tweened objects move in a curved or irregular way as you specify. To specify exactly how an object should move around during a tween, you can create a path called a *motion guide* for the object to follow during the tween. The following steps illustrate this simple process:

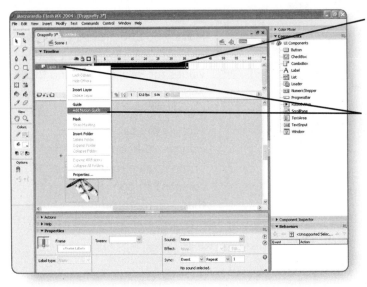

1. Create the motion tween as described in the earlier section "Creating a Motion Tween for a Layer."

2. In the Timeline, right-click on the layer and choose Add Motion Guide. A new layer appears with the name Guide: *layer name*, where *layer name* indicates the name of the layer for which you're adding the guide.

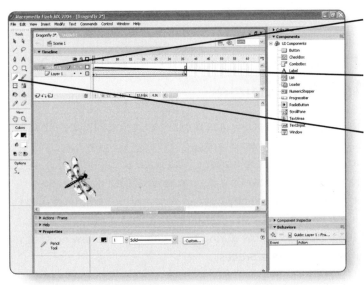

3. Click on the new guide layer in the Timeline.

4. Click on the first keyframe for the new guide layer.

5. Click on the Pencil tool in the Tools panel and choose the desired Options for the tool. You will use this tool to draw the motion guide—that is, the path that the object will follow during the tween.

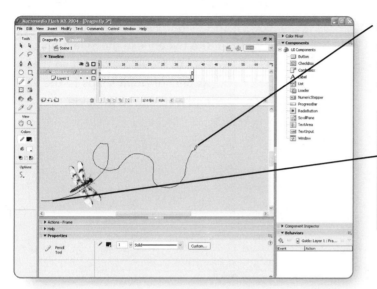

6. Draw the path you want the object to move along. This path can be straight, zigzagged, curved, or even looped.

TIP

Extend the path beyond the Stage if you want the tweened object to enter and/or leave the Stage.

NOTE

You can use the Pen, Pencil, Line, Circle, Rectangle, or Brush tools in the Tools panel to draw the motion guide.

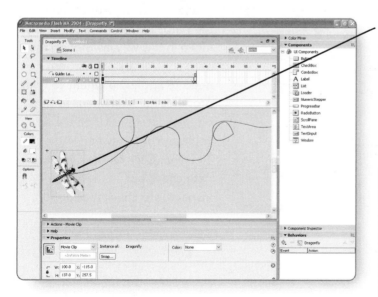

7. In the starting keyframe for the tween, use the Selection tool to move the object so that its anchor point (the circle in the center of the selected instance) snaps to the start of the motion guide.

TIP

Remember to check the Snap option in the Property Inspector when you create the tween to make it easier to snap an object to the motion guide.

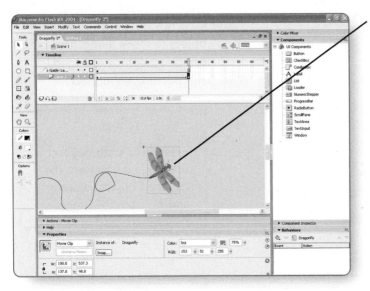

8. In the ending keyframe of the tween, use the Selection tool to move the object so that its anchor point snaps to the end of the motion guide.

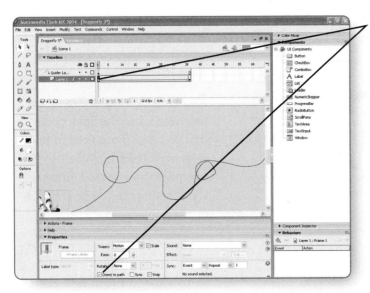

9. In this instance, I want the dragonfly to appear as if it's really flying. If it were, its body would turn as it turns around the path. To make the dragonfly move in this way, as though the path controls its orientation, I need to apply the Orient to Path property for the tween. To turn on this feature, click on the first keyframe of the tween in the Timeline. Click on the Orient to Path check box in the Property Inspector to check that option.

NOTE

If you play back the movie with the motion guide by pressing Enter, the motion guide will still appear onscreen. When you publish the movie, the motion guide will disappear. To preview how the movie will look when published, press F12.

You may find it difficult to visualize the impact of the Orient to Path check box. To help, look at a frame from a movie without the option enabled and then consider the same frame with the option enabled.

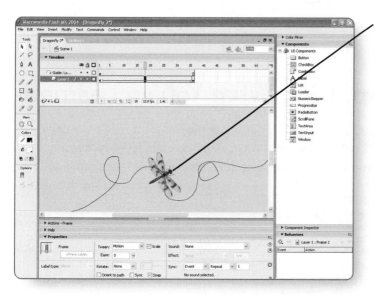

This example illustrates animation *without* Orient to Path enabled.

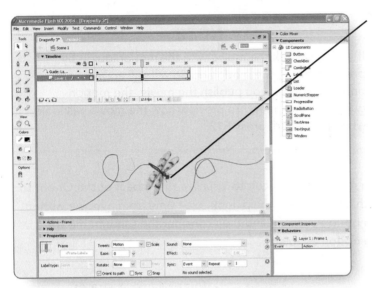

This example illustrates animation *with* Orient to Path enabled.

Applying What You've Learned

Now, you can pull together all the different motion tweens and create an animation in which one object moves along a motion guide, changes colors, rotates, and fades out. For simplicity, you work with only one object, and it does everything at once in a four-second movie:

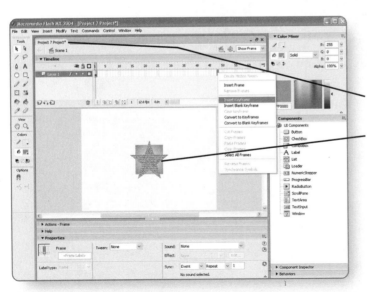

1. Create a new movie.

2. Draw an object in the first frame, or import an object to use as a symbol and place an instance on the first frame.

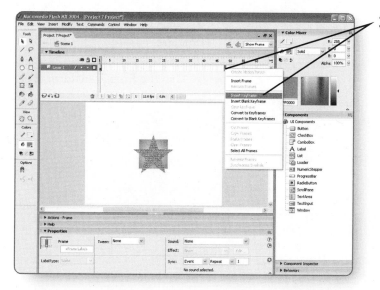

3. Add a keyframe at frame 48.

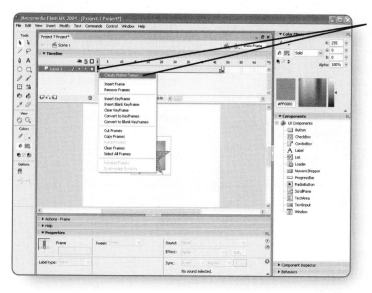

4. Right-click on frame 1 and then click on Create Motion Tween. You can now specify what will happen during the motion tween.

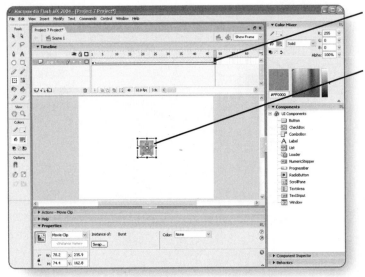

5. Click on frame 38 in the Timeline.

6. Use the Free Transform tool to resize the object.

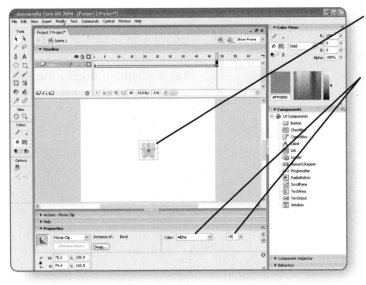

7. Use the Selection tool to select the instance in frame 38.

8. Apply the desired Color transform settings in the Property Inspector.

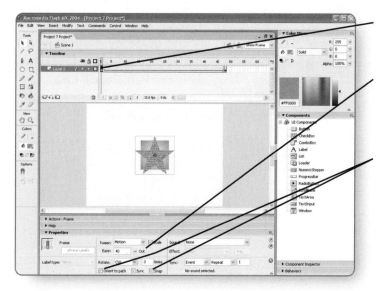

9. Click on frame 1 in the Timeline.

10. Specify the desired Ease, Rotate, and Rotation Count settings.

11. Check the Orient to Path and Snap check boxes.

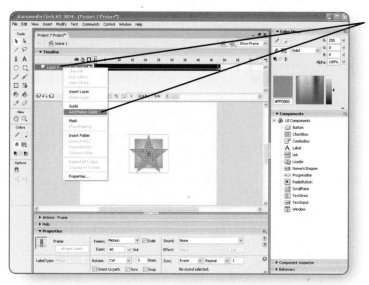

12. Right-click on Layer 1 in the Timeline and click on Add Motion Guide.

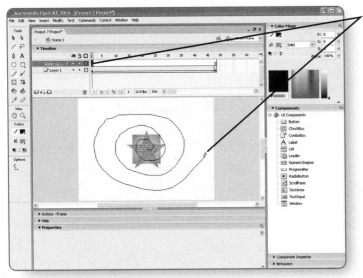

13. Click on frame 1 in the motion guide layer and draw a path for the object to follow by using the Pen, Pencil, Line, Circle, Rectangle, or Brush tool in the Tools panel.

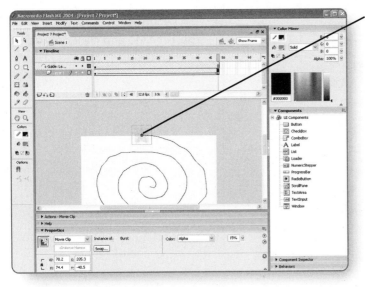

14. In the frames 1 and 38, use the Selection tool to move the object to snap to the starting and ending points of the path, respectively.

15. Play the movie.

8

Animation with Shape Tweening

Shape tweening in Flash MX 2004 enables you to create animation with a different look. Whereas motion tweening generally takes an object from one location to another and allows for some changes to the shape (such as height, width, or skew), shape tweening morphs an object into something completely different. A circle gradually morphing into a triangle illustrates the concept of shape tweening.

In this chapter, you will learn how to do the following:

- Understand how shape tweening works.
- Create a basic shape tween.
- Apply a shape tween with more complex shapes.
- Use shape tweening with text.
- Use shape hints to control the tween.
- Tween with a Timeline effect.

What Is Shape Tweening?

Shape tweening resembles motion tweening. In motion tweening, you create an object, tell Flash where to move the object, and Flash handles the rest. With shape tweening, you create the starting object, create the ending object, and you let Flash fill in the shape changes in between the two. A shape tween can be as simple as a circle becoming a square or as complex as a row of boxes becoming letters in a word. Basically, any shape or object can be tweened into another.

NOTE

Shape tweens are often referred to as *morphs*.

Making a Basic Shape Tween

A simple shape tween morphs one shape into another, also changing appearance properties such as a fill color or line style. These steps illustrate how to create a simple shape tween between objects you draw with the Flash drawing tools.

1. Create a new movie and add a layer to hold the shape tween, if needed.

NOTE

As with motion tweening, create each shape tween (tweened object) on a single layer for best results. Otherwise, Flash may confuse other objects on the layer with the shape being tweened. This situation can result in odd behavior in the finished movie.

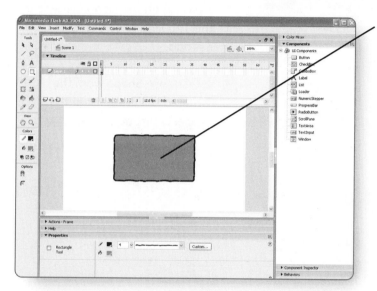

2. In the first keyframe, draw an object by using the desired stroke and fill colors.

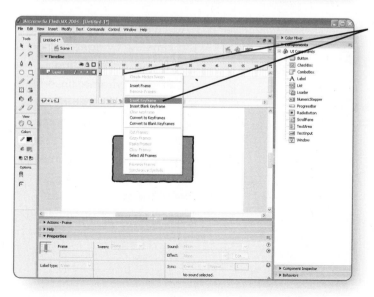

3. Insert a keyframe where you would like the tween to begin.

> ### TIP
>
> A tween need not begin on the first frame in a layer. When you create either a motion or shape tween, you can insert a keyframe anywhere on the Timeline to establish the beginning of the tweened sequence.

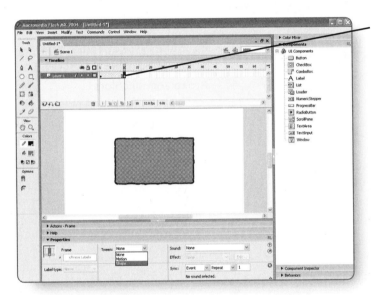

4. Click on the new keyframe in the Timeline to select it, if needed.

5. Choose Shape from the Tween drop-down list in the Property Inspector.

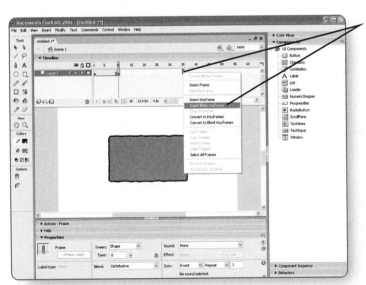

6. Add a new, blank keyframe in the Timeline by right-clicking on the frame and selecting Insert Blank Keyframe. (Insert Blank Keyframe is located below Insert Keyframe on the shortcut menu. Be sure that the keyframe you insert is blank.) The Timeline will display a dashed line between the two keyframes, indicating an incomplete tween.

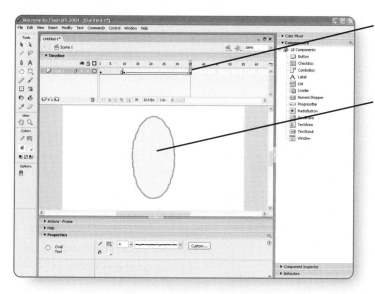

7. Click on the new keyframe in the Timeline to select it, if needed.

8. In the keyframe, draw another object—the one that identifies the new shape the object will take on during the tween—with the desired stroke and fill settings. The Timeline will display a solid arrow to indicate that the tween has been completed.

9. Press Enter to play the movie.

TIP

Flash MX 2004 provides feedback to help you with tween problems. The Timeline flags an incomplete tween with a dashed line between keyframes. (An arrow indicates a complete tween.) When you see the dashed line, look at both the first and last keyframes in the tweened sequence to try to discover the problem. In some instances, Flash also displays a warning icon to the right of the Ease drop-down list in the Property Inspector. Clicking on this icon reveals a message with troubleshooting help.

Shape Tweening Complex Shapes

Basic shape tweening works with only simple items. Complex shapes, objects, imported graphics, and text must be simplified into pieces to enable shape tweening to work properly. To convert an object to its component parts (or convert imported graphics to fills, right-click on the object and click on Break Apart or use the Selection tool to select the object and press Ctrl+B (⌘+B for the Mac). The following steps show you how to apply a shape tween to an imported graphic.

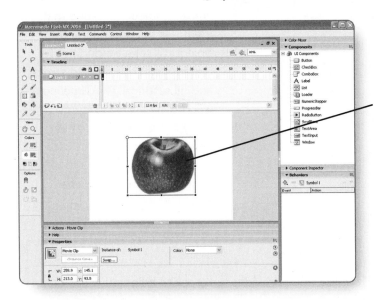

1. Create a new movie and add a layer to hold the shape tween, if needed.

2. Import the graphic to the Stage by using the File, Import, Import to Stage command. Size and position the graphic as desired.

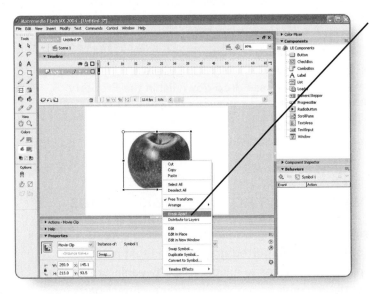

3. Right-click on the imported graphic and then click on Break Apart. This step converts the graphic to a fill so that Flash can tween the graphic.

NOTE

When using the Break Apart command on a graphic, you want it to be converted to a fill. Depending on the graphic, you may need to repeat the command two or three times. You will know that you've used the command enough times when the graphic becomes covered with selection shading.

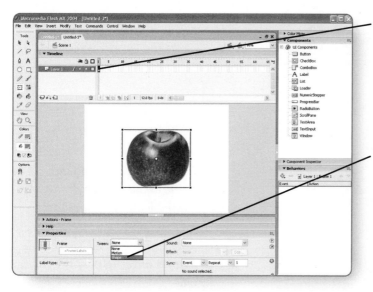

4. Click on the first keyframe for the tween in the Timeline. (You can first insert a new keyframe after frame 1 if you want to start the tween at a point later in the movie.)

5. Choose Shape from the Tween drop-down list in the Property Inspector.

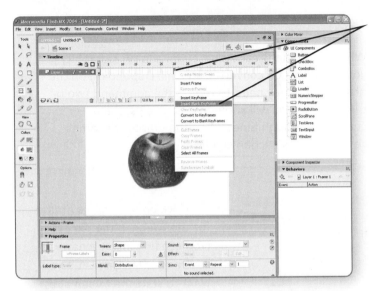

6. Add a new, blank keyframe at the desired location by right-clicking on a frame and then clicking on Insert Blank Keyframe. A dashed line indicating an incomplete tween will appear.

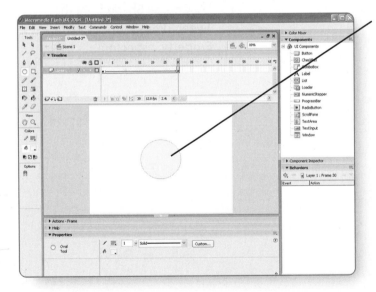

7. Add the final shape or graphic in the new keyframe. An arrow indicating a complete tween will appear.

8. Press Enter to play the movie.

If a warning icon appears in the Property Inspector after Step 5, you typically don't have to worry. If you click on that warning icon, you will see a message that Flash will not tween layers with symbols on them. This isn't entirely true. Flash will instead tween the symbol in a very modified way, and will change the fill at the last instant. This is one of the limitations of using imported graphics in a shape tween. Whenever possible, draw directly on the Stage to create the object you want to tween.

Tweening Text

Working with text in a shape tween is a little more complex than changing a square into a circle. You must break apart the text twice. The first time separates the single text block into many blocks, one for each letter. The second time you break apart text, each of the letters becomes a fill that looks just like the text character, but is, in fact, just a graphic.

Tweening Shapes to Characters

A simple way to work with text in a shape tween is to morph shapes into individual letters, or vice versa. These steps show you the easy process via a simple example—morphing circles into characters.

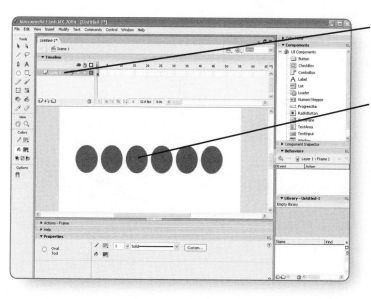

1. Create a new movie and add a layer to hold the shape tween, if needed.

2. In the first keyframe (or a later keyframe that you've inserted if you want the tween to begin later in the movie), create one shape for each letter in the word you'll include in the tween. This example shows six ovals, as the sequence will tween to a six-letter word.

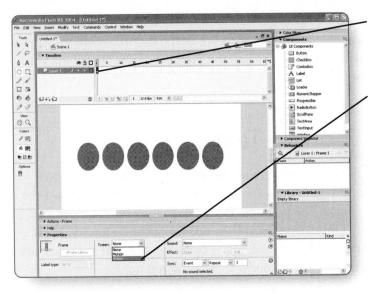

3. Click on the first keyframe of the tween in the Timeline, if needed.

4. Choose Shape from the Tween drop-down list in the Property Inspector.

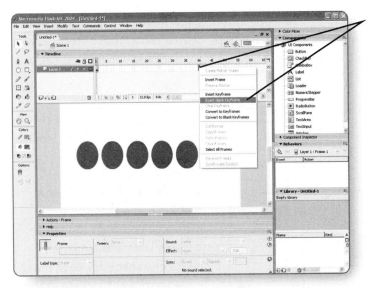

5. Insert a blank keyframe at the frame where you want the tween to end.

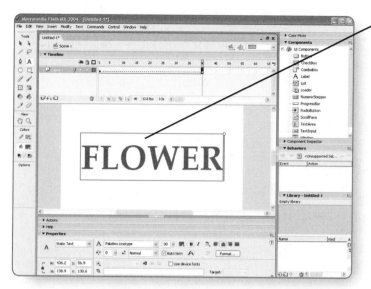

6. Use the Text tool to create a word (in the new keyframe) that has the same number of letters as the number of shapes you created in Step 2. This example shows a six-letter word.

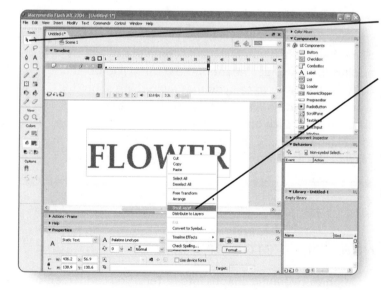

7. Click on the Selection tool in the Tools panel.

8. Right-click on the text and then click on Break Apart to break the word into multiple 1-letter text blocks. (You also can press Ctrl+B or ⌘+B for the Mac.) Each letter should be selected.

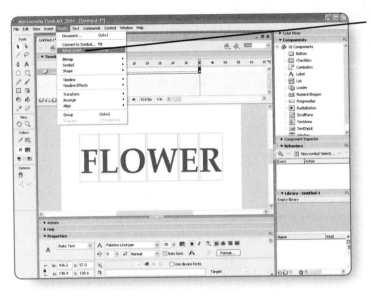

9. Choose Modify, Break Apart (or press Ctrl+B or ⌘+B) to change the each letter into a graphic.

10. Press Enter to play the movie.

CAUTION

Sometimes, when you finish an incomplete tween by adding the last piece needed, the dashed line does not become an arrow to tell you that everything should work. When you have what you think is a complete shape tween, click on a different frame in the Timeline, and Flash should be forced to update the display. Or try playing the movie to see if all items display properly.

Tweening Words or Phrases

In addition to tweening shapes into letters, you can tween one word into another and then even tween the second word into a third. You could use this technique in opening credits for your Flash movie, with a name like *Jones Price* changing to *presents*, which then changes to *Flash Animation*. Or you can use shape tweening with text to create captions or headings that change as the movie contents change. For example, captions like *Company History*, *Innovation*, and *Products* might appear as the movie progresses.

TIP

Work to make tweens subtle and gradual to blend into the rest of the movie. If the changes are too abrupt or complex, they can distract from the content or subject matter that the movie is trying to convey.

The following steps illustrate how to use shape tweening between words and phrases:

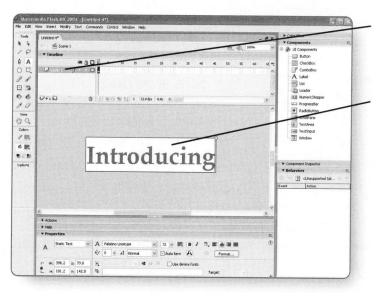

1. Create a new movie and add a layer to hold the shape tween, if needed.

2. In the first keyframe (or a later keyframe that you've inserted if you want the tween to begin later in the movie), use the Text tool to enter the desired word or phrase.

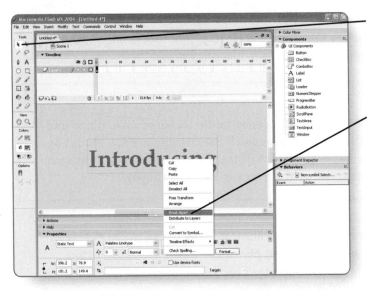

3. Click on the Selection tool in the Tools panel. Use it to move the text into the desired position.

4. Right-click on the text, and then click on Break Apart to break the word into multiple 1-letter text blocks. (You also can press Ctrl+B or ⌘+B for the Mac.) Each letter should be selected.

5. With the letters still selected, choose Modify, Break Apart. The letters will be converted to graphics for tweening.

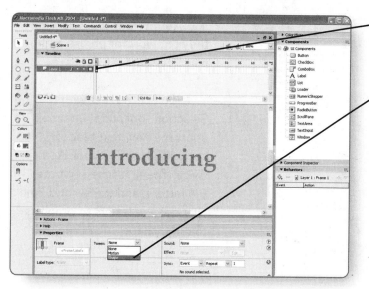

6. Click on the first keyframe of the tween in the Timeline, if needed.

7. Choose Shape from the Tween drop-down list in the Property Inspector.

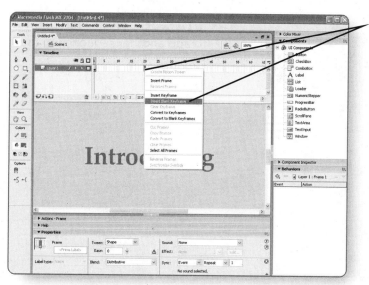

8. Insert a blank keyframe at the frame where you want to change the text.

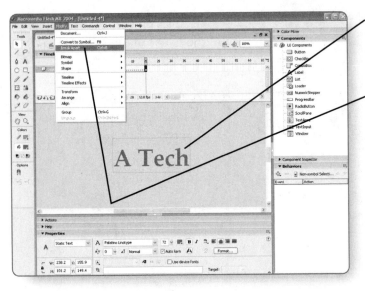

9. Use the Text tool to create the next word or phrase in the new keyframe.

10. Select the text with the Selection tool and then break apart the new text block by choosing Modify, Break Apart twice. The first time separates the letters, and the second time changes the letters to graphics that the shape tween can use.

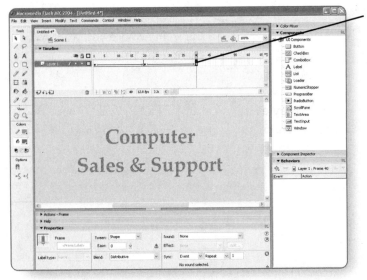

11. Repeat Steps 8 through 10 to add another sequence to the tween, if desired.

12. Press Enter to play the movie.

> **TIP**
>
> When you are creating shape tweens with text, the text can be in different fonts, colors, and sizes. Just change these properties before you break the text apart. After you have selected Break Apart on the letters to change them into graphics that Flash can use in the tween, you cannot change the font, and changing the size is difficult. For interesting effects, vary the location, size, colors, and fonts to see what sort of neat transitions you can create.

Working with Shape Hints

You may have noticed that when you play back a movie with a shape tween, some unexpected things happen. For example, a rectangle shape might rotate as it becomes an oval. The tweening tool thinks that this event should happen, but it just doesn't look right. What can you do to stop the rotation?

The wonderful people at Macromedia anticipated problems like this one. They even added a feature that can mitigate problems with shape tweens: you can add *shape hints* to keyframes to show that a specific point on the shape in the first keyframe will become a specific point in the shape in the last keyframe. For example, to stop the rotation of the rectangle into the square, you can place a hint in the middle of the top side of the rectangle in the first frame and place a hint at the top point of the oval in the last keyframe.

Follow these steps to add shape hints to a tween that you've created:

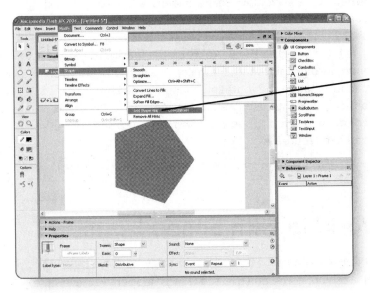

1. Select the first keyframe in the tween in the Timeline.

2. Choose Modify, Shape, Add Shape Hint. This step adds a hint—a small, red circle labeled *a*—to the keyframe.

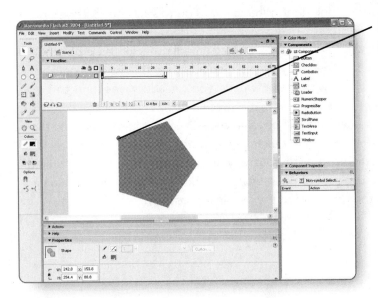

3. Drag the hint to the desired location on the shape.

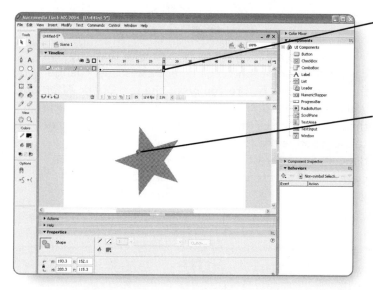

4. Click on the last keyframe in the tween in the Timeline. You will see that another red hint will appear on that frame.

5. Drag the hint on this frame to the desired location on the shape.

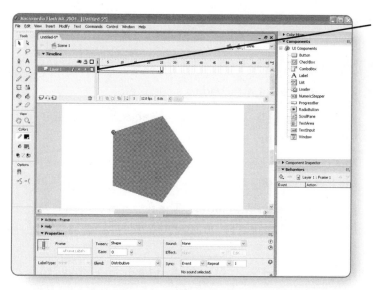

6. Click on the first keyframe for the tween.

7. Press Enter to play the movie.

TIP

When you are creating shape tweens with text, the text can be in different fonts, colors, and sizes. Just change these properties before you break the text apart. After you have selected Break Apart on the letters to change them into graphics that Flash can use in the tween, you cannot change the font, and changing the size is difficult. For interesting effects, vary the location, size, colors, and fonts to see what sort of neat transitions you can create.

NOTE

Hints are a great tool. There are, however, a few important things to remember

- Hints apply to a single tween from one keyframe to the next.

- Hints can be placed only in keyframes.

- Red hints are not attached to a curve.

- Hints appear yellow when properly placed on a shape in the first keyframe of a tween.

- Hints appear green when properly placed on a shape in the last frame of a tween.

- Hints are labeled with letters. The first hint added is *a*, the second is *b*, and so on. You may include up to 26 hints per tween sequence.

- Hints are paired. Hint A in the first keyframe moves to Hint A in the last keyframe. In the next tween, Hint B in the first keyframe moves to Hint B in the last keyframe.

When you need to remove a shape hint, you can easily do so:

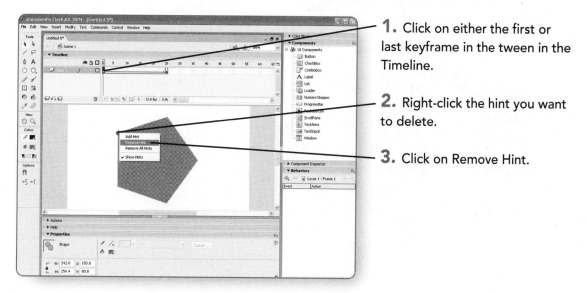

1. Click on either the first or last keyframe in the tween in the Timeline.

2. Right-click the hint you want to delete.

3. Click on Remove Hint.

NOTE

Click on Remove All Hints, instead, to remove all the hints in the movie.

Using a Timeline Effect

If tweening sounds like too much work, rest assured that Flash MX 2004 includes a few shortcuts. You can apply a Timeline Effect to help you apply a variety of tween settings in a single dialog box. The Timeline Effects primarily perform shape tweening, but some, like the Explode effect, include some motion. Follow these steps to apply a Timeline Effect:

1. Create a new movie and add a layer to hold the Timeline Effect tween, if needed.

2. In the first keyframe (or a later keyframe that you've inserted if you want the tween to begin later in the movie), use a Tools panel tool to create the object to tween.

3. Select the object by using the Selection tool.

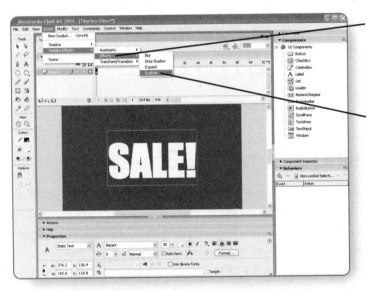

4. Choose Insert, Timeline Effects. Then choose either the Effects or Transform/Transition choice.

5. Click on the desired Timeline Effect in the submenu that appears. A dialog box with settings for the selected Timeline Effect will appear.

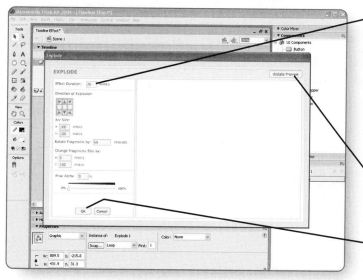

6. Specify settings for the effect, including how many frames you want the effect to last, rotation and size settings, and so on. The available settings will vary depending on the effect you selected in Step 5.

7. Click on Update Preview to verify that you like the impact of your choices.

8. Click on OK. Flash will apply the changes required by the effect and update the movie file accordingly.

9

Masking

Masking makes Flash more flexible. With masking, you can create a number of neat effects. If Flash is like theater on the web, consider masking to be high drama. You can affect the visibility of a bitmap in ways that create surprising looks, particularly when applying tweening options to a mask.

In this chapter, you will learn to do the following:

- Understand what a mask is and how to use one.
- Create a simple mask.
- Create masks that work with moving and animated content.
- Use movie clip symbols in masks.

What Is a Mask?

Creating a *mask* is like creating a window through which you can view the Stage. You create a mask on a new layer, specifying what portion of the layer below the mask will be hidden, and what portion the mask will allow to show through. You can think of a mask via this example. Take a piece of paper and cut an oval in it. Now lay the piece of paper on a favorite photo; the paper now works like a mask, hiding some parts of the image and revealing others.

In Flash, you can create masks to hide extraneous objects or content on the Stage. Using masks along with static and moving content expands the possibilities for adding focus and excitement into the movies you create. You can create lots of neat and sophisticated effects by creating masks like the ones explored in this chapter. With a little creativity, you should be able to apply the concepts presented here to create amazing movies.

Adding a Mask to a Movie

You need to plan exactly how you want to create a mask. Decide what you want hidden on the Stage, what you want visible, and how the area of visibility should look in terms of shape and size. For example, you can mask part of a graphic imported into Flash. Or you may decide you need a mask that moves like a spotlight, revealing different parts of the Stage as the animation plays.

The rest of this section explains how to create various types of masks, including those that move or work with moving content.

Creating a Static Mask over Static Content

The simplest kind of mask consists of an unmoving mask layer over static content on the layer below. Try your hand at creating a simple mask by following these steps:

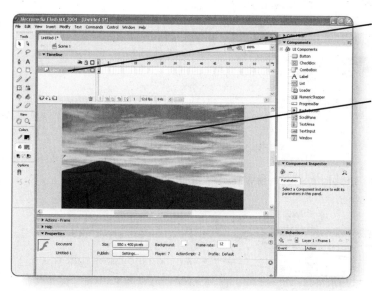

1. Create or open a movie and add a layer to hold the masked content, if needed.

2. Import or create the graphic to be masked in the first frame. Determine what parts of the graphic will be visible to the user.

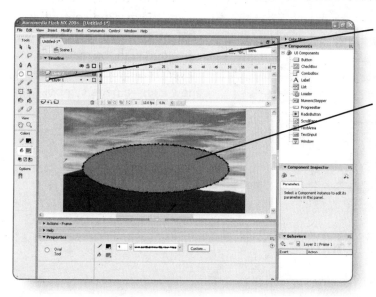

3. Insert a new layer in the Timeline by clicking the Insert Layer button.

4. On the new layer (Layer 2 in this example), draw a shape that outlines the area the mask will show. You can use the Rectangle tool, Oval tool, Pen tool, or Pencil tool to draw this shape.

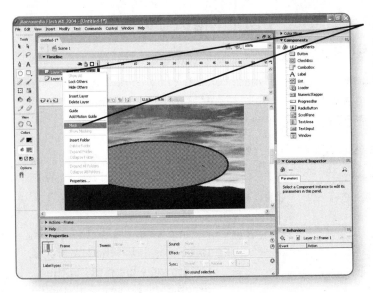

5. Right-click on the layer on which you just drew the object and choose Mask. The mask will be created immediately.

You should notice a few things about the mask you just created.

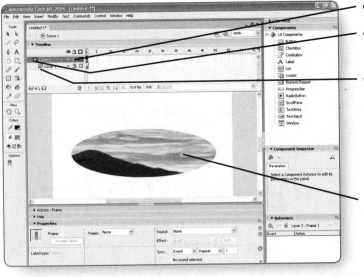

- Both layers are locked.

- An icon indicates that the new layer is a mask.

- Layer 1 (or the layer that holds the masked content) is indented, showing that it is grouped with the masking layer. This layer also has a new icon—a page symbol.

- On the Stage, only the unmasked portion of Layer 1 is visible.

Creating a Moving Mask over Static Content

The prior mask was static—it didn't move over the image content. Now, let's add a motion tween to the mask so that the mask moves over the static content on the Stage. Follow these steps to create a moving mask:

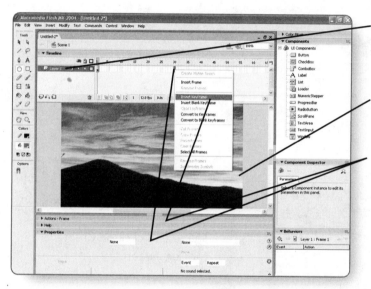

1. Create or open a movie and add a layer to hold the masked content, if needed.

2. Import or create the graphic to be masked in the first frame.

3. Insert a new keyframe at a later frame (frame 30 in this example). This step creates a static picture that lasts the designated number of frames.

TIP

Don't forget that when you're building more complex functionality like a mask into a movie, you can assign more descriptive layer names. In this instance, descriptive layer names help you tell at a glance whether or not you're working on the layer that holds the mask.

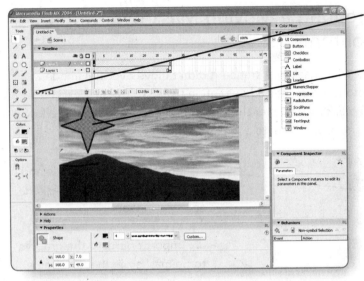

4. Add a new layer by clicking the Insert Layer button.

5. In the first frame of the new layer, draw the mask shape, through which part of the layer below will be visible.

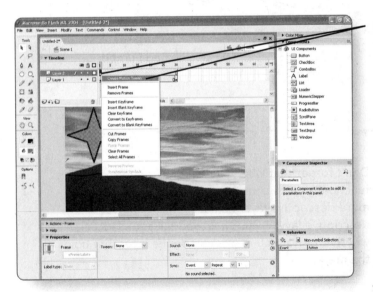

6. Right-click the first frame on the layer holding the mask shape and click on Create Motion Tween.

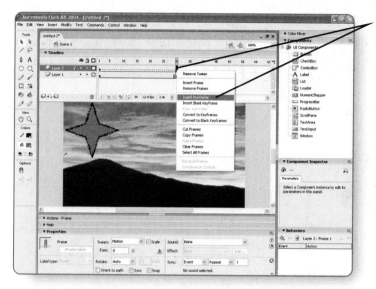

7. Add a keyframe on the new layer at the same frame number as the keyframe you added in Step 3 (frame 30 in this example).

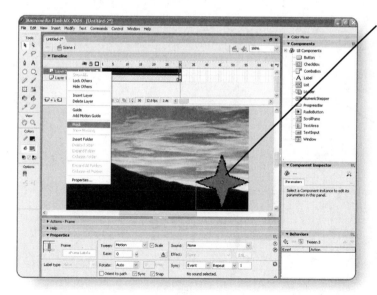

8. Move the mask shape to the desired ending position on the Stage in the new keyframe.

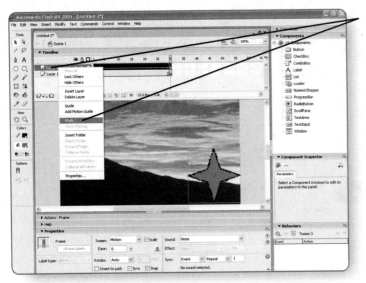

9. Right-click on the layer holding the mask object in the Timeline and choose Mask from the menu.

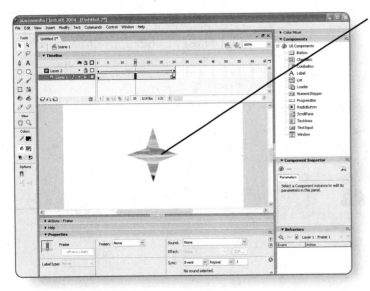

When you play the movie, the mask will move over the picture. Nifty, huh?

> **NOTE**
>
> Masks work only when the masked layer and the masking layer are locked, so you must remember that if you unlock either layer to edit it, you need to lock it again so that the mask displays properly.

Creating a Static Mask over Moving Content

You also can create masks that work with content in the opposite way—the mask remaining static while the content behind it moves. For example, you can use this technique to create a scrolling marquee effect. The mask can reveal text that scrolls or moves behind the mask. Follow these steps to create moving content beneath a static mask.

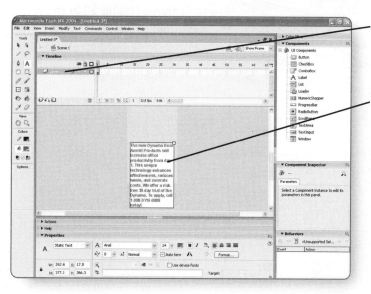

1. Create or open a movie and add a layer to hold the masked content, if needed.

2. Import or create the graphic to be masked in the first frame. This example shows text that will be "scrolled" behind the mask. To create this effect, add the text box at the bottom of the Stage. To create text that move horizontally through the mask, create the text block to the right of the Stage.

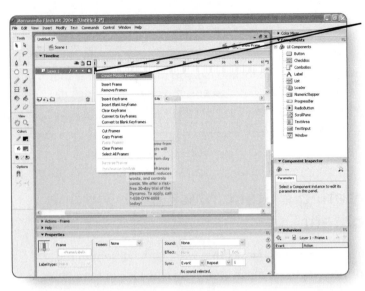

3. Right-click the first frame on the layer holding the content to animate and click on Create Motion Tween.

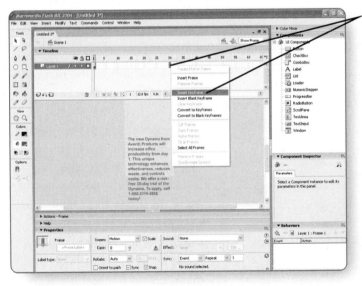

4. Insert a new keyframe at a later frame (frame 30 in this example).

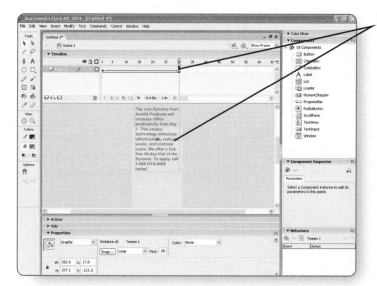

5. Click on the new keyframe and move the object to the desired finish position for the animation.

NOTE

You also can create multiple tweened segments and mask over the entire sequence. If you use this technique, it helps to click on the Onion Skin or Onion Skin Outlines button at the bottom of the Timeline so that you can create one or more mask objects to reveal the moving content at the desired points along the way.

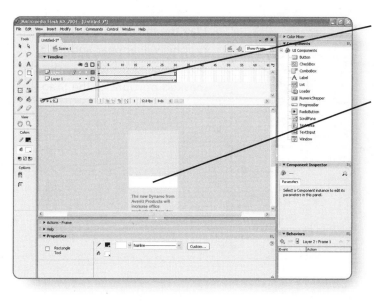

6. Add a new layer to the Timeline by clicking the Insert Layer button.

7. In the first frame of the new mask layer, draw the mask shape.

TIP

When you're creating a static mask, you can draw numerous shapes on the mask layer to add interest.

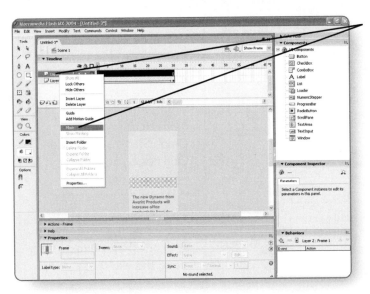

8. Right-click on the layer holding the mask object in the Timeline and click on Mask.

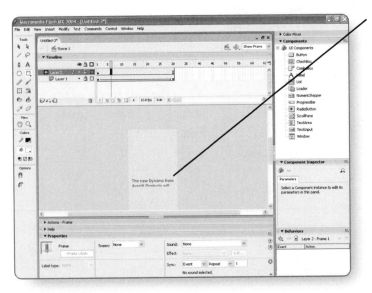

Play the movie. The moving graphic will appear and disappear as it travels under the masked portions of the Stage.

> **TIP**
>
> If the animation progresses too quickly or too slowly, remember that you can change the frame rate for the movie in the Property Inspector. Click on the Selection tool and then click on the Stage to display the movie properties.

Adding a Second Layer under a Mask

Any mask that you create can mask the content from multiple layers. This can help you make your movie file even more complex and interesting. After you create a mask over static or moving content, follow these steps to add a second layer with static or moving content under the mask:

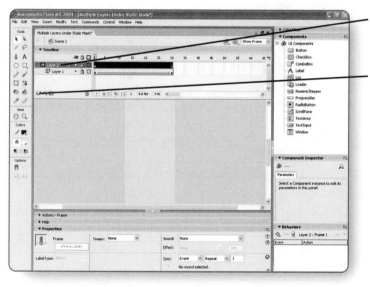

1. In the movie holding a mask, select the mask layer.

2. Click the Add Layer button. A new layer should be inserted above the mask layer.

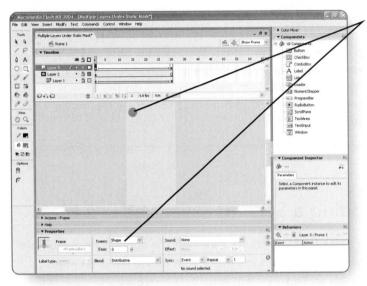

3. Create the desired content on frame 1 of the new layer and animate the content if desired. In this case, I've added a drawn object with a shape tween.

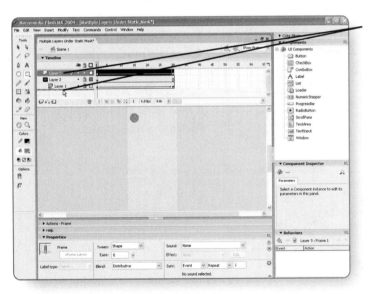

4. Drag the new layer under the masked layer in the Timeline. When you release the mouse button, the layer will become indented, indicating that it, too, will be masked by the mask layer.

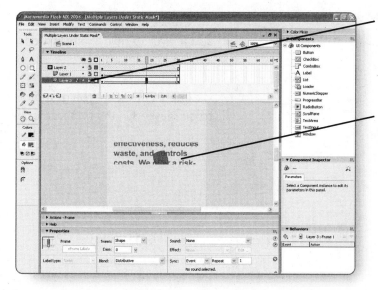

5. The newly-moved layer will not be locked, so you must lock it to enable it to work with the mask.

When you play the movie, both layers of content will appear and disappear as they move under the mask.

Creating an Animated Mask over Animated Content

You can really make things interesting by having an animated mask moving over an animated picture. In this example, you will see how to apply a shape tween to the masked object and a motion tween to the mask.

NOTE

One drawback to using masks is that a mask layer cannot have a motion guide associated with it, so you cannot easily create an animated mask that follows a preset path. The easiest way to work around this limitation is to break up the animation into several different tweens, each with simple movement from one point to another.

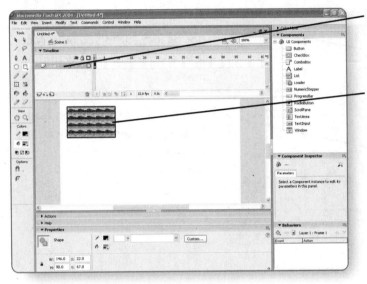

1. Create or open a movie and add a layer to hold the masked content, if needed.

2. Import or create the graphic to be masked in the first frame.

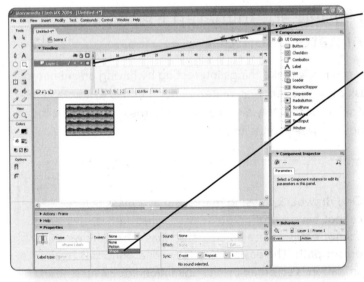

3. Click on the first frame in the layer.

4. Choose Shape from the Tween drop-down menu in the Property Inspector.

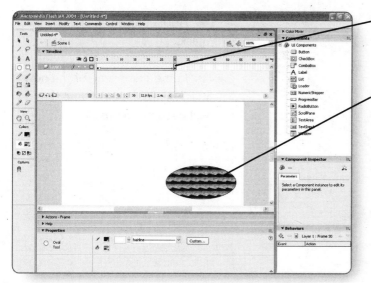

5. Add a blank keyframe at a later frame (frame 30 in this example).

6. In the new keyframe, draw the ending shape for the shape tween in the desired position.

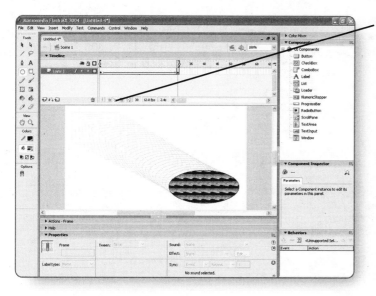

7. Turn on Onion Skins or Onion Skin Outlines and move the brackets so that you can see the movement of the elements in the movie. This will help you determine how the mask should overlap the animated object.

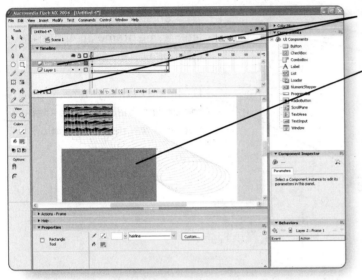

8. Add a new layer to hold the mask.

9. In the first frame of the new mask layer, draw a shape that will become the mask.

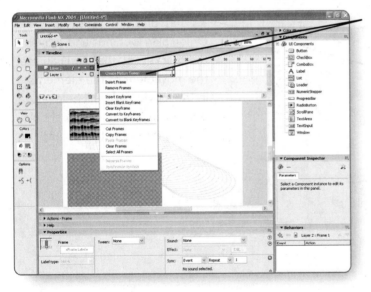

10. Right-click the first frame on the mask layer and click on Create Motion Tween.

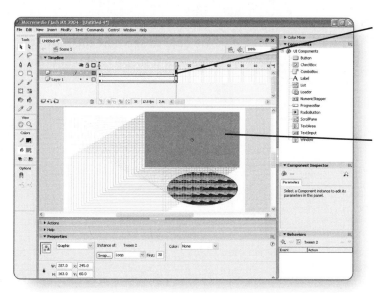

11. Add a keyframe to the same frame as the one to which you added a blank keyframe in Step 6 (frame 30 in this example) on the mask layer.

12. In the new keyframe, move the mask shape to the desired ending location.

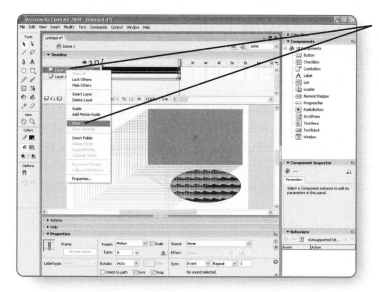

13. Right-click on the mask layer in the Timeline and click on Mask.

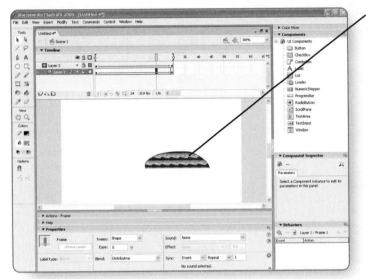

When you play the movie, you'll be able to see how the moving mask and shape tween interact.

Using Movie Clip Symbols with Masks

If you've already created an animated movie clip symbol, you can use it with either a static or a moving mask. Simply position the movie clip symbol on the Stage as desired. Then add the static or moving mask as described in earlier sections. Press F12 to preview the interaction between the symbol and the mask.

PART III

Finishing Touches

This section explains how to publish your Flash movies and also provides information about HTML that will enhance your success of including your movies on Web pages. The final chapter also introduces ActionScript and behaviors, providing foundation information for scripting in Flash MX 2004 and adding interactivity into your movies.

10

Adding Sound and Embedded Video

Used well, sound and video lend an additional dimension to your Flash MX 2004 movies. Sound can add warmth, feeling, or humor. Video can add realism and accuracy. On the other hand, sound and video can be distracting or slow down movie performance if overdone, so use these elements wisely in a movie.

In this chapter, you learn how to do the following:

- Understand sound basics and types.
- Import sounds into Flash.
- Add sounds to the Timeline.
- Work with sound and buttons.
- Modify, customize, and compress sounds.
- Import embedded video.

Understanding Sound Basics in Flash

Flash does not enable you to create sounds. You import sound files into Flash and then work with the imported files. If you want to create sound files, you can use basic software (like Sound Recorder in Windows or the sound recording program that came with your computer system's sound card), a sound source, and a microphone to record your own sound files. Or you can use a looping program like Acid Pro or Fruity Loops to create sound files. This chapter assumes you have created sound files or have licensed them from an online source for import into Flash.

When you include sound in a Flash movie, you need to achieve the best possible balance between sound quality and file size. Sound will greatly increase the size of an exported Flash movie. A sound file that is too large can prevent a movie from being displayed in the browser.

When digital sound is adapted from its analog form, it must be sampled. *Sampling* involves taking multiple snapshots, or *samples,* of a sound wave for a given amount of time. After several snapshots are collected, they are reassembled as a replication of the original sound. This process digitizes the sound. A higher number of snapshots results in better-quality sound.

Flash supports several file formats for digital sound files. Some sound formats are platform specific, and others include some compression applied to the original sound:

- **MP3 (Motion Picture Experts Group, level 3).** The standard file type for sound on the Internet. Critics dislike the quality of MP3 files, which are compressed; however, you are still able to customize the resulting output.

- **WAV (wave).** The native Windows sound file type; not usable in the Mac version of Flash. Wave files are typically larger than MP3s, even after compression.

- **AIFF (Audio Interchange File Format).** Developed by Apple Computer and used on the Mac OS platform only; the format of a great deal of professional music. QuickTime 4 or higher enables an AIFF file to be imported on a Windows system.

- **QuickTime.** Enables compatibility with other sound file formats, such as AIFF and AU. You can download it for free at http://www.apple.com/quicktime/download/.

Many sound files on the Web are produced in mono rather than stereo (meaning they are designed for just one channel instead of two), which is okay for use in Flash. Both speakers are activated by a mono file—they are simply playing the same sound, contrary to suspicions that only one speaker plays.

Importing a Sound File

Before you can use a sound file in a movie, you must first import the sound file into the Library. Follow these steps to import a sound file and make it available for use in a Flash movie:

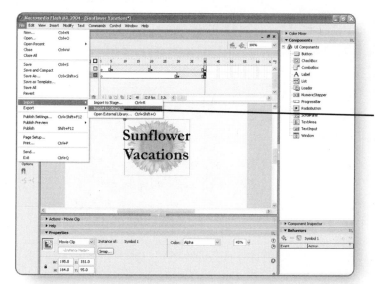

1. Choose File, Import, Import to Library. The Import to Library dialog box will open.

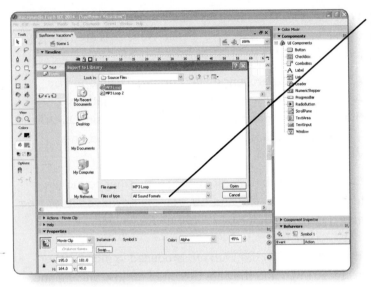

2. Select All Sound Formats from the Files of type drop-down list.

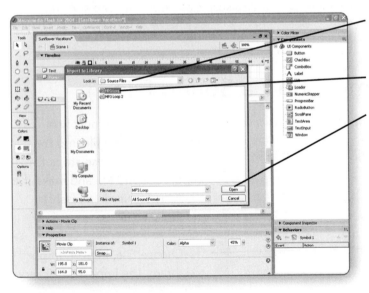

3. Browse to the disk and folder holding the file.

4. Click on the file to import.

5. Click on Open. Flash will import the sound into the Library.

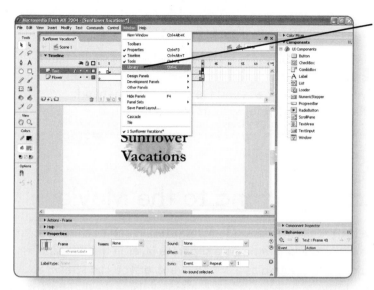

6. Choose Window, Library to open the Library panel. You will see the imported sound file in the panel.

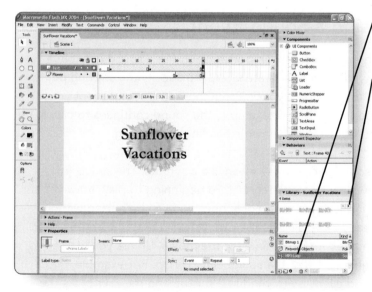

7. Click on the sound file in the Library panel.

8. Click on the Play button. Flash will play back the sound file, so that you can verify that you've imported the correct one.

CAUTION

Importing a sound file works best when the sound file is stored on your system's hard disk, not on a network. If you try to import a sound file stored on a network, Flash may crash your system.

Adding Sound to the Movie

The most basic way to add an imported sound to a movie is to insert it into a keyframe on a separate layer in the Timeline. You can add a sound as a *sound event,* or you can *stream* a sound. The remainder of this section explains these different approaches.

Using a Sound Event

When you insert an imported sound as a sound event in a keyframe on a separate layer, you specify the starting point for the sound playback. From there, the sound event acts independently. For example, the sound continues to play in its entirety even if the movie has finished playing.

A sound event works much like a symbol. The sound downloads completely before beginning to play; however, the sound is downloaded only once and can be reused without greatly increasing its file size. Downloading the entire sound can affect the load time for the movie. Unless you use sound events carefully, the sound can overlap. For example, if a sound event is attached to a button and the user clicks the button five times in quick succession, five instances of the sound begin to play, and each plays in its entirety. You can imagine what this situation might sound like.

Generally, if the sound is short and you are using it more than once (in a loop or for a button sound, for example), you should create a sound event.

Use the following steps to add an imported sound as a sound event in a movie:

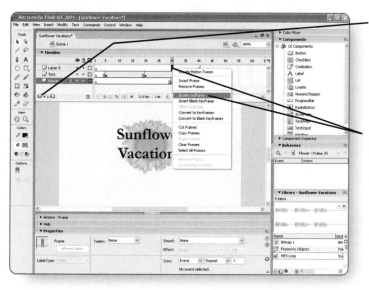

1. Click on the Insert Layer button to add a new layer to hold the sound. You should add each inserted sound on a separate layer.

2. On the new layer, insert a keyframe where you would like to add the sound event. In this example, I want the sound to start playing at frame 30, the same frame where a sunflower graphic appears, so I've inserted the keyframe at frame 30 of the new layer.

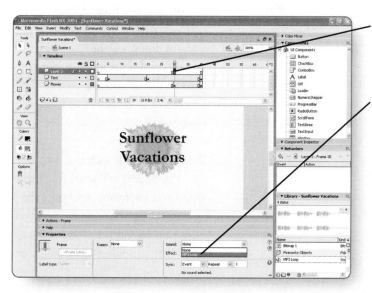

3. Click on the new keyframe on the layer that will hold the sound event.

4. Open the Sound drop-down list in the Property Inspector and click on the sound to add. Alternately, you can drag the sound file from the Library to the Stage. The Timeline will illustrate a wave form for the inserted sound.

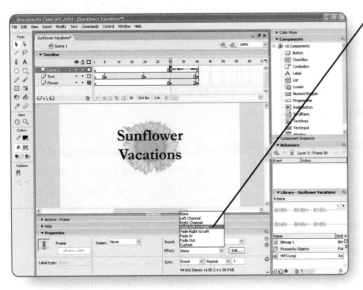

5. With the keyframe where you inserted the sound still selected, choose an effect for the sound from the Effect drop-down list. For example, the Fade Left to Right choice shown here will make the sound fade from the left channel to the right channel of system speakers during playback.

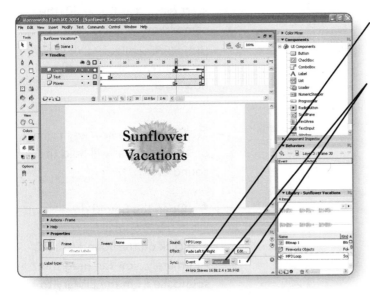

6. Leave Event selected in the Sync drop-down list.

7. If you want the sound to play back endlessly, choose Loop from the Sound Loop drop-down list. Otherwise, leave Repeat selected there and enter the desired number of times to repeat the sound (up to 999) in the Number of times to loop text box.

When you play back the movie file, the sound will start from the specified keyframe and play the specified number of times. It will continue playing until it finishes, even if the movie finishes earlier.

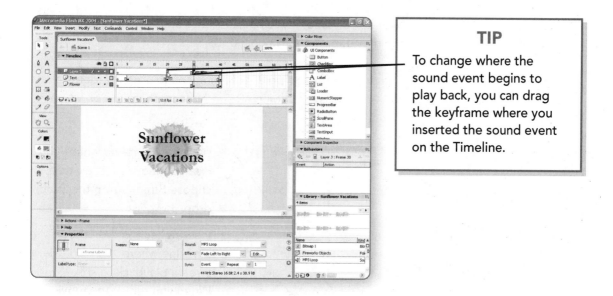

Streaming Sound

When you *stream* an inserted sound in a movie, you can specify both an exact starting point and an exact ending point on the Timeline.

Streaming sound offers both benefits and limitations. Streaming does allow precise control over when the sound file begins to play—theoretically. Playback begins when just a few seconds of the sound file have been downloaded. If the sound file plays more quickly than the download, gaps occur. Also, sound takes precedence during downloading. The Flash Player tries to continue playing the sound file smoothly at the expense of the animation. If problems occur, the Flash Player drops frames in an attempt to keep up, the results of which can be a choppy movie. If the sound is called to play again, the download process starts over because the sound is not stored in the computer's memory.

That being said, consider streaming sound if the sound plays for a longer amount of time, if you need more precise control over its playtime, if you need for it to start at the beginning of the movie, or if it plays only once.

The process for adding a streaming sound is nearly identical to the process for adding a sound effect. There are only two key differences:

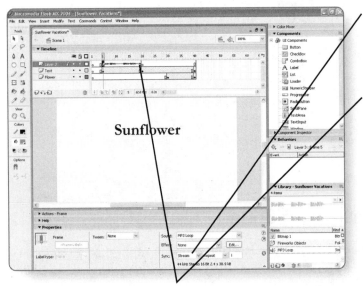

- With the keyframe where you inserted the sound selected, choose Stream from the Sync drop-down list.

- Insert a keyframe on the Timeline where you want the stream playback to stop. When you replay the movie, the streamed sound will play only through the specified frame.

NOTE

The Sync drop-down list in the Property Inspector also contains Start and Stop choices. The Start option is similar to the Event option in that the sound runs separately from the Timeline. Unlike the Event option, the Start option does not allow more than one instance of a sound to play until the preceding instance of the sound has finished playing completely. This feature is useful for a longer sound that takes a while to play, because it prevents the sound from overlapping itself. You can attach the Stop option to a keyframe to make the sound stop. This action stops only one sound file, however. If you want all sounds to stop, use the ActionScript command stopAllSounds.

Working with Sound and Buttons

When you create a button symbol (see "Creating a Button" under "Creating Symbols" in Chapter 5), you can add a sound to a button state in the button symbol's own Timeline. Choose short sounds, appropriate for "clicks," to add to buttons. Use these steps to assign a sound to a button symbol that you're editing or creating:

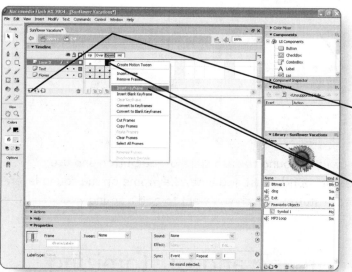

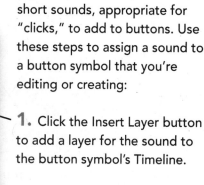

1. Click the Insert Layer button to add a layer for the sound to the button symbol's Timeline.

2. Decide to which state of the button you want to add sound. Sound is commonly added to the Down state so that the sound plays as the button is clicked. Insert a keyframe on the new sound layer at the frame for the state (Down, for example) to which you want to add the sound.

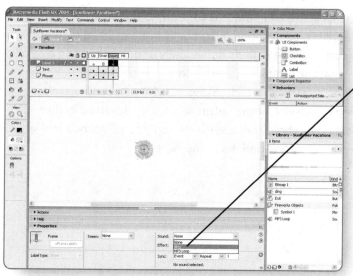

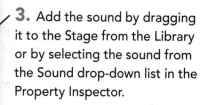

3. Add the sound by dragging it to the Stage from the Library or by selecting the sound from the Sound drop-down list in the Property Inspector.

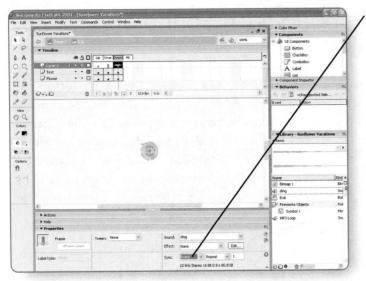

4. Choose Event from the Sync drop-down list in the Property Inspector. You can then continue editing the button symbol as needed.

You can add sound to each state of the button and use different sounds. Just add a new keyframe on the sound layer for each state to which you want to add a sound.

Modifying and Customizing Sound

Flash has some nice features for editing sounds. The settings you apply to each sound individually are exported with the movie. If you edit sounds individually and then change overall sound settings in the Export dialog box, the individual changes, when exported, take precedence over the global settings. Likewise, if the settings are only adjusted in the Export dialog box, those settings apply to all sounds in the movie, reducing variations in the output.

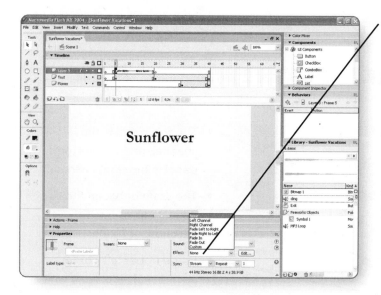

Now let's review the various sound effects available in the Property Inspector. (Click on the first keyframe where you inserted a sound in a layer to display the sound properties in the Property Inspector.) You can add one of seven different effects to an inserted sound, including Custom, which allows you to create your own effects:

- **Left Channel**. Plays the sound file only in the left channel.

- **Right Channel**. Plays the sound file only in the right channel (as you might have guessed).

- **Fade Left to Right**. Sound begins playing in the left channel and gradually gets softer in the left channel as it gets louder in the right channel. The sound concludes with full volume in the right channel and silence in the left channel.

- **Fade Right to Left**. The same process occurs as in the preceding bullet, beginning in the right channel and ending in the left channel.

- **Fade In**. Play begins with no volume and gradually increases to full sound.

- **Fade Out**. Play begins at full volume and gradually decreases to no volume.

- **Custom**. This option allows you to create edit points in the sound and change volume levels in the right and left channels.

If you click on the Edit button beside the Effect drop-down list, the Edit Envelope dialog box opens. You can use this dialog box to apply a completely custom effect to the sound's playback.

Let's take a closer look at the components of the Edit Envelope dialog box.

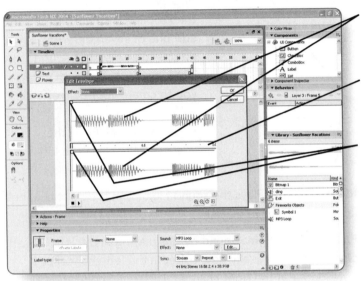

- The top panel is the left channel, and the bottom panel is the right channel.

- The scale between the two panels represents time in seconds, or frames.

- In the upper-left corner of each panel, you see a white square with a black line along the top of the sound image. This line represents the volume level. Effects that alter volume levels, such as those involving fades, alter this line.

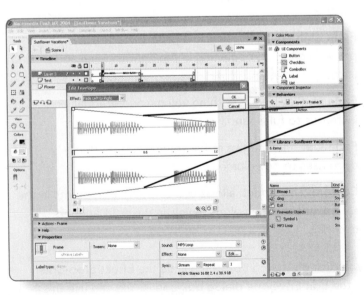

- The top of each panel represents full volume, and the bottom of each panel represents silence.

- Fade Left to Right, for example, shows the left panel at full volume with the volume line decreasing to full silence. The right panel begins at full silence and increases gradually to full sound, as shown in the previous figure.

Now that you've seen how the elements in the Edit Envelope dialog box work, let's see how to use those elements to create a custom effect:

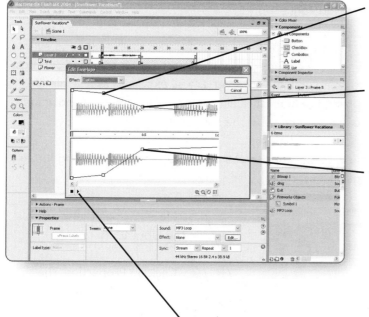

- Drag a white square on a volume line to move it, thus changing the volume for that point during playback.

- Click on the volume line to add an additional square (anchor). You can add up to eight anchors per volume line.

- When you add a new anchor square to one channel, Flash automatically creates one in the same position on the other channel so you can make needed volume changes on the second channel.

- Click on the Play button in the lower-left corner to preview your changes.

After you specify the desired settings in the Edit Envelope dialog box, click on OK to apply those changes to the sound.

Applying Compression to a Sound

Undoubtedly, you have had the experience of making a photocopy of a copy rather than of the original. The more steps away from the original, the poorer the quality of your results. The same philosophy applies to sound. If at all possible, you should begin with an original file of high quality that has not been compressed. Let Flash handle the compression for you.

Sound comprises the bulk of the exported file size, so you should not skip this process. A large sound file can have dramatically detrimental results on animation, particularly when played back by an older computer or downloaded via a slow Web connection.

You can set compression options individually for sound event sounds; the exported sounds will retain the specified settings. Streaming sounds, however, are all exported as a single file, applying the highest quality setting applied to any individual streamed sound to all the sounds in the group.

Follow these steps to change the compression setting for an imported sound file:

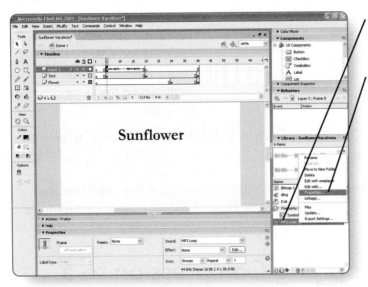

1. Right-click on the sound file in the Library.

2. Click on Properties. The Sound Properties dialog box will open.

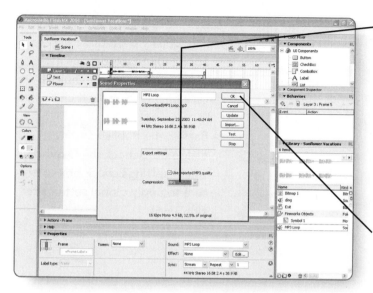

3. Choose the desired compression setting from the Compression drop-down list. (If a Sample rate drop-down list appears, make a choice from that list as desired.) Check the information at the bottom of the dialog box to ensure your compression choice is having the desired effect.

4. Click on OK to apply the compression choice.

Flash will export the sound according to the selections made on the Compression drop-down list. If you choose Default from this drop-down list, Flash will compress the sound file according to the global settings in the Publish Settings dialog box. Using global settings is okay if all the sounds in your movie should be exported according to the same specifications.

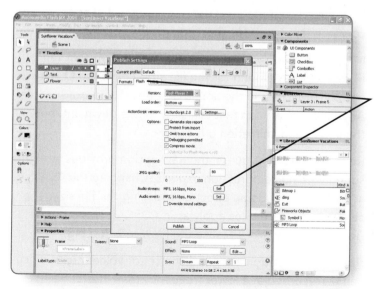

Choose File, Publish Settings to open the Publish Settings dialog box.

Click on the Flash tab. The Audio Stream and Audio Event options buttons appear at the bottom of the tab. Click either Set button to open the Sound Settings dialog box so you can change the global settings for audio streams or events.

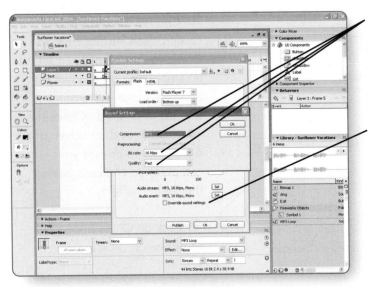

Use the Compression, Bit Rate, and Quality drop-down lists to adjust sound export quality. After you make your choices, click on OK to apply them.

Back in the Publish Settings dialog box, check the Override sound settings check box to be sure to apply global settings to all sounds.

Now that you know where to find compression settings in Flash, let's look at the different types of compression:

- **Default**. As discussed, this selection applies the global settings created in the Publish Settings window to all sounds.

- **ADPCM**. ADPCM, or Adaptive Differential Pulse Code Modulation, is sometimes used as a method of speech compression. Use it for short sounds (like button clicks).

- **MP3**. A commonly used compression standard that tends to give the best sound for the file size. Leave the Quality option set to Fast in the Sound Settings dialog box. Anything higher than that can slow things down and get the sound and animation out of sync.

- **Raw**. As you might guess, the Raw option provides straight sound with no compression exports. Changing the Quality setting can have some effect on reducing the file size. The same sample rate rules apply as in ADPCM. This option is usually not practical because the file size is too big.

- **Speech**. This option is a good choice for voice tracks. Voice can be recorded at a lower frequency than music soundtracks (11KHz or lower usually sounds good).

The Sound Properties dialog box also enables you to specify a sample rate, in kiloHertz, along with a Compression type. Choose one of the following sample rate, as dictated by download speeds and the sound quality requirements for your movie:

- **5KHz**. The lowest possible setting for recognizable speech

- **11KHz**. The lowest setting you should use for music; 25 percent of the standard rate for CDs

- **22KHz**. A common choice for Web playback; 50 percent of the standard CD rate

- **44KHz**. The standard audio rate for music CDs

Finally, the Sound Settings dialog box enables you to specify a Bit rate, in kbps (kilobits per second). The higher the setting, the higher the sample rate. 64 kbps will yield a recognizable sound that downloads fairly quickly over a slow connection. However, for better quality, you can opt for 128 kbps.

Troubleshooting Sound

As you have probably discovered by now, including sound in a Flash movie is not always a precise science. Differences in computers and connection speeds, file size, and compression methods, for example, can cause problems with your movies.

Cutting silence from your sound files helps reduce file size. Silence is exported as actual sound, so it can add to the size of your file. Get rid of whatever you do not need.

If playback looks choppy, consider selecting Auto High from the Quality drop-down list on the HTML tab in the Publish Settings dialog box. The default High setting continually attempts to render the animation at the highest possible quality. The Auto High setting, however, plays the animation at high speed until a problem occurs and then lowers the picture quality in an attempt to keep everything synchronized. You should test the Auto High setting because some versions of Flash Players seem to have difficulty with it.

Another option is changing the frame play rate. The default is 12 frames per second. Keep in mind that a faster frame play rate results in faster play of those animation cells I mentioned earlier, so test for quality playback after dropping the frame rate.

Importing Embedded Video

You learned in Chapter 5 how to create a movie clip symbol that contains its own animation. But what if you want to include a digital movie in your Flash movie? You can import a digital video file (typically in the .mov or .avi formats) into your Flash movie and then insert the file onto its own layer for playback. You need to install the free QuickTime player, particularly on a Windows system, before you can import and embed digital video in Flash. Go to http://www.apple.com/quicktime/download/ to obtain the QuickTime player.

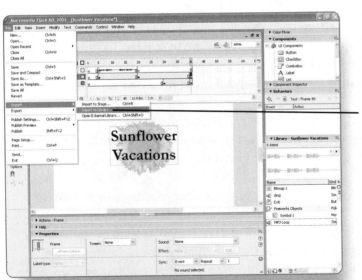

The following steps explain how to import and embed digital video in Flash:

1. Choose File, Import, Import to Library. The Import to Library dialog box will open.

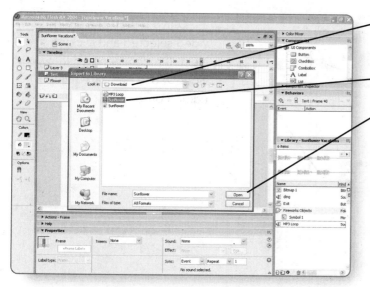

2. Browse to the disk and folder holding the file.

3. Click on the file to import.

4. Click on Open. Flash will launch the Video Import wizard to help import the sound into the Library.

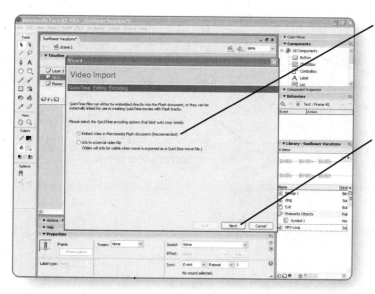

5. Click on the desired import option: Embed video in Macromedia Flash document or Link to External video file. The former option is most flexible.

6. Click on Next.

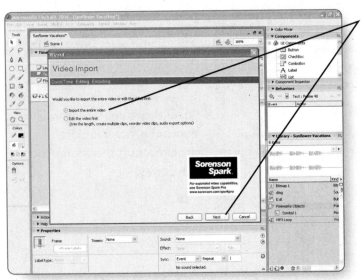

7. Leave Import the entire video selected and click on Next. (I recommend editing your video with a dedicated video editing program.)

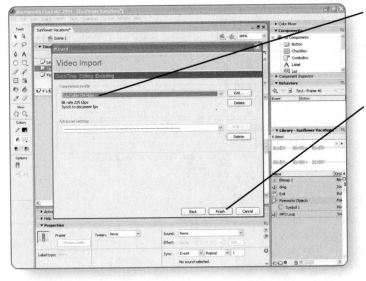

8. Choose a Compression profile to specify how fast an Internet connection your audience members will be using.

9. Click on Finish. The wizard will close, and Flash will finish importing the file.

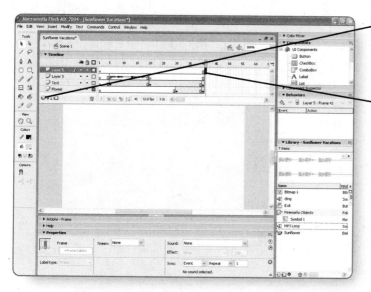

10. Click on the Insert Layer button to add a new layer to hold the video.

11. On the new layer, insert a keyframe where you would like to add the video. In this example, I want the video to start playing at frame 41, when the other elements of the movie have concluded.

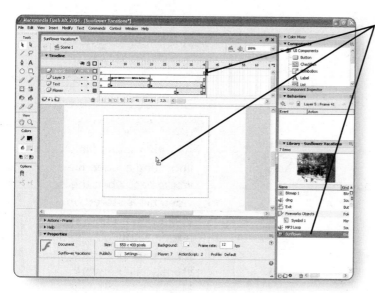

12. Click on the new keyframe on the layer that will hold the video and drag the video from the Library to the Stage.

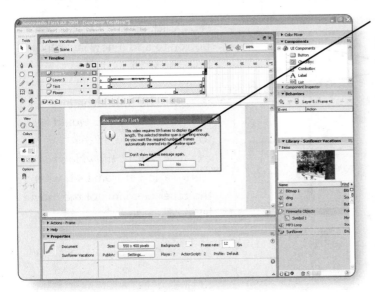

13. If Flash prompts you to add additional frames to the movie to accommodate the inserted video, click on Yes.

When you play back the movie file, the embedded video file will play starting from the keyframe where you inserted it.

CAUTION

As with a sound file, importing a video file works best when the video file is stored on your system's hard disk, not on a network. If you try to import a video file stored on a network, Flash may crash your system.

11

Publishing in Flash

Now that you have learned to create animation projects with Flash MX 2004, you should learn how to present the finished movies to your audience. Most Flash movies are published on the Internet on Web sites. Other movies are distributed via digital media for stand-alone viewing. To learn how to publish these movies online, you will cover the following topics in this chapter:

- The different formats in which Flash can publish.
- Why some formats are preferred over others.
- How do to create a basic HTML page.
- How to use HTML and Flash together.

Understanding Publishing and Movie Formats

Publishing a Flash movie converts the content you have created in the working project file (the .FLA file) to the finished movie file (often in the .SWF Flash movie format, which works with the Flash player). Viewers can download the Flash Player via a link on the Flash Player home page at http://www.macromedia.com/software/flashplayer/. Of course, you may need to publish a Flash movie in another final format.

Flash MX 2004 can publish movie files in a number of formats, including:

- **.SWF**. Files for a Flash Player
- **.HTML**. The format for a basic Web page that will contain the Flash movie
- **.GIF**. Static or animated GIF files, viewable in most browsers and imaging programs
- **.JPEG**. Static image files, viewable in most browsers and imaging programs
- **.PNG**. Another type of static image often used on Web pages
- **.EXE**. A self-contained Microsoft Windows program that includes a Flash player and the movie
- **.HQX**. A self-contained Apple Macintosh program that includes a Flash Player and the movie
- **.MOV**. Apple QuickTime movies

Each of these file types offers benefits and limitations. The files types can be categorized into four groups:

- **Interactive movie**. SWF, MOV, EXE, and HQX files fall into this category. These types of files include animation, and can include user interactivity if you build it into the project with ActionScript. The SWF files require a Flash player or Flash plug-in for a Web browser for viewing. QuickTime MOV files require the Apple QuickTime player or plug-in for your Web browser. The EXE and HQX files have all the information needed to play the movie, including Flash Player. Publish to the SWF format when the published movie is to be viewed on the Internet. The stand-alone file types (EXE and HQX) run completely on their own. For example, if you place a stand-alone movie on a CD-R, you can double-click on the file icon in a folder window, and the movie will play—no Internet connection is needed.

- **Non-interactive movie**. These movies, including animated GIF files, play continuously without user interaction. Animated GIF files can be viewed in browsers without a plug-in or special player, but are usually *very* large.

- **Static picture**. GIF, JPEG, and PNG files are created from only the first frame of the Flash movie or a keyframe with the label #Static. Although not interactive or dynamic, these pictures are useful in Web development. You can create an image to use as a background for a Web site in Flash, export the image as a GIF or JPEG file, and use it in the Web site's HTML files.

- **Helper file**. HTML files created by Flash assist in the process of moving your movie to the Web. These files do not contain the movies themselves, but contain information telling a Web browser how to display the Flash files.

Specifying Publishing Options

In addition to choosing the format for a published movie, you can choose a variety of other settings that affect the size and quality of the published file(s). Because of the sheer number of possible combinations, this section shows you how to find the available options. You should check the Publish Settings before each publishing operation. Then you'll be sure that the files published meet your needs.

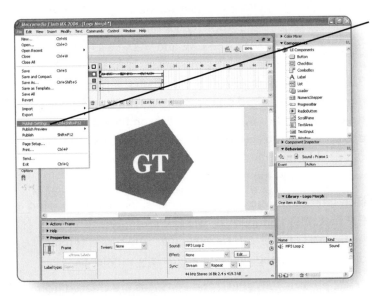

You choose publishing options in the Publish Settings dialog box. Open this dialog box by choosing File, Publish Settings or by pressing Ctrl+Shift+F12 (Command+Shift+F12 on the Mac).

After you choose the desired settings in the Publish Settings dialog box, you can:

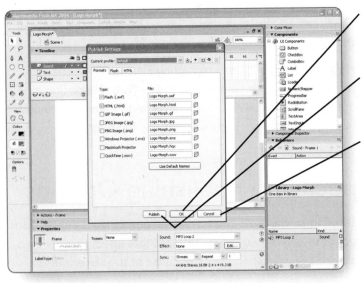

- Click on OK to close the dialog box and apply the settings.

- Click on Publish to publish the movie project by using the specified settings.

- Click on Cancel to close the dialog box without saving the settings.

Now explore the settings in the Publish Settings dialog box.

Formats

The Formats tab enables you to select each type of file you want to publish. You can generate multiple files each time you publish the project.

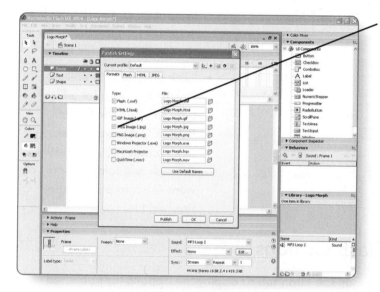

Simply check the checkbox for each type of file you want to publish in the Type column.

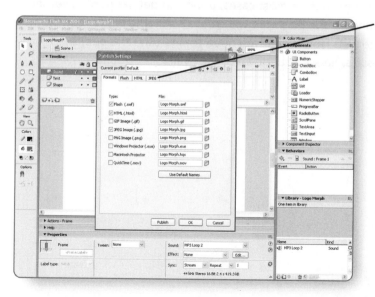

When you check a file type on the Formats tab, a new tab with the settings for that particular file type will appear in the Publish Settings dialog box. For example, if you check the JPEG Image choice on the Formats tab, the JPEG tab will appear. (The rest of this section will show the dialog box with the tabs for all publishing formats.)

In addition to choosing the formats to publish on the Formats tab, you can:

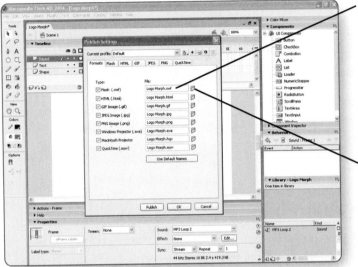

- Edit the name for each published file as desired in the applicable text box in the File column. Click on Use Default Names to revert the text boxes to the default file names, which are the same as the Flash project file name.

- Click on a Select Publish Destination icon for a file type to open the Select Publish Destination dialog box so that you can specify the disk and folder where you want Flash to publish the finished file.

Flash Options

Click on the Flash tab to display the options for published Flash movies. In most cases, using the default publish settings found on the Flash tab will create a suitable file for use on the Internet. However, if you need to fine-tune the published results, here's a rundown of the available options:

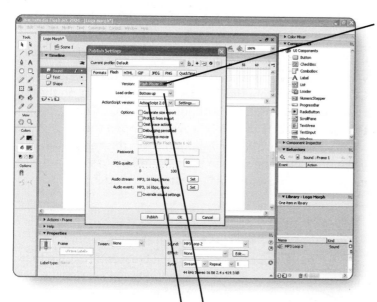

- **Version**. Choose the Flash Player version that viewers must have installed to play back the movie. Flash MX 2004 can publish movies playable in all seven Player versions. However, features that have been added to newer versions of Flash and Flash Player do not appear in movies published for older versions of the player. For example, most ActionScript does not work in versions earlier than Version 5.

- **Load Order**. When a Flash movie is being downloaded over a slow connection, this option determines whether the movie should load from the bottom of the frame up (Bottom Up, default) or from the top of the frame down (Top Down).

- **ActionScript Version**. Choose which ActionScript version Flash should use in the published movie.

TIP

There are two schools of thought that exist with regard to publishing for a particular Flash Player version. Some developers believe that you should always use the newest technology and force users to upgrade Flash Player if necessary. Although it is an inconvenience for users, this strategy enables the developer to use the newest tools and features in Flash. Or you can publish for the lowest-level player that implements the features you need in your movie. Then users probably do not need to upgrade Flash Player, although the movie may not do everything that was intended. (continues)

TIP (continued)

If you choose to publish for the latest Flash Player version and are generating HTML, choose the Flash Only template (from the Template drop-down list on the HTML tab in the Publish Settings dialog box). This template instructs the Web browser to open the Macromedia Flash Player 7 plug-in. With this template, if the browser cannot open the plug-in because it is not installed, the browser tries to install the plug-in.

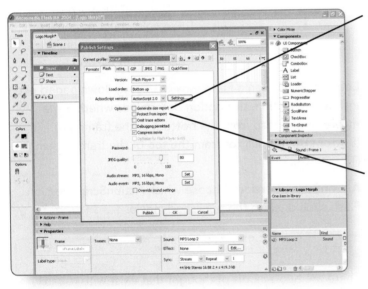

- **Generate size report**. This option creates a text file that details how much room in the SWF file is devoted to each frame and the elements in each frame. (You will look at a report file later in this chapter.)

- **Protect from import**. This option prevents users from loading the SWF file into Flash MX 2004 and treating it as their own work. Commercial entities that have an Internet presence do not necessarily want to share all their proprietary information. For example, a company that sells access to Flash games online would not want anyone to be able to download a Flash movie file that contains a popular game, open the file in Flash MX 2004, add a few features, and sell it themselves. You probably should turn on this setting.

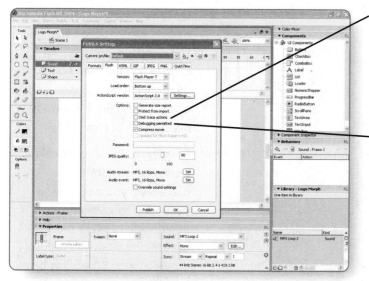

- **Omit trace actions**. ActionScript uses the Trace() command, which prints a string of text. Omit Trace Actions disables this debugging feature.

- **Debugging Permitted**. This option enables the ActionScript debugging. When you are working on complex programming, the option to debug your work is invaluable.

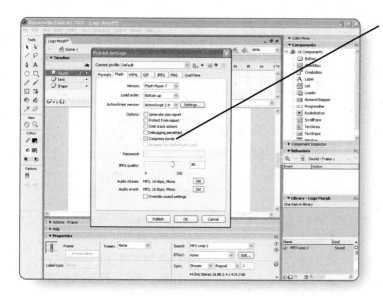

- **Compress movie**. Check this checkbox to compress the SWF file so that it can download more quickly. Compressing the Flash movie is a good practice to follow when you are publishing to the Web. Compression creates a much smaller file that downloads more quickly to convey the same information. This is important because you cannot predict the speed at which a user is connecting to the Internet. A large file combined with a slow connection speed means movie playback will be choppy at best.

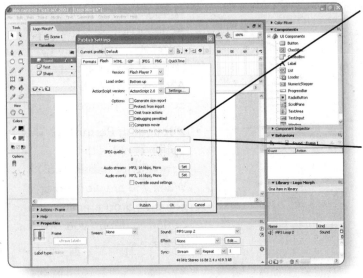

- **Optimize for Flash Player 6 r 65**. If you choose Flash Player 6 from the Version drop-down list, this setting becomes active. Check it to optimize the Flash movie for revision 65 of Flash Player 6.

- **Password**. If you check the Debugging permitted checkbox, you can enter a password to prevent unauthorized users from peeking into how a Flash movie works. When this box is blank, no password is set.

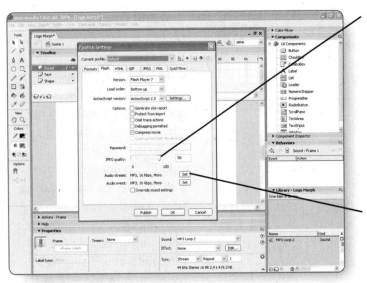

- **JPEG quality**. Drag the slider to set the desired quality for compressing bitmap images included in the Flash movie. Higher-quality (or better-looking) pictures require more space, which creates a larger movie. Highly compressed images should create a smaller movie.

- **Audio stream**. The Set button displays options for audio streams. Refer to Chapter 10 for information on these settings.

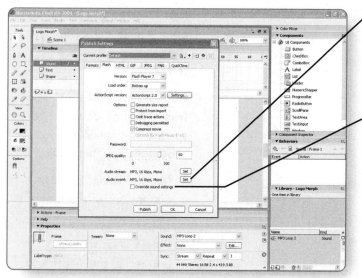

- **Audio event**. You set these options by clicking the Set button. Refer to Chapter 10 for information on these settings.

- **Override sound settings**. When this option is checked, Flash overrides the settings for each individual sound inserted into the movie and instead uses the audio options you set on this tab of the Publish Settings dialog box.

HTML Options

If you have checked the HTML checkbox on the Formats tab of the Publish Settings dialog box, the HTML Options tab appears. This tab contains settings that assist in putting your movie on the Web. (See the later "HTML Basics" section for more details about the Web concepts introduced here.)

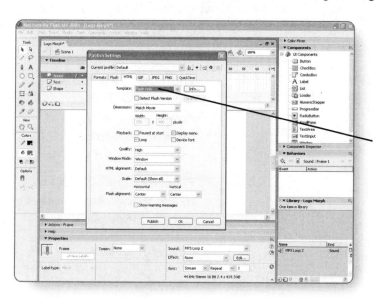

- **Template**. Choose a template from this drop-down list to determine what is included in the published HTML file. Flash Only is the default selection and a good choice, as mentioned earlier. Several options are available here, including QuickTime and Flash for Pocket PC 2003.

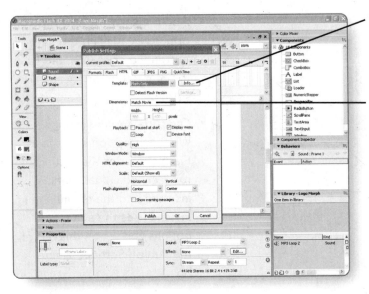

- **Info**. Click on this button to open a dialog box that describes the selected template.

- **Dimensions**. Make a choice from this drop-down list to specify how the Web browser should display the movie:

  - **Match Movie**. Uses the dimensions of the movie you created.

  - **Pixels**. Uses the size entered in the Width and Height boxes to set the size of the movie in pixels. The movie is expanded or shrunk as necessary.

- **Percent**. Determines the size of the movie as a percentage of the browser window. Enter the Width and Height as numbers between 1 and 100, where 100 fills the browser window completely.

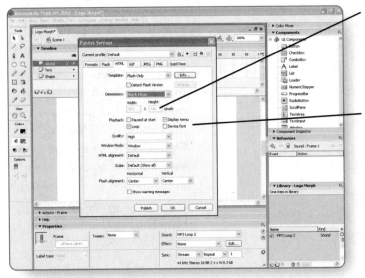

- **Width and Height**. If you choose either Pixels or Percentage from the Dimensions drop-down list, enter the desired sizes here.

- **Playback**. Check choices here to add special characteristics with the movie playback:

- **Paused at start**. Prevents the movie from playing automatically. Instead, the movie loads and pauses on the first frame of the first scene.

- **Loop**. Loops the movie back to the beginning upon completion, playing over and over.

- **Display menu**. Determines whether a menu should appear when a user right-clicks on your Flash movie. If this box is unchecked, a menu with only one item, About Macromedia Flash Player 7, appears.

- **Device font**. This option enables Flash to substitute system fonts found on all computers for any font the user may not have.

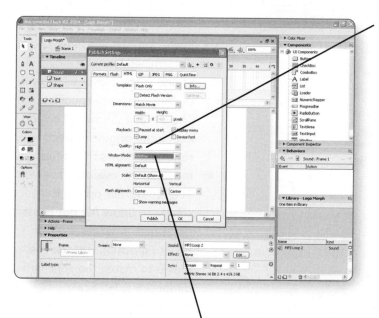

- **Quality**. When the movie plays, you see a trade-off between the speed and the quality of the playback. In some instances, speed is more important than quality. Use this option to tell Flash how high the image quality should be. Low-quality movies play quickly, but do not look perfect. Best-quality movies may look fantastic, but might stall during playback as the computer is forced to do image processing.

- **Window Mode**. This option controls how the HTML file opens in the Microsoft Internet Explorer 4.0 browser with the Flash ActiveX control.

- **Window**. Plays the movie in its own browser window.

- **Opaque Windowless**. Forces the movie to the foreground of the window it is in, hiding anything behind it.

- **Transparent Windowless**. Applies to movies that have transparent areas. In this mode, the Web page's background is visible through any transparent area of the movie.

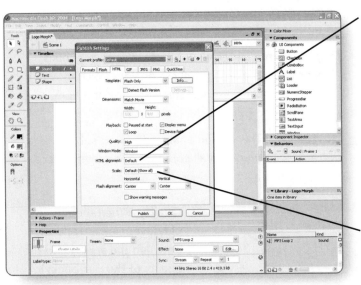

- **HTML Alignment**. Choose a setting from this drop-down list to specify how the movie should be aligned on the Web page. The Default option centers the movie in the browser window. All other options place the movie on the appropriate side of the browser window, cropping the other sides if necessary.

- **Scale**. Your choice here determines how the movie is scaled in the player window if dimensions were specified. The Default (Show All) option keeps the original aspect ratio and shows the entire movie in the available space. The No Border option is similar to Show All, but crops the movie if necessary. The Exact Fit option distorts the movie to match the specified dimensions. No Scale prevents the movie from scaling.

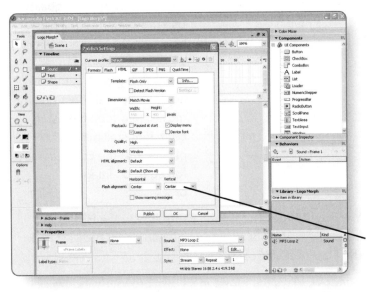

- **Flash alignment**. The Horizontal and Vertical choices you make here determine where the movie is placed in the player window.

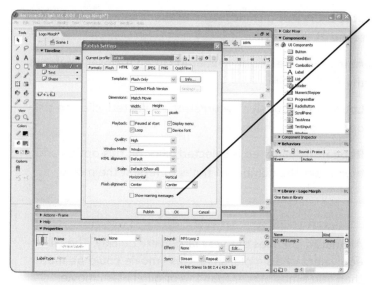

- **Show warning messages**. When this option is checked, Flash will alert you when a problem occurs with any settings, such as if two settings conflict.

GIF Options

Most Web graphics were created in one of two formats: GIF or JPEG. Unlike JPEG images, GIF images can include animation and transparent areas. When you plan to publish a GIF file from your movie project file, first choose the desired options on the GIF tab of the Publish Settings dialog box.

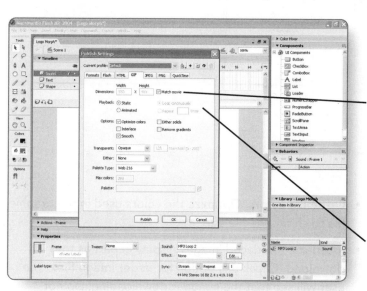

- **Dimensions**. When Match movie is checked, the GIF's dimensions match those of the original movie. Uncheck Match movie if you want to enter the another Height and Width in pixels.

- **Playback**. Your choice here determines whether the image file will include animation:

- **Static**. Creates a static image of the first frame of the first scene of the movie.

- **Animated**. Creates an animated GIF that closely matches the Flash movie.

- **Loop Continuously**. If Animated is selected, click on this option to loop the movie.

- **Repeat**. If Animated is selected, click on this option and then enter the number of times to repeat the movie.

CAUTION

Animated GIF files get very large very quickly. The GIF equivalent of a simple, small Flash movie could be more than 100 times bigger than the original Flash movie.

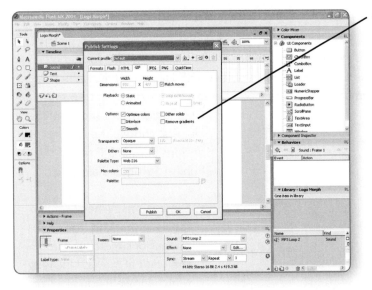

- **Options**. Your Options choices affect the look of the image, including its color.

- **Optimize colors**. Optimize the colors used in the graphic file to shrink the file size.

- **Interlace**. Interlaced images display in part as they download. Check this option for larger image files. The user will see that the image is downloading. Do not interlace animated GIF files.

- **Smooth**. Smoothing an image creates a higher-quality image at the expense of file size.

- **Dither solids**. This option applies dithering to solid colors in the image. Dithering enables the image to appear to contain colors that are not on the image's palette.

- **Remove gradients**. When gradient fills are published to a GIF file, a loss of image quality occurs, and you will see a dramatic increase in the file size. Checking this option replaces all gradient fills with a solid fill of the first color in the gradient.

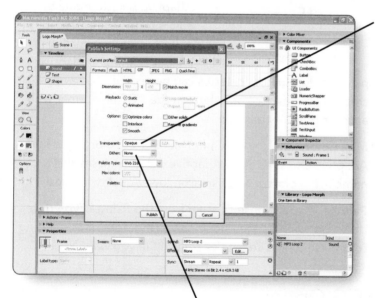

- **Transparent**. Make a choice from this drop-down list to determine whether the background should be transparent. *Opaque* yields a solid background. Choose *Transparent* to make the background fully transparent. Choose *Alpha* to set partial transparency and then enter a number between 0 and 255, where 0 is transparent and 255 is opaque.

- **Dither**. Make a choice here to decide how colors that are not on the color palette are handled. *None* turns off dithering, and any colors in the file not in the color palette are replaced with the closest match. Although this technique creates smaller files, these files usually look less than acceptable. *Ordered* dithering creates decent-looking colors with minimal increases in file size. Select *Diffusion* to produce the largest, best-looking images.

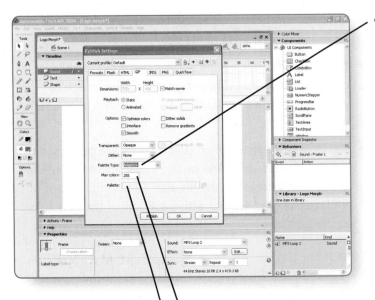

- **Palette Type**. Choose the palette type used in the image. The default, Web 216, works well in most situations by creating good-quality images with a standard 216-color palette. The Adaptive palette determines which colors are necessary for the image and creates an accurate palette and a larger GIF file. The Web Snap Adaptive palette matches colors to the Web 216 palette, creating smaller images than pure adaptive palettes do. Custom palettes can be used if you have created your own color palette in the ACT file format with another graphics program.

- **Max Colors**. Set the maximum number of colors used in the Adaptive and Web Snap Adaptive palettes. A smaller number of colors creates smaller, lower-quality images.

- **Palette**. If you choose Custom from the Palette Type drop-down list, click on the folder icon to the right of this setting to browse to and select the palette file you want to use.

JPEG Options

JPEGs are 24-bit colored images that use compression to ensure smaller image files, making them ideal for publishing on the Web. The JPEG tab of the Publish Settings dialog box offers only a few options to consider when you are publishing to a JPEG file.

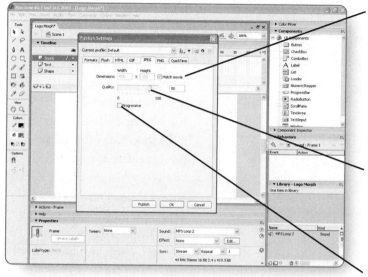

- **Dimensions**. As with GIF images, you can check the Match Movie checkbox to generate a JPEG image that matches the size of the original movie, or clear the checkbox and then enter the desired Height and Width.

- **Quality**. Use the slider to specify the desired balance between file size and image quality. The default value of 80 works well.

- **Progressive**. Check this checkbox to have the image display as it loads rather than appearing only after the entire image is downloaded. This option is similar to the interlacing option used with GIF images.

PNG Options

The PNG tab in the Publish Settings dialog box offers many of the same options as for GIF images. Choose settings here when you want to publish the Flash project as a PNG file.

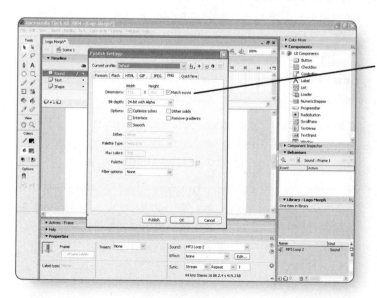

- **Dimensions**. When Match movie is checked, the published file's dimensions match those of the original movie. Otherwise, you can uncheck Match movie, and then enter the desired Height and Width in pixels.

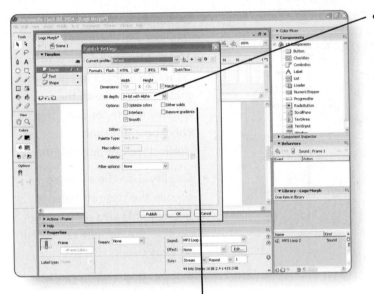

- **Bit Depth**. Your Bit depth choice specifies the number of bits per pixel used in the image, which relates to the number of colors available for use in the palette. The higher the bit depth, the bigger the published file. A bit depth of 8-bit creates 256 color images, while 24-bit bit depth allows thousands of colors. Selecting a bit depth of 24-bit with Alpha creates images that can contain thousands of colors and transparency. The Dither and Palette Type options only become active when you choose 8-bit from the Bit depth drop-down list.

- **Options** Your Options choices affect the look of the image, including its color

  - **Optimize colors**. Optimize the colors used in the graphic file to shrink the file size.

  - **Interlace**. Interlaced images display in part as they download. Check this option for larger image files. The user will see that the image is downloading. Do not interlace animated GIF files.

  - **Smooth**. Smoothing an image creates a higher-quality image at the expense of file size.

  - **Dither solids**. This option applies dithering to solid colors in the image. Dithering enables the image to appear to contain colors that are not on the image's palette.

  - **Remove gradients**. When gradient fills are published to a GIF file, a loss of image quality occurs, and you can see a dramatic increase in the file size. Checking this option replaces all gradient fills with a solid fill of the first color in the gradient.

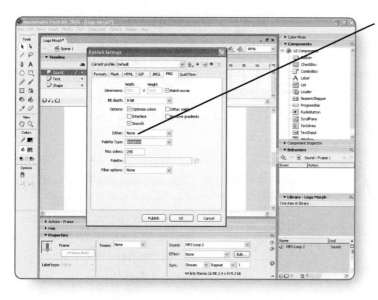

- **Dither**. Select an option to decide how colors that are not on the color palette are handled. Selecting None turns off dithering, and any colors in the file not on the color palette are replaced with the closest match. Although this option creates smaller files, they usually look less than acceptable. Ordered dithering creates decent-looking colors with minimal file size increases. Selecting Diffusion produces the largest, best-looking images.

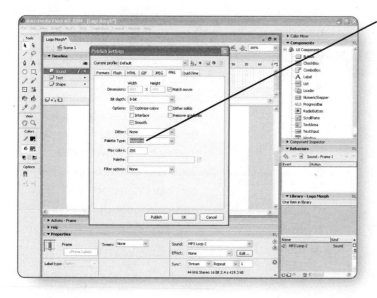

- **Palette Type**. Choose the type of palette used in the published image. The Web 216 palette works well in most situations by creating good-quality images with a standard 216-color palette. The Adaptive palette determines which colors are necessary for the image and creates an accurate palette and a larger file. The Web Snap Adaptive palette matches colors to the Web 216 palette, creating smaller images than pure adaptive palettes. Custom palettes can be used if you have created your own color palette in the ACT file format with another graphics program.

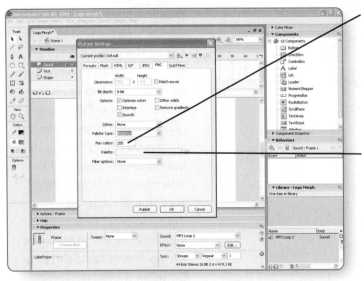

- **Max Colors**. Enter the maximum number of colors that can be used by Adaptive and Web Snap Adaptive palettes. A smaller number of colors creates smaller, lower-quality images.

- **Palette**. If you choose Custom from the Palette Type drop-down list, click on the folder icon to the right of this setting to browse to and select the palette file you want to use.

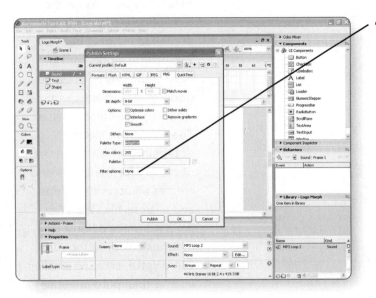

- **Filter Options**. Filtering analyzes the image and attempts to compress the image. Each of the Filter options choices applies a different method to compress the image. Play with the various choices to see which one works best for a particular image.

QuickTime Options

The QuickTime movie format created by Apple requires either a QuickTime player or browser plug-in installed on the computer. When Flash publishes to a QuickTime movie, it creates a QuickTime track that contains the entire movie. If the Flash movie contains a QuickTime movie (as an imported symbol, for example), each included QuickTime movie is placed on its own track. You can set a number of options for publishing to a QuickTime movie on the QuickTime tab of the Publish Settings dialog box:

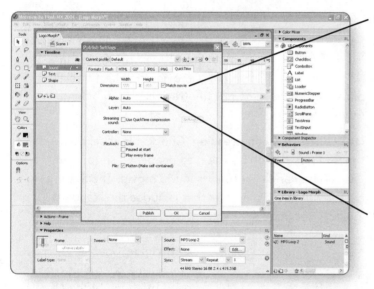

- **Dimensions**. As for publishing to other file formats, the dimensions of the published movie can be set to match the original movie (check Match Movie). Or clear the Match Movie checkbox and enter the desired Width and Height dimensions.

- **Alpha**. Your Alpha choice applies to the Flash track created in the QuickTime movie. If the movie includes several tracks, this setting affects how the Flash movie track interacts with them. If other tracks are in the movie, the Auto option makes the Flash track transparent if it is on top of any other tracks; if the Flash track is the only track in the movie, it is opaque. The Copy option makes the Flash track opaque. Alpha Transparent makes the Flash track transparent so that other tracks can be seen through it.

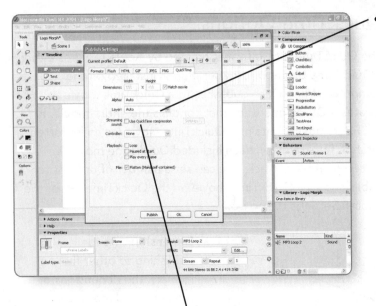

- **Layer**. Your Layer drop-down list choice controls whether the Flash track in the QuickTime movie is on top of or underneath other tracks in the movie. The Top option places the Flash track on top of other tracks, and Bottom places it under the other tracks in the movie. The Auto option places the Flash track in relation to any QuickTime movie tracks in the movie. If objects in the Flash movie are on top of the QuickTime movie, the Flash track is placed on top; otherwise, the track is placed behind the other tracks.

- **Use QuickTime compression**. Check this checkbox and use the Settings button beside it to enable Flash to have QuickTime handle all sounds in the movie. The Settings button opens a dialog box that includes the standard QuickTime sound settings.

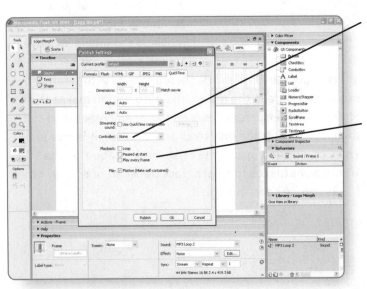

- **Controller**. Choose the QuickTime controller type used by the published movie: None, Standard, or QuickTime VR.

- **Playback**. Choose whether to include any special characteristics with the movie playback:

  - **Loop**. Check this box to have the movie loop.

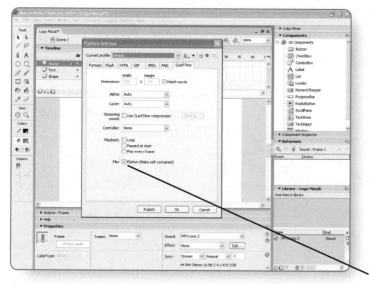

- **Paused at Start**. If this option is checked, the movie pauses at the first frame.

- **Play Every Frame**. When this option is enabled, it plays every single frame in the movie rather than the usual practice of skipping frames when necessary to maintain the pace. With this option enabled, sound does not play.

- **File**. Checking the Flatten option copies any external movie objects into the QuickTime movie rather than relying on links.

NOTE

To publish a Flash movie to the QuickTime format, you may need to have the version on the Flash options tab set to Flash Player 6 or earlier. If you try to publish a movie targeted to Flash Player 7 as a QuickTime movie, you may get an error message indicating "The installed version of QuickTime does not have a handler for this type of Macromedia Flash movie."

Publishing a Movie

After you've used the Publish Settings dialog box to choose desired publishing formats and options for those formats, you can publish the movie. Here are the overall steps for publishing a movie project file:

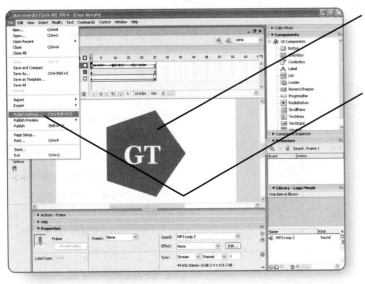

1. Open the movie project file to publish. If the file was already open, save any recent changes.

2. Choose File, Publish Settings. The Publish Settings dialog box will open.

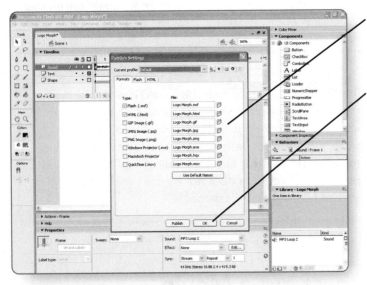

3. Choose publishing formats and settings as described in the previous section.

4. Click on OK. (Or you can click on Publish and then click on OK; skip Step 5 if you do so.)

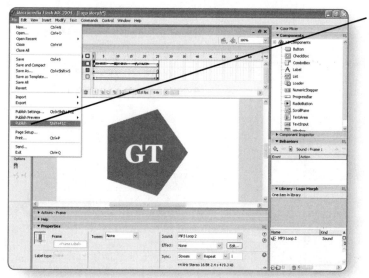

5. Choose File, Publish. Flash will publish your movie in the specified format(s).

To preview an exported file, double-click on the file icon in a folder window for your operating system.

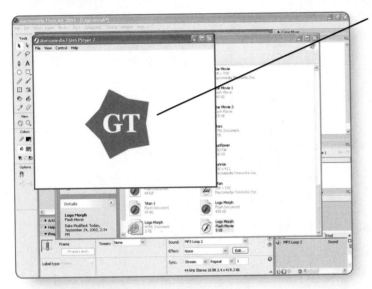

The exported file will open in a Player window or your Web browser. Simply close the window when you've finished reviewing the exported file.

After you generate a movie, HTML, or graphic file, you need to publish it to the Web server or other location where the viewer can access the file. Those publishing instructions vary depending on the type of Web server you are publishing to. You can use an FTP client like cuteFTP or Fetch to copy both the HTML and the SWF files to the server. For help with the specifics, consult your Internet Service Provider or Webmaster.

Looking at a Size Report

If you check the Generate size report option on the Flash tab of the Publish settings dialog box, Flash creates a report to detail the size of each element in the movie. Flash publishes the report as a text file (.txt) in the same folder as the published movie.

All the information in the size report is intended to help isolate areas of the movie that could be changed to make the final, published movie smaller. You should look at a frame or tween that is much larger than the other frames or tweens to determine whether you can do anything to simplify it. One big space-saver is to make sure that any shape used more than once is converted to a symbol and that instances of that symbol are used wherever possible.

You can double-click on the icon for the size report file in a folder window to open the report. (In Windows, it will open in the Notepad applet.) Here's what the report will tell you:

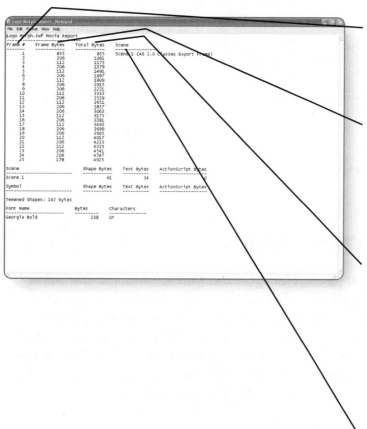

- **Frame #.** The first column shows the frame numbers for the movie, starting at one and continuing through each scene.

- **Frame Bytes**. The second column lists the amount of space in the file devoted to the contents of each frame. The first frame holds 855 bytes, the second 206 bytes, and so on.

- **Total Bytes**. The third column displays the cumulative total number of bytes needed for the movie up to that frame number. At Frame 3, the movie has 1173, which is the sum of Frame 1 (at 855 bytes), Frame 2 (206 bytes), and Frame 3 (112 bytes).

- **Scene**. Lists the scene being reported on.

The following sections of the report offer additional information:

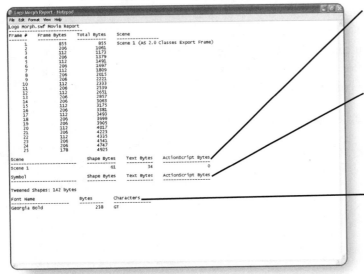

- The scenes in the movie, sizes of the shapes used in the scene, and the size of the text in the scene.

- The symbols used in the movie, including tweens; the sizes of each symbol in bytes; and the size of the text used in the symbol.

- The name of the font that was used, the size of the string in bytes, and the text in the string.

HTML Basics

HTML is short for HyperText Markup Language, the language of the Internet. All Web browsers understand a flavor of HTML, although each browser behaves differently. Microsoft Internet Explorer and Netscape Navigator interpret the same tag and possibly display slightly different results. This section introduces you to some HTML basics, so you can understand how the HTML files generated by Flash work.

> **NOTE**
>
> HTML is a subject for an entire book. This chapter touches on a few basic topics. For a more in-depth discussion, check out *Learn HTML in a Weekend,* 4th Edition, by Steve Callihan from Premier Press. You can check the numerous online resources for learning HTML including:
>
> - http://www.w3.org (The World Wide Web Consortium)
>
> - http://hotwired.lycos.com/webmonkey/
>
> - http://webreference.com/html/
>
> - http://www.htmlgoodies.com/

HTML Structure

HTML files are text files that have a basic structure. You can open HTML files in your favorite text editor (such as Notepad) or in special HTML editors, like Macromedia's Dreamweaver MX 2004. HTML is a *tagged* structure. Special tags surround the text and graphics to be displayed; the tags tell a Web browser how to display the text.

You use almost all HTML tags in pairs, meaning that you must include both an opening and closing tag for each tagged part of the document. Angle brackets, < and >, identify each tag, as in <HTML>. An added forward slash (/), as in </HTML>, indicates a closing tag. Get into the habit of always closing HTML tags; you will soon learn the few that do not get closed. Leaving the wrong tag open causes big problems in some browsers, and that open tag can be hard to find in a long page of code. HTML tags are not case-sensitive, but most Web developers tend to use all upper- or lower-case letters in tags just for good form and easier reading.

<HTML>

The HTML tag tells the Web browser that the file holds HTML content. All HTML files have an opening tag

```
<HTML>
```

near the beginning of the file (it may include additional specification information) and a closing tag near the end:

```
</HTML>
```

<HEAD>

The header block, denoted by the <HEAD> tag, can contain such information as the document's title, any scripting, and Meta information (including keywords and description) that can be used by search engines.

<TITLE>

The contents of the title tag appear in the Web browser's title bar. Locate this tag within the <HEAD> tag.

<BODY>

The body section follows the header section and contains the bulk of the information in the HTML file. As previously mentioned, HTML is vast enough to fill its own book with information and several books, including those recommended, exist as resources for you. Text in the body tags can be formatted much like text can be formatted in a word processing program. Do some research on Cascading Style Sheets to learn the preferred methods.

TIP

Flash MX 2004 supports a subset of CSS tags found in cascading style sheets. The TextField.StyleSheet class in ActionScript enables you to use the CSS styles. Search for "css" in the Flash Help system to learn more about using this advanced HTML development technique.

<H1>, <H2>, <H3>, <H4>, <H5>, and <H6>

Heading tags display the text contained inside of them as section headers. <H1> tags contain large text, and each subsequent numbered header has smaller text.

<P>

Paragraph blocks contain text that should be grouped together and followed by a line break. Because the text in an HTML file is displayed continuously, except when line breaks are intentionally placed, this tag is helpful.

One of the few unpaired tags (there is no closing </BR> tag), <BR> forces the end of a line.

<A>

Anchor tags create hyperlinks, or links, between pages. Anchor tags can contain several attributes. The most important attribute for an anchor tag is the HREF, or the URL that the link connects to. This sample anchor tag takes users to http://www.premierpressbooks.com when they click on the words *Premier Press Web Site*.

```
<A HREF="http://www.premierpressbooks.com">Premier Press
Web Site</A>
```

<IMG>

This tag inserts an image and takes several attributes:

- **SRC**. The URL of the graphic file
- **ALT**. A text string that is displayed either when the image cannot be loaded or when the user hovers the mouse cursor over the image for a moment
- **WIDTH**. The width of the image in pixels
- **HEIGHT**. The height of the image in pixels

HTML in Practice

Now that you've been introduced to some of the commonly used HTML tags, you can put them into practice by editing an HTML file that you've published from Flash. Open the file in Notepad, or your favorite text editor or browser.

Add in tags and text as desired. For example, here I've added <H1>, <H2>, and <P> tags and text.

After you make the desired changes in the HTML file, be sure to save your changes. Close the file.

To view the HTML file with your changes, double-click on the file icon in an operating system folder window.

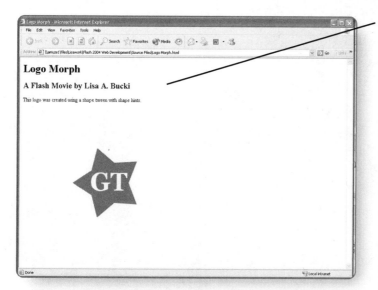

When the file opens in your system's Web browser, you will see the new information that you added.

Of course, the tags presented in this section do not represent all of HTML, by any stretch of the imagination. Plus, using a dedicated Web page development program like Dreamweaver MX 2004 opens up even greater possibilities for using your Flash movies in Web pages. I hope this chapter has whetted your appetite for publishing your Flash movies to the Web.

NOTE

In Microsoft Internet Explorer, you can select Source (or Page Source) from the View menu to see the source code for the current page or right-click on the page and choose View Source from the context menu. Look at the code for some of your favorite pages, see how the HTML is written, and experiment.

12

Using Simple ActionScript

You have come to the conclusion that you will need to get yourself on the Internet and that a Web page will be the best way to do this. Now you need to get started with FrontPage, Microsoft's tool for creating Web pages. In this chapter, you'll learn how to do the following:

- Start FrontPage 2003.
- Run commands from menus, toolbars, and dialog boxes.
- Effectively use the new Task Pane feature.
- Navigate through the different FrontPage design views.
- Obtain help when needed.
- Exit FrontPage 2003.

What Is ActionScript?

Flash enables you to create anything from a simple animation to a complex interactive game. The choice is up to you. However, to talk to Flash and tell it how you want it to respond to the user requires speaking to Flash in a language it understands. The language that Flash MX 2004 understands and can work with is ActionScript 2.0. The full-featured ActionScript scripting language allows the programmer to control objects and movies and to enable a Flash movie to respond to the user.

This chapter covers a few basic elements of a programming language. Programming languages like ActionScript enable you to develop a program in smaller pieces called *functions*. Breaking up the program into small parts provides several benefits. For example, the code can be organized into logical pieces. If the program will perform several different actions, the manner to carry out each of those actions can be placed in its own function. Also, code used multiple times can be placed in a function. Any changes that must be done to the logic in a frequently used piece of code, therefore, need to be updated only once if a problem appears.

Another advantage of using functions is that they can be given information to use when they are called. The information passed to a function is an *argument*. Arguments can be extremely helpful. For example, one of the functions of most calculators is to compute the squares of numbers, such as "two squared equals four." The calculator program probably has a Square() function that takes a number as an argument. The Square function then multiplies the number by itself and gives the resulting number as a return value. Return values are another benefit of functions because you can have a function calculate an answer based on input and give the answer back through a return value.

Keeping these concepts in mind, let's look at a few building blocks of ActionScript.

ACTIONSCRIPT AND JAVASCRIPT

ActionScript is loosely based on JavaScript. If you have used JavaScript in Web site development, you should be able to learn how to use ActionScript relatively quickly. The new version of ActionScript, 2.0, offers even greater compatibility with other object-oriented programming languages like Java and JavaScript. (Object-oriented programming languages take a modular approach to programming.) The syntax for ActionScript is almost identical to that of JavaScript, which can make reading and understanding code much easier. However, JavaScript supports a number of procedures that ActionScript does not, and some ActionScript elements behave differently than their JavaScript counterparts.

You use the Behaviors panel to assign the behavior. When you assign a behavior, you also specify configuration settings for the behavior and the event that triggers the behavior, such as a mouse click. Use the following steps to add a behavior to an instance:

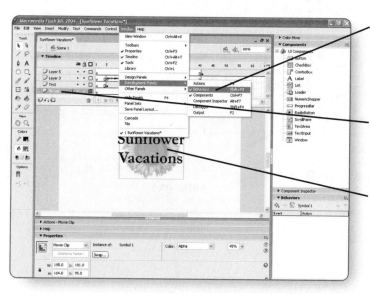

1. If the Behaviors panel isn't already open, choose Window, Development Panels, Behaviors to open it.

2. Click on the layer and frame that hold the instance to which you want to add a behavior.

3. Select the instance to which you want to add the behavior.

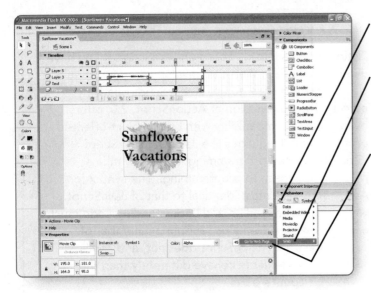

4. Click on the Add Behavior button in the Behaviors panel.

5. Point to the category that holds the behavior to assign. A submenu will appear.

6. Click on the behavior to assign. A dialog box with settings for configuring the behavior will open.

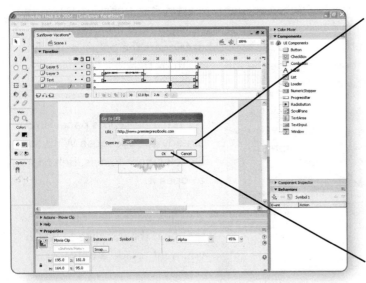

7. Specify settings for the behavior as desired. (Of course, the settings will vary, depending on the behavior selected.) The Go to URL behavior requires that you specify a target URL and the browser window that the target Web page will Open in. (The "_self" choice means that the target will open in the same Web window that holds the Flash movie.)

8. Click on OK to apply the settings.

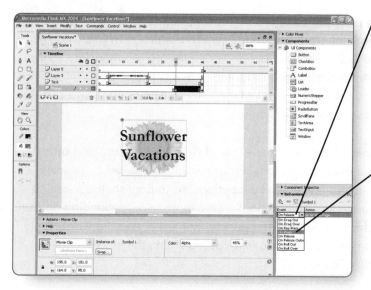

9. To change the event which triggers the behavior during playback of the published movie, click on the Event column cell for the behavior in the Behaviors panel. A drop-down list arrow will appear.

10. Open the drop-down list and then click on the desired event.

The behavior has now been added. You can press F12 to preview the movie in your system's Web browser and test the behavior.

Basic Programming Concepts

If behaviors do not meet your needs and you need to start writing scripts in ActionScript 2.0, then read on. While learning programming requires a time investment, the resulting Flash movies will better serve your goals and the needs of your audience. A few universal concepts apply in programming, no matter what language you use, and this section presents a few of those concepts.

All programming languages have a language structure called *syntax*. Programmers need to follow the syntax so that the computer can understand what the programmer wants it to do. Computers can understand only certain instructions given to them in the binary language (using ones and zeros). Programming languages provide a simple way to give the computer instructions. (The translation from the programming language to binary takes place behind the scenes.) In this way, the program code can be read and understood by a person who knows the language in which the program was written. The ActionScript structure is simple: You can associate scripts in ActionScript with different elements in the movie, including each keyframe, each instance of a button symbol, and certain instances of other symbols.

Spoken languages have lots of rules for their use and often have many exceptions. Programming languages have fewer rules, but few (if any) exceptions. As in English, the meaning of a statement in ActionScript may change, depending on the order of its words, the punctuation used, and the words themselves. The following list highlights the key rules in ActionScript:

- Statements in ActionScript end with a semicolon.
- ActionScript statements are grouped together into functions.
- ActionScript uses curly braces, { and }, to hold the contents of a function.

Functions can use certain information to determine what the function should do. Information used by a function in this manner is a *parameter*.

- Parameters are pieces of information passed to a function.
- Parameters are passed to functions in parentheses.

ActionScript cares about the case of words in only a few instances, when it is working with a short list of words reserved for use by ActionScript. You should use these special, reserved words, or *keywords*, in the correct case, which is all lowercase. Other words—for example, variable names—do not depend on case, so as far as ActionScript is concerned, **BoB** and **bob** are the same. Working with a program is much simpler, of course, if you use case consistently throughout the program.

- ActionScript is typically not case-sensitive.

- Keywords should always be used in the correct case— lowercase.

The period, or dot, has special meaning in ActionScript. When you have an object, you can access the properties of that object by using the period. I cover this concept later in this chapter.

One other important item to consider is the comment. A comment is a note to the programmer that ActionScript does not need to know about. Comments are preceded by two forward slashes (//) and apply until the end of the line. Anything inside a comment is ignored by Flash and ActionScript and exists only to explain to a programmer what is happening.

ACTIONSCRIPT KEYWORDS

ActionScript uses only 32 keywords. Some you rarely use, although others may appear quite often in your code. Keywords cannot be used as variable names or as function names. See the ActionScript Dictionary in Flash help to learn more about using specific keywords. The keywords are shown in this list:

- break
- case
- class
- continue
- default
- delete
- dynamic
- else
- extends
- for
- function

- get
- if
- implements
- import
- in
- instanceof
- interface
- intrinsic
- new
- private
- public

- return
- set
- static
- switch
- this
- typeof
- var
- void
- while
- with

ActionScript and the Actions Panel

In Flash MX 2004, just about everything you can create has properties you can access through various panels. ActionScript is no different. You can open the Actions panel by selecting Window, Development Panels, Actions or by pressing F9. This panel, which appears by default under the Stage work area, is complex. Review how this panel works and then cover some of the basic concepts of ActionScript.

In Flash MX 2004, the Actions panel uses a single view. (In previous Flash versions, it had Normal and Expert modes.) Here are the key features of the Actions panel:

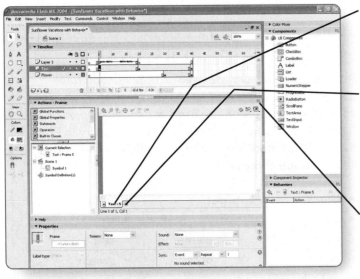

- **Navigation tab**. Shows you the layer name and frame number for the currently displayed script.

- **Pin active script**. Click on this button to pin the selected script so that its tab is visible in the Actions panel, no matter what you select in the Stage.

- **Panel Options Menu button**. Click on this button to open the Options menu for the Actions panel, which contains a number of options specific to working with ActionScript.

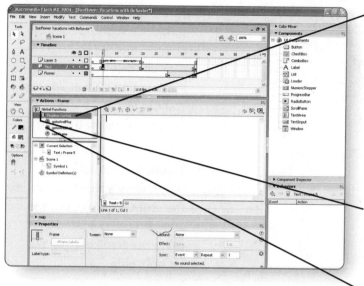

- **Actions Toolbox**. This hierarchical list contains the different tools in ActionScript that can be used in your movie. Clicking on a heading expands the heading and shows the items in a list under that heading. Double-clicking on an item adds it to the list.

- **An open heading is shown as an open book**. Clicking on an open heading hides its contents.

- **A circle with arrow icon identifies each item**. Double-clicking on an item adds it to your script.

- **A closed heading appears as a closed book**. Clicking on a closed heading displays its contents.

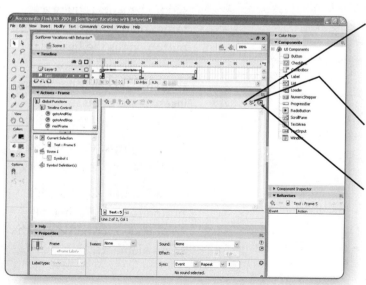

- **Reference**. Open the Help panel description of the selected tool in the Actions Toolbox by clicking on this button.

- **Debug Options**. Click on this button and then click on the desired debug setting.

- **View Options**. Click on this button and then click on the desired view choice.

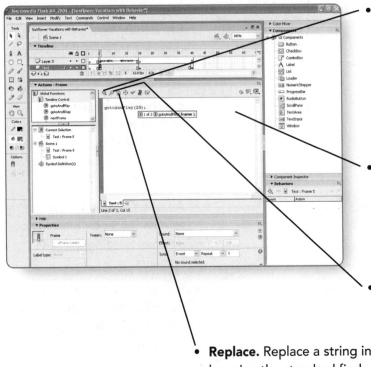

- **Add a new item to the script.** Click on this button, point to a category, and then click on the element to insert in the submenu that appears. You can use this button, rather than using the Actions Toolbox.

- **Script.** This area lists the script. Only a short portion of the script is visible, but the area can be navigated by using the scroll bars on the far right side.

- **Find.** Find a string in the Script by using the standard Find dialog box.

- **Replace.** Replace a string in the script with another string by using the standard find-and-replace dialog box.

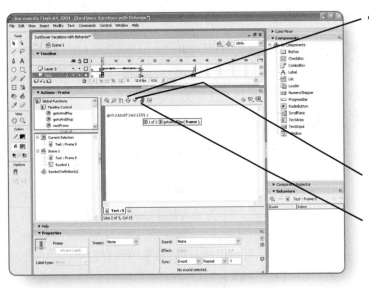

- **Insert a target path.** Some script elements require a target path as an option. This button opens the Insert Target Path dialog box so that you can easily create and insert these paths as parameters for functions.

- **Check Syntax.** Click on this button to find coding errors.

- **Auto Format.** Click on this button to have Flash apply color-coded formatting to the script elements.

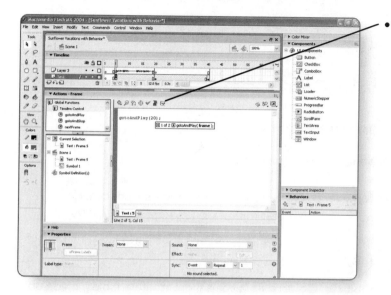

- **Show Code Hint**. Click on this button to display a yellow pop-up code hint for the current statement. The code hint explains how to supply a parameter or other required information in the statement.

Understanding Programming Building Blocks

To become better acquainted with ActionScript and how it works as a language, you need to spend some time learning the vocabulary. This section describes the components of ActionScript in greater detail.

Constants and Variables

Almost all programming languages call for the use of variables and constants. Constants are a simple way to keep track of things that do not change while the program (or script) is running. In math, for example, *pi* is a constant (a number that always is 3.14[…]), as well as the number of sides in a triangle. Constants represent known quantities. Variables, in contrast, change during the time a program runs. For example, when you open your Web browser and type the URL of a site you want to visit, the string you type is stored in a variable and used by the program. Later, you might type another address, and that value is stored in the same variable.

Let's look at how Flash uses variables.

Variable Types

Flash uses three types of variables:

- **Numbers**. *Numbers* are either integers or decimal numbers. Some examples are 12, 10.5, and 9999.99.

- **Strings**. *Strings* are text strings, like "Flash is cool." Most feedback to the user occurs by using strings.

- **Objects**. *Objects* are a special group of variables, made up of other properties and methods. *Properties* are variables that help describe the object, and *methods* are functions that the object can do or that other elements can do to the object. You refer to objects in two different ways. Object definitions describe what is in an object, and some instances of an object follow the definition, but contain information specific to a certain instance of it. For example, you could create an online store with a catalog. One object you might need is a *Product*, which contains the information for an item sold on the site. The object might contain several properties, including an SKU number, a name, a description, a price, and the number available. One method might be UpdatePrice, which changes the price of the instance of the Product you are working with. One instance of a Product might be this book, in which the SKU is the ISBN number, the name is the title, and the description is "The best Flash MX book you can get," for example. Objects can be a tricky concept.

Fortunately, ActionScript makes things easy by keeping track of a variable's type for you. Most of the time, you do not need to worry about the variable type. On the rare occasion that you do need to ensure that a variable is a certain type, you can use one of two special functions: Number and String. Number takes a variable and returns a number. String takes a variable and returns a string.

Variable Scope

Scope, which is important when you are working with variables, refers to where the variable exists and when it can be used. Flash uses three possible scopes: Local, Timeline, and Global.

Local variables are available in the same part of the program in which they are declared. Local variables exist between curly braces. Often, a variable is needed in only a specific function. Because variables consume memory when they are used, it makes sense that variables that are needed in only one area of code are created in only that area of code.

Because you can access Timeline variables from anywhere in the Timeline, you have a simple way to access variables that are used often, but at the cost of memory usage.

Global variables can be used from anywhere in the script. This variable type is handy for information you need available from every section of the script.

Using Variables

Now, try an example of using variables.

NOTE

The code samples in this chapter help familiarize you with ActionScript and scripting in Flash. These examples do not do much, if anything, but they help you understand some interesting and important concepts.

First, create (or *declare*) a variable in the first keyframe of Layer 1 in a new movie. You then set the value of the variable and change the value.

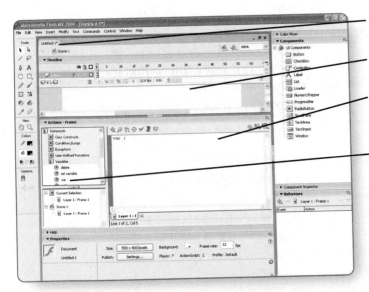

1. Create a new Flash file.

2. Click on the Stage.

3. Open the Actions panel, if needed.

4. In the Actions Toolbox, find Statements, Variables, var. Add var to the script by double-clicking on it. You can now name and configure the variable.

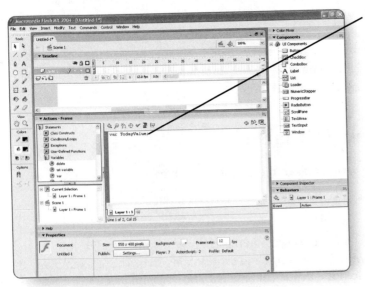

5. Type a name for the variable before the semicolon in the statement. Variable names must be one word. Of course, the word can be a long concatenation of several words, as long as it has no spaces. You can declare several variables at one time by separating them with commas. If the script area highlights the line of code in red, a problem has occurred. In this case, you either have a space in the variable name or have used one of a dozen reserved words called *keywords*.

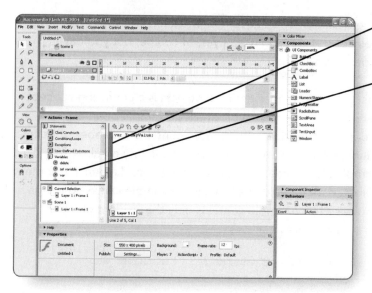

6. Click on the next blank line of the script.

7. In the Actions Toolbox, find Statements, Variables, set variable. Double-click on set variable to add the set variable statement to the script.

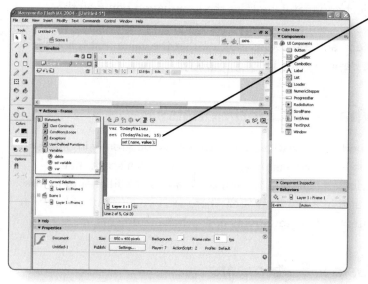

8. As prompted by the code hint that appears, type the variable name, a comma, a space, and the desired value for the variable.

Congratulations! You have now written some code. The code does not do anything useful yet, of course, but you have made a start.

Most people find that defining objects is a confusing concept the first time around. An often-used example of an object is a student. The Student object often contains a number of items, including a student number (a Social Security number, for example), last name, first name, address, and a bunch of other characteristics. Looking at a limited example can keep things simple, so this example contains only the student number, name, and address.

```
Student = { StudentNumber:12345, FirstName:'Bob',
LastName:'Jones',
Address:'123 Main St.' };
```

The curly braces in this example indicate that Student is an object and that it contains the information between the braces. Commas separate the different properties of the object, and the colons indicate that the value that follows is the desired value for the property.

What Are Conditionals?

Conditionals enable a script to behave differently in different situations. For example, if you're creating a script that performs a calculation, you could add a conditional to ignore input that is not a number. There are two types of conditional statements: if statements and switch statements.

Basic If Statements

The If statement is the simplest conditional statement to understand. The format is

```
if (x == 5)
{
y = 10;
}
```

> **TIP**
>
> Find the if element in the Statements, Conditions/Loops list of the Actions Toolbox.

Examining this code, you see a few interesting points. First, the structure of an if statement is the word *if* followed by a conditional statement in parentheses. If the statement in parentheses is true, if x is equal to five, the code between the curly braces runs. If not, the code in the curly braces is skipped. Notice the double equal signs in the condition. That's not a typo. In ActionScript, a single equal sign sets the variable on the left to the value on the right. A double equal sign is used for comparing two values. Triple equal signs (===) comprise a strict equality comparison in which the data types of the variables being compared are not converted to a similar data type.

The legal comparison operators include:

Comparison Operator	Symbol
Equal to	==
Strict equality	===
Greater than	>
Less than	<
Not equal to	!=
Test strict inequality	!==
Greater than or equal to	>=
Less than or equal to	<=

> **NOTE**
>
> With an if statement, many programmers would argue that the curly braces are not needed for a 1-line if statement. Technically, in the preceding case, you could leave out the braces. However, bugs are often created by programmers who leave out the braces and then return to add more lines to the body of the if statement. In good programming practice, you include the braces whether they are needed or not.

A more complex if statement is the if[…]else statement.

```
if (x == 5)
{
y = 10;
}
else
{
y = 20;
}
```

> **NOTE**
>
> To create this statement, first insert the if element and add parameters, click on the next blank line, and then insert the else if statement and complete it.

In this statement, if x equals 5, then y is set to 10. If x is not equal to 5, then y is set to 20. This is a simple extension of the if statement.

Switches

Switches are a slightly more complex type of conditional statement that allows for numerous possible cases. A switch tests a value against several cases and runs the code for a case if the case and the value are the same. A new reserved word, break, jumps out of the switch statement. Here is some sample code you can analyze.

```
var MyVar;
var x;
set (MyVar, Number((InputTextField.text)));
switch (MyVar){
case 1:
        x = 1;
        break;
case 10:
        x = 5;
case 11:
        x = 10;
        break;
default:
        x = 0;
        break;
}
```

This example is a little complex, so take it slowly. An assumption made in this example is that a text box is set up to be an input field with the variable name InputTextField. When the movie runs and the user makes an entry into the text field, the value is stored as MyVar. The switch statement then tests the value of MyVar against each of the cases listed. If MyVar equals 1, the x variable is set to 1 and the break jumps you out of the switch statement. If MyVar equals 10, x is set to 5 and the break jumps you out of the switch statement. If MyVar equals 11, x is set to 10 and the break jumps you out of the switch statement. If the Variable does not match any other cases, the default case is run, setting x to 0 and then the break jumps you out.

CAUTION

Make sure you include break with each switch statement. Otherwise, the script may not function correctly. You should always double-check switch statements to avoid this type of omission.

Looping Constructs

Loops enable a script to repeat a task numerous times. ActionScript uses these types of loops:

- for
- for[...]in
- while
- do[...]while

For Loops

For loops are a great way to perform a task a set number of times. *For* loops set up a counter and increase the value of the counter each time through the loop. The following examples include two new concepts: the ++ operator, which adds 1 to the variable that precedes it, and the trace function, which prints the string between the quotes as an argument in the Output panel.

```
for(i = 0; i < 10; i++) {
}
        trace("the counter = " + i );
```

This example runs 10 times, increasing the value of i by one each time as long as i is less than 10, and creates the following output.

```
counter = 0
counter = 1
counter = 2
counter = 3
counter = 4
counter = 5
counter = 6
counter = 7
counter = 8
counter = 9
```

> **NOTE**
>
> In addition to the ++ operator, the — operator
> decreases by 1 the variable that precedes it.

For[...]in Loops

For[...]in loops are fantastic for working with objects. You can
iterate through each property in an object and manipulate
that property. In the following example, you create an object
named CatalogItem and print each of the properties and their
values.

```
CatalogItem = { SKU:'12345', name:'Book', price: '19.95'
};
trace("A CatalogItem has the following properties: ");
for (property in CatalogItem);
{
trace(property + "  :  " + CatalogItem[property]);
}
```

This code produces the following output.

```
A CatalogItem has the following properties:
SKU  :  12345
name :  Book
price :  19.95
```

While Loops

While loops are another tool for repetitive tasks. These loops
use a test condition and run as long as the condition is true.

```
var VarAttempt;
set (VarAttempt, 0);
while (VarAttempt < 3)
{
trace ("Number of attempts is " + VarAttempt);
VarAttempt++
}
```

This example results in the following output.

```
Number of attempts is 0
Number of attempts is 1
Number of attempts is 2
```

While loops do not run if the condition is false the first time it is hit, which is different from Do[...]while loops, which always run at least once.

Do[...]while Loops

Do[...]while loops are similar to While loops, but always run them through once before checking the conditional statement. Look at the following example and the resulting output.

```
var test1;
set (test1, 0);
do {
trace("test1 = " + test1);
test1++;
}while (test1<3);

var test2;
set (test2, 0);
do {
trace("test2 = " + test2);
}while (test1>3);

test1 = 0
test1 = 1
test1 = 2
test2 = 0
```

Notice that the second Do[...]while loop ran once, even though the condition statement is false.

> **CAUTION**
>
> When using any type of loop, you can create an *infinite* loop, or a loop that never ends because of a mistake in either the end condition or the iterator. Infinite loops create all sorts of problems, including crashing Flash. Be careful to double-check to ensure that at some point, no matter what happens, the loop ends.

Arrays

Arrays are special types of variables that contain several values. Arrays are useful in a number of circumstances. A new operator associated with arrays, the array access operator, is a pair of brackets ([]). Arrays contain a set number of elements, and each element is accessed via its index. Indices are numbers, starting at 0. You can create an array in several ways, and the choice of which is chosen depends on circumstances. The following example creates two arrays and then uses trace to print the contents of each one.

```
var test1;
myArray = new Array(3);
myArray[0] = "Hello";
myArray = "There";
myArray = 10;
for (I=0; I < myArray.length; i++) {
trace("myArray[" + i + "] = + myArray[i];
}
myArray2 = new Array (1, 2, 3, 4, 5, "done");
for (I=0; I < myArray2.length; i++) {
trace("myArray2[" + i + "] = " + myArray2[i];
}
```

- Lines 1 through 4 create an array that can hold three elements. The first element has an index of 0, as shown in Line 2.

- You also can initialize the array with the values of the elements, as in Line 8.

- Arrays are objects with properties. One of these properties is length, which contains the number of elements in the array. Lines 5 and 9 use the length property.

This short script, when run, will display the values of the three elements in myArray and the six elements in myArray2, as follows:

```
myArray[0] = Hello
myArray = There
myArray = 10
myArray2[0] = 1
myArray2 = 2
myArray2 = 3
myArray2 = 4
myArray2[4] = 5
myArray2[5] = done
```

Applying What You've Learned

Those are the building blocks for ActionScript. In the remainder of this chapter, we'll explore some code examples to practice what you've learned.

Let's return to an example mentioned earlier in this chapter, the calculator function Square(). The Square function returns the square of an argument. To create an example that is meaningful, you need to do several things:

- Create a text box where the user can enter a number.

- Create a button so that the user can click to calculate the square of the number that is entered.

- Create another text box to display the answer.

- Define a variable so that when the user clicks on the button, the code gets the number in the first text box, squares it, and puts the result in the second text box.

Follow these steps to build this movie project:

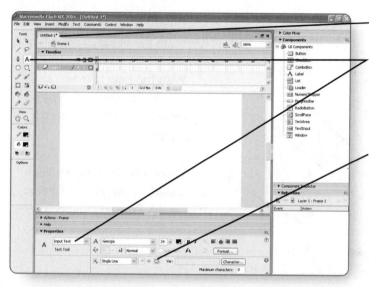

1. Create a new Flash file.

2. Select the Text tool in the Tools panel. Choose Input Text from the Text Type drop-down list in the Property Inspector.

3. Still in the Properties panel, make sure that the Show border around text option is selected.

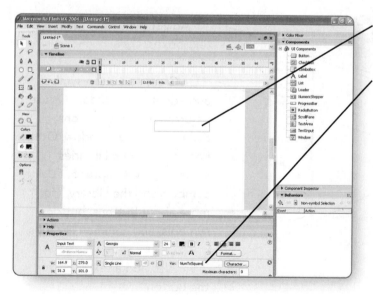

4. Draw a small text box on the Stage.

5. With the new text box selected, type a name (such as NumToSquare) in the Var text box in the Property Inspector. You will use this variable name in the ActionScript you write.

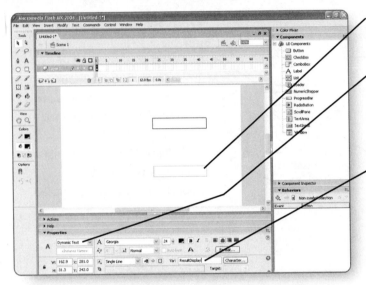

6. Create another text box, lower on the Stage.

7. With the new text box still active, change the Text Type to Dynamic Text in the Property Inspector.

8. Enter a variable name (such as ResultDisplay) in the Var text box in the Property Inspector.

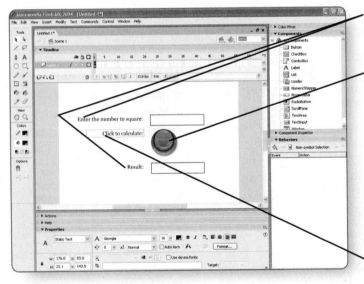

9. Add static text to label the text boxes.

10. Create a button symbol and add it to the Stage. Or use a button from the Buttons common library (Window, Other Panels, Common Libraries, Buttons). See Chapter 5, "Using Symbols and the Library," for more about buttons, button symbols, and common libraries.

11. Also add a text label for the button.

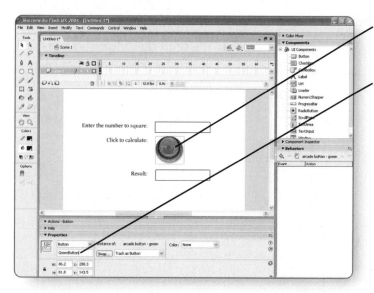

12. Use the Selection tool to select the button on the Stage.

13. Type a name for the button instance in the Instance Name text box of the Property Inspector. You will use this name to verify that you're adding the ActionScript to the button. Leave the button selected on the Stage.

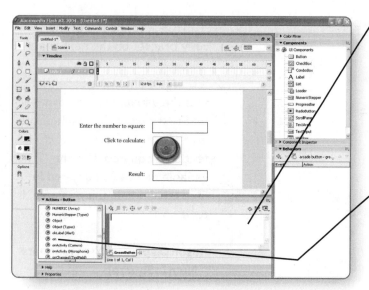

14. Open the Actions panel. You may need to hide the Property Inspector to give yourself enough room to work. Verify that the Navigation Tab in the Actions panel shows the name you assigned to the button instance.

15. You need to specify an *on handler* to work with the button. The on handler specifies what mouse or other action (applied to the button) will trigger the included script statements. To add this handler, click on Index in the Actions Toolbox, scroll far down the list, and double-click on *on*. ActionScript will insert the code, and prompt you to specify the specific event that applies.

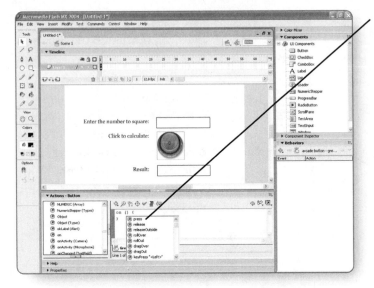

16. Double-click on press in the drop-down list. This will insert the press event between the parentheses.

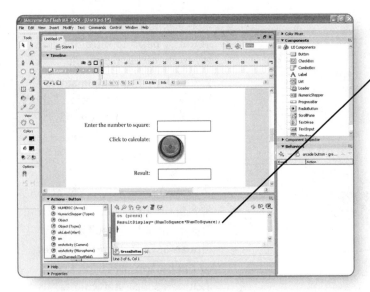

17. Click to the left of the curly bracket on the next line.

18. Now enter the code that sets the variable for the dynamic text text box to the result of the user's entry in the input text text box, squared. Use the variable names you entered in Steps 5 and 8. In this example, I type:

ResultDisplay = (NumToSquare * NumToSquare);

where ResultDisplay is the variable name for the results box and NumToSquare is the variable name for the input box. This tells the code to multiple the value entered into the input text box by itself, and then to set the value of the ResultDisplay variable to the result. (Hint: this is another form of syntax for setting a variable.)

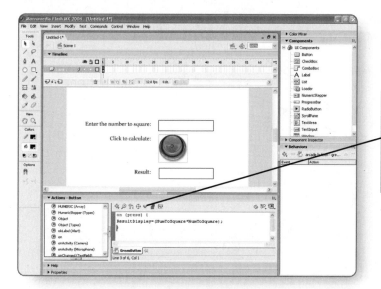

19. Press Enter to move the curly bracket to its own line, for good form.

TIP
Click on the Check Syntax button to check for coding errors.

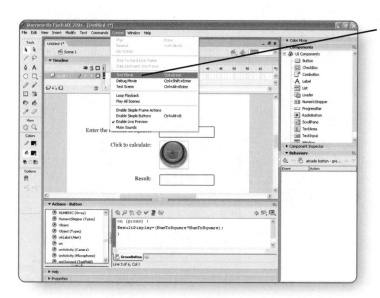

20. Choose Control, Test Movie.

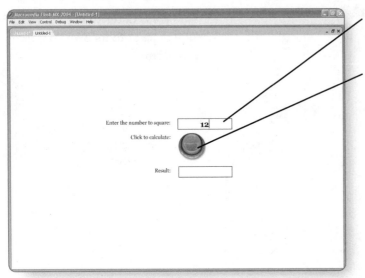

21. Type a number in the input field.

22. Click on the button.

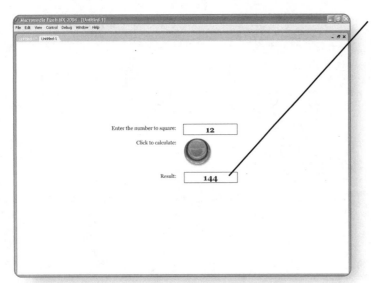

The dynamic text text box will display the result.

Congratulations! You have finished your first program in ActionScript, as well as concluding your progress through this book. You now have a good foundation to begin building Flash movies.

A

Installing Flash MX 2004

Before being able to use Flash MX 2004, you need to install it. To install Flash MX 2004, you need to purchase the Flash MX 2004 CD-ROM or download the 30-day trial version from the Macromedia's Web site (http://www.macromedia.com/software/flash).

In this chapter, you'll learn how to do the following:

- Identify the system requirements for Flash MX 2004.
- Install Flash MX 2004 on a Windows computer.

Identifying System Requirements

Flash MX 2004 is designed to function on both Mac and Windows operating systems. However, in order to make Flash MX function, your computer should match the requirements listed in the following sections.

For Windows Users

A Windows computer should match the following requirements:

- 200MHz Intel Pentium Processor
- Windows 98 SE, Windows Me, Windows 2000, or Windows XP
- At least 64MB of available system RAM (128MB is recommended)
- 110 MB of hard disk space
- 1024 X 768, 16-bit (thousands of colors) color display or better
- CD-ROM drive

For Mac Users

A Mac computer should match the following requirements:

- Power Macintosh G3 processor
- Mac OS X 10.1.5 or higher or Mac OS X 10.2.6 or higher
- At least 64MB of available system RAM (128MB is recommended)
- 110 MB of hard disk space

- 1024 X 768, 16-bit (thousands of colors) color display or better

- CD-ROM drive

Installing Flash MX 2004 on a Windows Computer

After you install Flash MX 2004 on your system, you can start creating optimized and interactive Web graphics. To install Flash MX 2004 on a Windows-based computer, follow these steps:

1. Insert the Flash CD-ROM in your system's drive. A folder window with the installer icon should open.

2. Double-click on the install_flash_2004.exe file icon. The welcome dialog box will open.

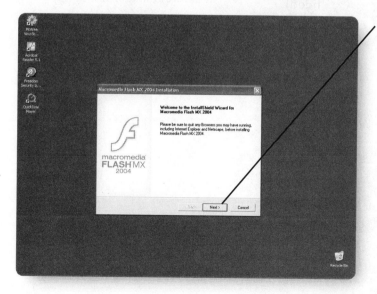

3. Click on Next. The License Agreement dialog box will open.

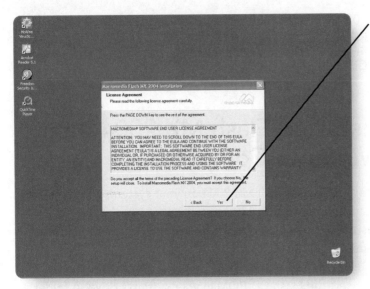

4. Click on Yes. The Choose Destination Location dialog box will open.

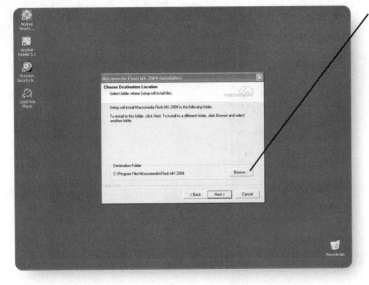

5a. Click on Browse to specify a different install location.

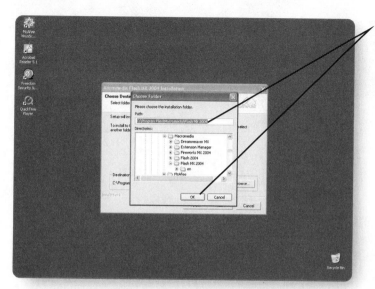

The Choose Folder dialog box will open. Select the desired install folder and then click on OK to continue.

OR

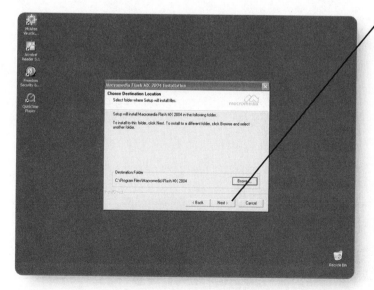

5b. Click on Next. The Install Macromedia Flash Player dialog box will open.

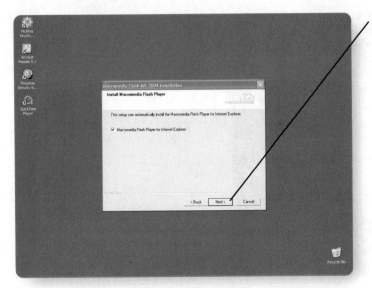

6. Click on Next. The Start Copying Files dialog box will open.

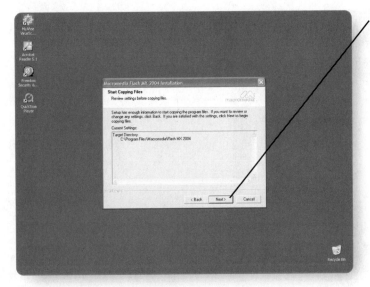

7. Click on Next. The Setup Status dialog box will open. When the install process finishes, the InstallShield Wizard Complete dialog box will notify you.

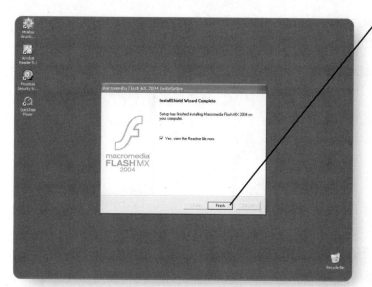

8. Click on Finish. The dialog box will close, and a folder window will display a shortcut icon for starting Flash. Another window will show the Readme file. Close the Readme file window.

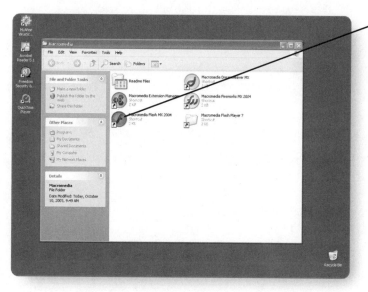

9. Double-click on the Macromedia Flash MX 2004 Shortcut icon. The Macromedia Product Activation dialog box will open.

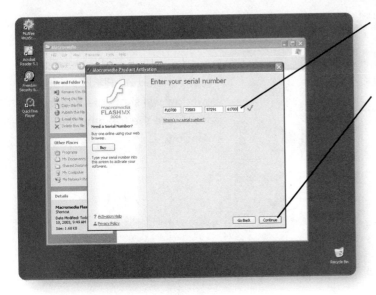

10. Enter your serial number, which is typically located on the sleeve for the install CD.

11. Click on Continue. Flash MX 2004 will start.

B

Customizing Flash MX 2004

You can control the appearance of the Flash MX 2004 user interface and choose default settings, such as specifying default colors. To do so, work with the Flash MX 2004 preferences. In addition, Flash MX 2004 enables you to adjust the Tools panel and create keyboard shortcuts to help you work faster.

In this chapter, you'll learn how to do the following:

- Set preferences.
- Change the tools on the Tools panel.
- Create a keyboard shortcut.

Setting Preferences

Flash MX 2004 enables you to set preferences to control its appearance, specify editing options, specify Clipboard options, and more. Use the Preferences dialog box to set these preferences. To view the Preferences dialog box, follow these steps:

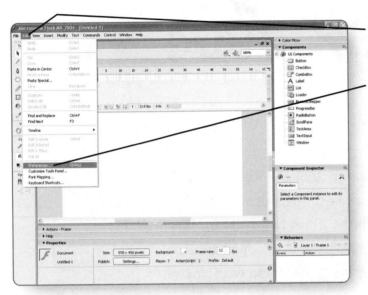

1. Click on Edit. The Edit menu will appear.

2. Click on Preferences. The Preferences dialog box will open.

TIP

You can also press Ctrl+U (⌘+U) to open the Preferences dialog box.

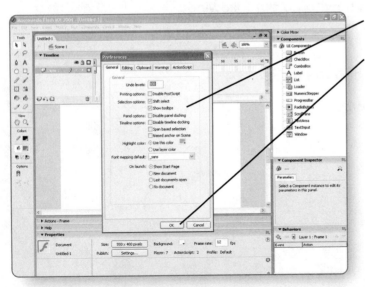

3. Choose settings as desired.

4. Click on OK. The Preferences dialog box will close, applying the new preference settings.

The Preferences dialog box contains several tabs, including the General, Editing, Clipboard, Warnings, and ActionScript tabs. Each tab contains a number of related options for customizing Flash. The following sections describe how to use each tab to specify various preferences.

Setting General Preferences

You use the General preferences tab to set the following:

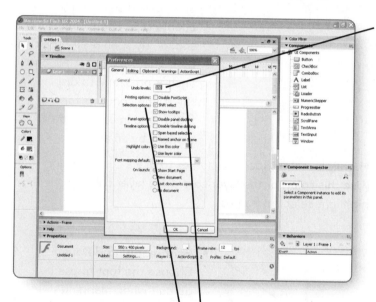

- **Undo levels.** Specify the number of actions that can be undone via the Undo command and the History panel. This value can be between 0 and 1009. Keep in mind, though, that specifying a large value, such as 999, in the Undo levels box requires more memory to store all the steps. So, you may still have adequate protection if you reduce this setting to 200 Undo levels. You must quit and restart Flash for any change to this setting to take effect.

- **Printing options.** Check the Disable PostScript checkbox if you want to prevent the use of the PostScript language during printing.

- **Selection options.** Check the desired options here to enable them. Shift select requires you to press Shift while clicking in order to select multiple objects. Show tooltips displays a yellow pop-up tip when you hover the mouse pointer over an onscreen element.

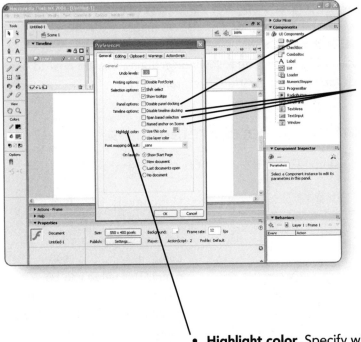

- **Panel options**. Check Disable panel docking when you want all panels to appear as floating windows onscreen.

- **Timeline options**. Check Disable timeline docking when you want the timeline to appear in a floating window onscreen. Check Span based selection to enable selecting a Timeline section by span rather than by frame. Also check Named anchor on Scene to display the frame contents for the first frame in each scene marked by an anchor.

- **Highlight color**. Specify whether to use a custom color (Use this color) or the layer color (Use layer color) to highlight selected frames.

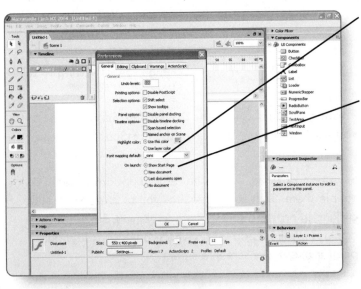

- **Font mapping default**. Choose the font to use by default when mapping missing fonts.

- **On Launch**. Click on the desired option button to specify whether Flash displays the Start page, a new document, the last open documents, or no document on startup.

Setting Editing Preferences

The Editing preferences tab contains options to control the Pen tool, vertical text, mouse behavior, and line placement when drawing.

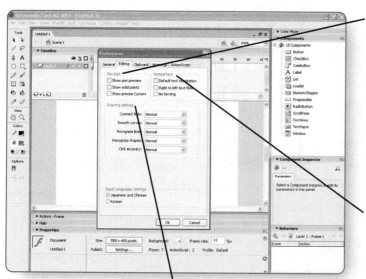

- **Pen tool**. Check the desired options. Show pen preview previews the line segments as you create them. Show solid points includes anchors along line segments. Show precise cursors replaces tool-specific icon pointers, such as the pen, with the crosshair pointer.

- **Vertical text**. Check the options to enable when you're creating vertical text. Default text orientation makes vertical text the default for all text you add. Right to left text flow moves the insertion point to the left (rather than right) when you press Enter. No kerning disables kerning in vertical text.

- **Drawing settings**. Choose the desired setting for each line type, shapes, or click accuracy.

Clipboard Preferences

The Clipboard preferences control how Flash handles graphics pasted from the Clipboard. This tab offers the following options:

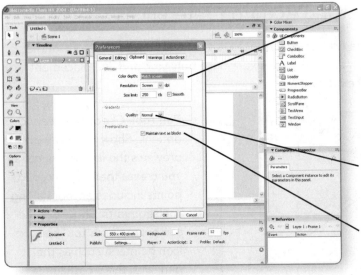

- **Bitmaps**. Choose the desired settings to specify the Color depth and Resolution for any graphic pasted into Flash. Also specify the Size limit for the pasted information, as well as whether Flash should Smooth outlines.

- **Gradients**. Choose the desired Quality setting for gradients in pasted objects.

- **FreeHand text**. Enable Maintain text as blocks when pasted if you want to be able to edit text pasted from a Freehand file.

Setting Warnings Preferences

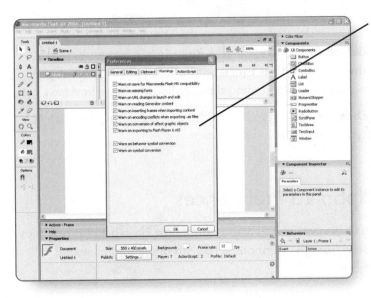

Check or clear the check box for an option here to determine whether that type of warning is enabled. When a warning type is enabled, Flash will display a dialog box any time you perform the action specified by the warning type. For example, when the Warn on symbol conversion type is checked (enabled), Flash will display a dialog box prompting you for confirmation when you convert a graphic to a symbol.

Setting ActionScript Preferences

Use the ActionScript preferences tab to manage how Flash converts and displays ActionScript code.

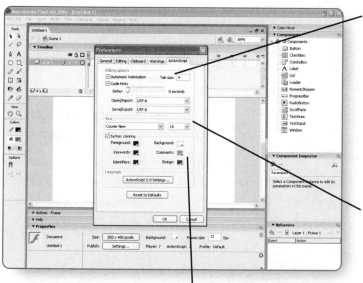

- **Editing options**. Choose whether Flash automatically indents (Automatic indention) code as you write it. Specify the desired default Tab size, whether or not Code hints appear, and the text encoding scheme used when you Open/Import or Save/Export script.

- **Text**. Choose the font and size to use for displaying ActionScript code.

- **Syntax coloring**. Check this option to enable automatic coloring of ActionScript code based on syntax and to choose the desired colors for various syntax elements.

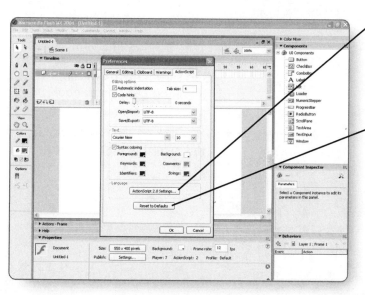

- **ActionScript 2.0 Settings**. Click on this button to open the ActionScript Settings dialog box, where you can add and remove Classpaths.

- **Reset to Defaults**. Click on this button to reinstate the default ActionScript preferences.

Customizing the Tools Panel

As you learned in Chapter 2, the Tools panel holds the tools you'll use frequently to create and manage the content in your Flash productions. You can use the following procedure to add and remove Tools panel choices as desired:

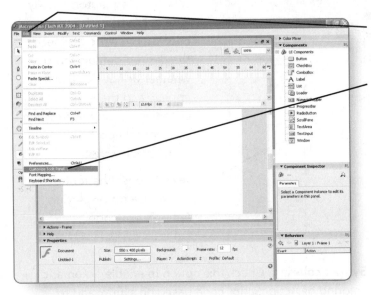

1. Click on Edit. The Edit menu will appear.

2. Click on Customize Tools Panel. The Customize Toolbar dialog box will open.

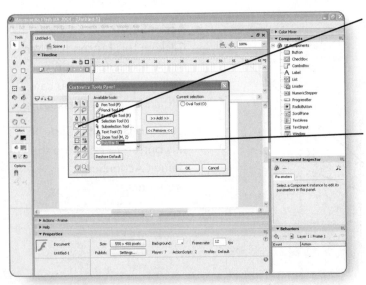

3. Click on the position where you want to add or change a tool in the toolbar at the left. A red selection box will appear around the tool.

4. Click on the tool to add in the Available tools list.

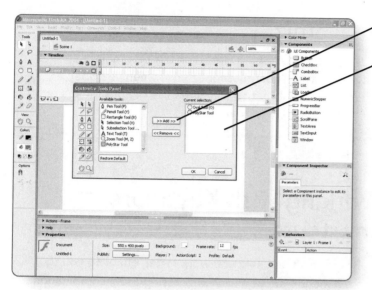

5. Click on Add.

The tool will be added to the Current selection list, which shows the tools for the Tools panel position you selected in Step 2. When the Current Selection list shows more than one tool for a Tools panel position, that position will have a pop-up menu from which you can select one of the listed tools.

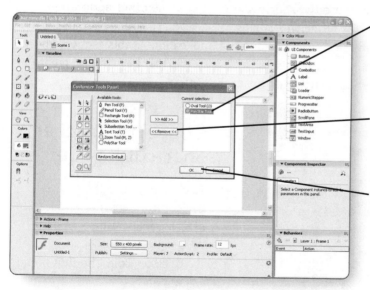

6. To remove a tool from a Tools panel position, click on the tool name in the Current selection list.

7. Click on Remove. The tool will be removed from the selected Tools panel position.

8. Click on OK. The Customize Toolbar dialog box will close, applying your changes to the Tools panel.

> **TIP**
>
> Use the Font Mapping choice on the Edit menu to indicate what substitute font to use when you open a flash document that specifies the use of a font that's not installed on your system.

Working with Keyboard Shortcuts

Keyboard shortcuts help you work faster, enabling you to access a menu item or a tool by pressing a key combination. Flash MX 2004 provides default keyboard shortcuts to access most of the menus and tools. In addition, Flash MX enables you to use the shortcut key set of some other application, such as FreeHand or Illustrator, if you're already proficient with the shortcuts from that application. In this section, you will learn to choose an alternate shortcut key set and create keyboard shortcuts to access tools.

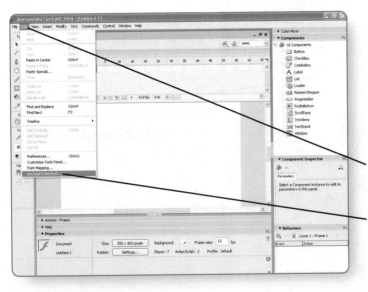

Choosing Another Shortcut Key Set

To choose to use the shortcut key set from another application in Flash, follow these steps:

1. Click on Edit. The Edit menu will appear.

2. Click on Keyboard Shortcuts. The Keyboard Shortcuts dialog box will open.

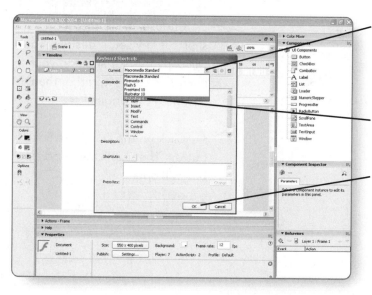

3. Click on the Current Set drop-down list arrow. The list of available shortcut key sets will open.

4. Click on the desired shortcut key set. The set will be selected.

5. Click on OK. The shortcut key set will become active in Flash.

Changing a Keyboard Shortcut

Flash enables you to create your own custom keyboard shortcuts for menu commands or the tools. If a shortcut already exists for a command, you can replace it. To change a keyboard shortcut, follow these steps:

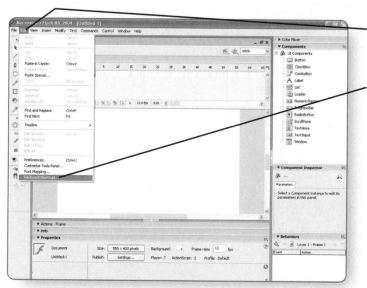

1. Click on Edit. The Edit menu will appear.

2. Click on Keyboard Shortcuts. The Keyboard Shortcuts dialog box will open.

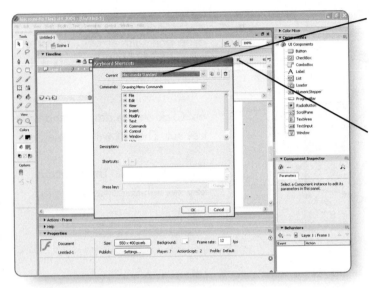

3. Choose an alternate shortcut key set, if desired. You will copy this set and add your new shortcut to it, rather than changing the original set.

4. Click on the Duplicate Set button. The Duplicate Set dialog box will open.

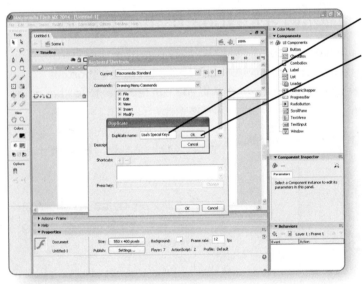

5. Type a name for the new set.

6. Click on OK. The new set will be selected in the Keyboard Shortcuts dialog box.

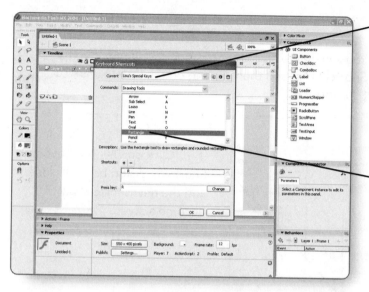

7. Choose a command category, such as Drawing Tools, from the Commands drop-down list. The commands in the category will appear in the list box below the Commands drop-down list.

8. Click on the command or tool for which you want to create a shortcut. The Add Shortcut (+) and Delete Shortcut (–) buttons will become active.

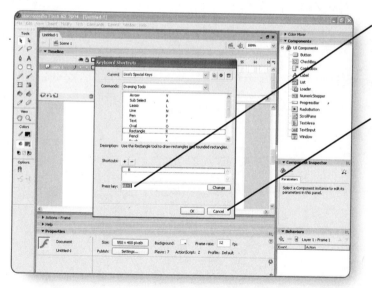

9. Select the current shortcut key in the Press Key box and then type a new shortcut key or combination.

10. Click on the Change button. The new shortcut will replace the old one.

TIP

You can delete an old shortcut by clicking on it in the Shortcuts list and then clicking on the Delete Shortcut (–) button.

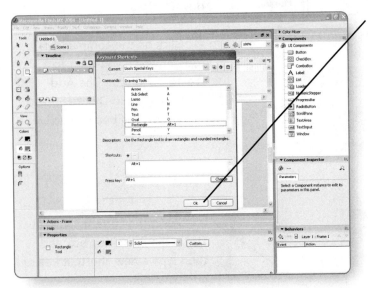

11. Click on OK. The Keyboard Shortcuts dialog box will close, and the new shortcut will become active.

C

Quick Reference Glossary

Knowing Your Workspace

It's essential to know your way around the Flash MX 2004 workspace as you continue to develop in Flash. Review key workspace parts in the list below.

- **Timeline**. You see this panel with one or more series of vertical rectangles whenever you open Flash. The rectangles are white with a gray rectangle in every fifth position. Use the Timeline to designate the amount of time each object appears in a particular position when you playback the movie.

- **Frame**. Each rectangle in the Timeline represents a frame. Frames represent points in time during movie playback.

- **Keyframe**. Keyframes mark a change in action, denoting a new occurrence in your movie. The typical procedure is "enter keyframe and add action or change."

- **Layers**. Each row of frames in the Timeline forms a layer. The layer names appear at the left side of the Timeline. Layers are used to organize and overlap various objects in your movie.

- **Stage**. The Stage appears below the Timeline. This large, white space is your work area, where you place the objects in the movie. There, you do everything from creating the symbols to be used to laying out the look of your movie.

Frequently Used Panels

Flash offers a variety of panels enabling you to set numerous options. You will use some panels, however, more regularly than others:

- **Property Inspector**. This panel appears below the Stage. If the Property Inspector does not appear, you can display it by choosing Window, Properties. When you're selecting anything on the Stage, the Property Inspector displays that object's particular properties so that you can edit those properties.

- **Actions panel**. You use this panel to add ActionScript to your movies. The panel, which has a toolbox that expands for navigation, works in Normal mode and Expert mode.

- **Color Swatches panel**. This panel provides swatches of set color choices, along with ready-to-use radial selections, that you can easily apply to a selected object.

- **Color Mixer panel**. This panel enables you to create custom colors, affecting the type of gradient applied and its alpha setting, for example.

Flash Functionality

- **Symbol**. You should convert the graphical objects in your movie to symbols. Symbols are more compact in size than the graphics themselves, enabling Flash to export smaller files.

- **Button**. This type of symbol provides a button that movie viewers can click to perform an action. You set up different states for the button.

- **Movie clipv** This type of symbol has its own timeline and can be independently animated.

- **GIF**. This commonly used image type can be animated or include transparency.

- **JPEG**. This is a commonly used image type.

- **Motion tweening**. Applying a motion tween enables you to specify how an object moves from one location to another during the movie.

- **Shape tweening**. This functionality morphs an object from one shape to another (and also works with text) during the movie.

- **Shape hint**. This feature is used with shape tweening to instruct Flash about how the shape change should occur.

- **Alpha**. This feature, found on the Color Mixer panel, controls the transparency of an object.

Components

Find the Components panel by selecting Window, Components. On this panel, Flash provides ready-to-use controls that you can drag to the Stage to enable the viewer to perform common tasks during movie playback.

- **CheckBox**. Adds to your movie a common check box where multiple selections can be made.

- **ComboBox**. Adds a combo box or drop-down box to your movie.

- **ListBox**. Adds to your movie a list box where items are viewable and scroll vertically.

- **PushButton**. Can serve numerous functions, such as a Submit button or Reset button, for example.

- **RadioButton**. Adds radio buttons to your movie, where only one selection can be made.

- **ScrollBar**. Adds the scrolling function (a good feature not to have to create from scratch).

- **ScrollPane**. Adds the scrolling function both vertically and horizontally.

D

What's Next?

Now that you have a solid grasp of the fundamentals of Flash, where do you go from here? There are a number of development possibilities. The next two sections can help you better define that path. "Helpful Resources" points out good places to look for information and "New Directions" provides examples of new development venues.

Helpful Resources

The Internet offers many different types of Flash resources, including Web sites, newsgroups, forums, and listservs. Macromedia also offers extensive information for developers.

To get started with the basics, go to the Macromedia Flash Support Center at http://www.macromedia.com/ support/flash. This Web page offers links to a variety of help, including Getting Started with Flash, Flash Concepts, and tutorials. If you want to delve into greater detail about a topic, start here.

If you want to learn from others and post specific questions, go to the Flash online forum at http://webforums. macromedia.com/flash/. This message forum provides a number of discussion categories, including:

- Flash General Discussion
- Flash ActionScript
- Flash Site Design
- Flash Data Integration

Browsing through information in this forums is a good way to broaden your knowledge of the Flash MX 2004 capabilities. You should also read about the kinds of issues other developers are interested in or struggling with. Forums also provide a place to post questions.

The Macromedia Exchange for Flash page found at http://www.macromedia.com/cfusion/exchange/ provides links to various items that developers have created for Flash, such as components, buttons, and templates. Most of these downloads are free for your use, but if a fee is required, clicking the link takes you to the author's home page. Extensions are a great way to enhance your Flash movies with new features.

If you learn best by examining example files, go to http://www.macromedia.com/devnet/mx/flash/sample_files/. There, you can download a variety of sample files for either the Windows or Mac version of Flash.

Finally, as your proficiency increases, visit http://www .macromedia.com/devnet/mx/flash. This page includes links to more advanced information about a variety of categories and techniques, such as ActionScript.

In addition to the information available on Macromedia's Web site, other good resources include:

- **Flash Kit**. Offers valuable resources, including a conference and an expo: http://www.flashkit.com.

- **Virtual-fx.net**. Offers many tutorials with a search feature as well as a variety of other resources: http://virtual-fx.net/vfx/index.php.

- **Flashmagazine**. Offers a variety of insight on what's happening in the Flash community: http://www. flashmagazine.com. Talk about extending the uses of Flash—this magazine keeps you informed. In particular, check out the Resource Links section of this site. It offers links to a variety of other resources where you can learn more about Flash topics.

New Directions

As you see as you begin to review some of these resources, Flash capabilities have grown exponentially. This section is meant to whet your appetite to discover some of Flash's new capabilities.

For example, you can now develop applications in Flash for PocketPCs, extending Flash's more common Web environment. This option was briefly discussed as a publish setting in Chapter 11. Imagine the possibilities! If this is an area of interest to you, be sure to research the benefits and limitations.

With the help of Macromedia Cold Fusion MX, you can add data exchange to your Flash application. You can see an example of an application of this nature by clicking the Reservations button at http://www.broadmoor.com. You can benefit from the intense functionality without the application having to make several trips to the server each time a new call is made.

These illustrations just touch on the many possibilities for development with Flash MX 2004. Hopefully your interest has been piqued. Enjoy yourself as you discover more and truly become an expert!

Index

A

\<A> tag, 271–272
Acid Pro, 216
ACT file format, 259
actions
   layers, 77
   undoing and redoing, 49
Actions panel, 15, 329
   Actions Toolbox, 283, 288
   adding new item to script, 284
   Auto Format button, 284
   Check Syntax button, 284, 303
   circle with arrow icon identifying each item, 283
   closed heading as closed book, 283
   Debug Options button, 283
   F9 keyboard shortcut, 282
   Find button, 284
   Insert target path button, 284
   Navigation tab, 282, 301
   open heading as open book, 283
   Options menu, 282
   Panel Options Menu button, 282
   Pin active script button, 282
   Reference button, 283
   Replace button, 284
   Script area, 284
   Show Code Hint button, 285
   View Options button, 283
ActionScript, 4, 241, 276
   Actions panel, 282–285
   arrays, 297–298
   based on JavaScript, 277
   case insensitivity, 280–281
   comments, 281
   comparison operators, 291
   conditionals, 290–294
   constants, 285–286
   curly braces ({ }), 280
   debugging settings, 283
   default preferences, 319
   Do[...]while loops, 296
   functions, 276, 280
   If statements, 290–292
   keywords, 280–281, 288
   labels for referencing frames, 126
   Linkage options, 98
   For loops, 294–295
   loops, 294–297
   naming conventions, 98
   preferences, 319
   programming building blocks, 285–296
   programming concepts, 279
   rules, 280
   special meaning for period or dot, 281
   statements, 280
   structure, 280
   switches, 292–293
   symbols, 98
   tools, 283
   variables, 285–290
   version, 245
   view selections, 283
   While loops, 295–296
ActionScript Settings dialog box, 319
Adaptive palette, 256
Add Motion Guide command, 160, 167
Add Motion Tween command, 140
ADPCM (Adaptive Differential Pulse Code Modulation) compression, 232
Advanced Effect dialog box, 158–159
AIFF (Audio Interchange File Format) files, 217
Alpha, 330
ALT attribute, 272
anchor points, snapping to motion guide, 161–162
anchor tags, 271–272

anchors, 109, 229
animated GIF files, 254
animated mask over animated content, 207–212
animated movies, controlling flow, 15
animating object along motion guide, 159–164
animation, 96, 241
    animated masks over, 207–212
    background image disappearing, 135
    basic, 128–133
    breaking into tweens, 207
    controlling motion changes, 131–133
    defining, 124
    ending point, 140
    every frame shown, 63
    frames, 60, 124–127
    keyframes, 125, 139, 165
    large sound files, 230
    last frame on layer didn't play, 135
    layers, 78, 130
    motion tweening, 138–142, 164–168
    movie clip symbol didn't play, 135
    movie creation, 128
    static mask over, 201–205
    troubleshooting, 135–136
    type between keyframes, 127
    unwanted, 136
    viewing movement, 61
animation cells, 124
Apple QuickTime player or plug-in, 241
Apple Web site, 234
Argosy Publishing Web site, 4
arguments, 276
array access ([]) operator, 297
arrays, 297–298
assigning, 277–279
audience identification, 8
Auto High option, 233–234

B

Bézier curves, 27–28
Back to Stage button, 59, 102, 115
background color, 54, 65, 67
background image disappearing in animation, 135
Backspace key, 49
Beach Background layer, 76
behaviors, 113, 277–279
Behaviors panel, 277–279
bitmap fills, 42–45
bitmaps, 42, 318
blank document, 54–55
blending mode and symbol instances, 113
body section, 270
<BODY> tag, 270

 tag, 271
Break Apart command, 174, 175, 179–180, 182
Break Apart (Ctrl+B (⌘+B)) keyboard shortcut, 174, 179–180, 182
break reserved word, 293
Broadmoor Web site, 334
Brush tool, 34, 161, 168
built-in components, 6
button instances, naming, 301
button symbols, 93–95, 225, 300
    assigning sound to, 225–226
    creation of, 102–104
    naming, 103
    saving, 104
    symbol-editing mode, 102–103
buttons, 94–95, 329
    adding sound to state, 225–226
    Down state, 102
    handler, 301
    Hit state, 102
    naming, 98
    Over state, 102
    states, 94, 102, 104
    text label, 300
    Up state, 102
Buttons common library, 300

C

case insensitivity, 280–281
CatalogItem object, 295
Check Spelling dialog box, 51
CheckBox component, 330
Choose Destination Location dialog box, 308
Choose Folder dialog box, 309
Circle tool, 161, 168
circles, drawing, 29–30
Clipboard preferences, 317–318
Close Panel command, 19
closing movies, 56–57
closing tags, 269
Cold Fusion MX, 334
Color Mixer panel, 41–42, 329
Color Swatches panel, 329
color tween, applying, 154–155
colors
    fills, 48
    for highlighting frames, 316
    layer outline, 86
    lines, 26
    lines, outlines and pen strokes changes, 43
    reusing, 44–45
    strokes, 26, 48
    text, 37
    tools, 48

ComboBox component, 330
comments, 281
common libraries, 117, 119
common operations, shortcuts for, 16–17
comparison operators, 291
complete tween, 173
complex shapes and shape tweening, 173–177
components, 16
Components panel, 330
compression
    ADPCM (Adaptive Differential Pulse Code Modulation), 232
    default, 232
    Flash movies, 247
    MP3, 232
    PNG files, 260
    QuickTime, 262
    Raw, 232
    sound, 229–233
    Speech, 232
    types, 232
conditionals
    If statements, 290–292
    switches, 292–293
constants, 285–286
content
    adding to movies, 129–131
    animated with animated mask, 207–212
    moving with static mask, 201–205
    static with moving mask, 197–200
    static with static mask over, 195–196
Control, Enable Live Preview command, 134
Control, Loop Playback command, 134
Control, Text Movie command, 303
Convert to Keyframe command, 135
Convert to Symbol command, 108
Convert to Symbol dialog box, 108
converting objects to component parts, 173–174
copying
    scenes, 72
    symbols between libraries, 117
Create Motion Tween command, 165, 198, 202, 210
Create New Symbol dialog box, 97, 99
    Advanced button, 98, 118
    Back to Stage button, 100
    Button option button, 103
    Graphic option button, 100
    Movie clip option button, 101
    Name text box, 100, 101, 103
CSS styles, 271
curly braces ({}), 280
curved lines, 27–28

custom
    palettes, 256
    tints, 157
Custom effect, 227
Customize Toolbar dialog box, 320–321
customizing
    sound, 226–229
    Tools panel, 320–322
cuteFTP, 266

D
decrement (—) operator, 295
default
    compression, 232
    fonts, 316
    keyboard shortcuts, 322
    workspace, 14–16
Delete key, 49
Delete Layer command, 81
deleting
    keyboard shortcuts, 326
    layers, 64, 81
    objects, 49
    scenes, 72
design process, 9
development process
    design process, 9
    gather requirements, 8–9
    mechanics of developing, 10
    review stage, 10–11
    to-do list, 7
digital movies, importing, 234–238
dithering, ordered, 255
dockable panels, 17
docking panels, 18
Document Properties dialog box, 65–67
documents
    opening, 16, 57
    properties, 20
    substitute fonts, 322
    switching between, 14
    template creation of, 55–56
Do[...]while loops, 296
Down state, 225
downloading
    Flash movies, 245
    sound effects, 220
drawing
    circles, 29–30
    freeform lines, 33–35
    ovals, 29–30
    polygons, 31–33
    rectangles, 30–31

settings, 317
squares, 30–31
straight-line segments, 26–27
tools, 25–35
Duplicate Set dialog box, 324
Dynamic text, 36–38

E

Edit, Customize Tools Panel command, 320
Edit, Find and Replace command, 52
Edit, Font Mapping command, 322
Edit, Keyboard Shortcuts command, 322, 323
Edit, Preferences command, 314
Edit, Undo command, 49
Edit, Undo Delete Layer command, 81
Edit command, 116
Edit in New Window command, 116
Edit in Place command, 116
Edit Scene button, 59
Edit Symbols button, 59, 114
editing
    movies, 61
    multiple frames, 62
    objects, 38–47
    preferences, 317
    symbol instances, 112–113
    symbols, 112, 114–116
    tools, 38–47
effects and sounds, 222
elements, associating scripts with, 280
embedded video, importing, 234–238
end of line, 271
.EPS format, 105
Equal to (==) operator, 291
Eraser tool, 45–46
erasers, 46
erasing, 45–46
.EXE format, 240–241
Explode effect, 189
Export dialog box, 226
exported file, previewing, 265–266

F

Fade In effect, 227
Fade Left to Right effect, 222, 227
Fade Out effect, 227
Fade Right to Left effect, 227
Fetch, 266
File, Close command, 57
File, Export Movie command, 42
File, Import, Import to Library command, 106, 217, 234
File, Import, Import to Stage command, 106, 174
File, New command, 54, 55

File, Open command, 57
File, Page Setup command, 67
File, Publish command, 265
File, Publish Preview, Default command, 111
File, Publish Settings command, 231, 242, 264
File, Save command, 56
file name for movie document, 65
file tab, 14
files, creation of, 17
fills, 29
    bitmap fills, 42–43
    changing, 44
    changing to gradient, 40–41
    colors, 48
    erasing, 46–47
    gradient fills, 40–41
    manipulating, 39–40
find-and-replace dialog box, 284
finding and replacing text, 52
Fireworks, 42
Fireworks PNG Import Settings dialog box, 42
Runfolder, 119
.fla file, 56
Flash 2004
    built-in components, 6
    features, 5–6
    installing, 307–312
    multiple languages, 5
    multiple platforms, 6
    overview, 4–5
    resources, 332–333
    scripting, 6
    setting preferences, 314–320
    startup options, 316
    system requirements, 306–307
    video, 5
Flash ActiveX control, 251
Flash Kit Web site, 333
Flash online forum, 332
Flash Player, 66, 223, 240–241, 245–246
Flash Player home page, 240
Flashmagazine Web site, 333
Folder layer, 86
folders
    for grouping layers, 64
    organizing layers, 87–88
    renaming, 87
font symbols, 93
fonts, 37, 268
    default, 316
    substitute, 322
For loops, 294–295
For[...]in loops, 295
formal and informal Web sites, 8

formatting
   paragraphs, 38
   tools, 26
forms, Submit button, 94
fps (frames per second), 54, 61, 66
frame rate, 54, 61, 66, 145
frames, 328
   anchoring markers, 62
   animation, 60, 124–127
   centering Timeline on, 61
   changing content, 133
   with content, 60
   controlling motion changes, 131–133
   editing multiple, 62
   every one in animation, 63
   five on either side of selected, 63
   frame number, 61
   graphical content, 15
   identifying on Timeline, 125–126
   labels, 126
   last not playing, 135
   managing, 15
   markers bracketing, 62
   moving objects outlines in group of, 62
   Onion Skin mode, 62
   onion skinning, 61
   in order, 60
   properties, 126–127
   resizing or rotating object without moving, 146
   selecting, 60
   sound, 127
   symbols, 110
   text, 15
   time from beginning of movie to, 61
   type of label, 127
   unused, 60
Free Transform tool, 38–39, 109–110, 113, 146–148, 166
freeform lines, drawing, 33–35
Fruity Loops, 216
FTP client, 266
functions, 276, 280

G
general preferences, 315–317
GIF files, 329
   dimensions, 253
   dithering, 255
   interlacing, 254
   looping, 254
   maximum number of colors, 256
   optimizing colors, 254
   palette type, 256
   playback, 253–254

   removing gradients, 255
   repeating, 254
   smoothing, 255
   static image of first frame, 254
   transparent background, 255
.GIF format, 240–241
global variables, 287
Go to URL behavior, 278
gradients
   changing fill to, 40–41
   quality settings, 318
   reusing, 44–45
graphic symbols, 93–94, 99–100
graphical content, 15
graphics
   converting to symbols, 105
   covered with selection shading, 175
   importing, 174
   importing as symbol, 105–107
   interlacing, 254
Greater than (>) operator, 291
Greater than or equal to (>=) operator, 291
guide layer, 160

H
<H1> - <H6> tag, 271
Hand tool, 47
<HEAD> tag, 270
header block, 270
HEIGHT attribute, 272
help, 16
Help panel, 16
Helper files, 241
History panel, 50
   level of undos, 315
   Replay button, 50
.HQX format, 240–241
HTML (HyperText Markup Language), 268
   ALT attribute, 272
   <BODY> tag, 270

 tag, 271
   closing tags, 269
   <H1> - <H6> tag, 271
   <HEAD> tag, 270
   HEIGHT attribute, 272
   <HTML> tag, 270
   <IMG> tag, 272
   opening tags, 269
   <P> tag, 271
   SRC attribute, 272
   structure, 269
   <A> tag, 271–272
   tags, 269

<TITLE> tag, 270
WIDTH attribute, 272
HTML files, 270, 272
   aligning on Web page, 252
   describing template, 250
   dimensions, 250
   Flash ActiveX control, 251
   forcing to foreground of window, 251
   Internet Explorer, 251
   location in player window, 252
   method of displaying, 250
   own browser window, 251
   playback characteristics, 250
   publishing, 249–253
   scaling in player window, 252
   size of, 250
   templates, 249
   transparent areas, 252
   viewing, 273
   warning messages, 253
.HTML format, 240–241
<HTML> tag, 270
hyperlinks, 38, 271–272

I

If statements, 290–292
images, 272. See also graphics
<IMG> tag, 272
Import Settings dialog box, 106
Import to Library dialog box, 42, 106, 217–218, 234
imported sound as sound event, 221–222
importing
   embedded video, 234–238
   graphic symbols, 94
   graphics, 174
   graphics as symbols, 105–107
   sound files, 216–220
incomplete tween, 172–173, 176, 180
increment (++) operator, 294–295
infinite loops, 297
Ink Bottle tool, 43, 45
input text, 36–38
Input Text command, 299
Insert, Layer command, 77
Insert, New Symbol command, 96, 99, 101, 103
Insert, Scene command, 72
Insert, Timeline, Create Motion Tween command, 140
Insert, Timeline Effects command, 190
Insert Blank Keyframe command, 130, 172, 176
Insert Frame command, 132
Insert Frame (F5) keyboard shortcut, 132, 133
Insert Keyframe command, 130
Insert Target Path dialog box, 284

Install Macromedia Flash Player dialog box, 309
install_flash_2004.exe file icon, 307
InstallShield Wizard Complete dialog box, 310
instances, adding behavior, 277–279
interactive movies, 71, 241
interlacing images, 254
Internet Explorer
   HTML files, 251
   viewing source code, 273
irregular areas, selecting, 24–25

J

JavaScript, 277
JPEG files, 256–257, 329
.JPEG format, 240–241

K

kbps (kilobits per second), 233
kerning text, 37
keyboard shortcuts
   changing, 323–326
   choosing another set of, 322–323
   default, 322
   deleting, 326
Keyboard Shortcuts dialog box, 322–326, 325–326
keyframes, 125, 165, 328
   adding, 129–131, 176
   animation, 139
   controlling motion changes, 131–133
   guide layer, 160
   identifying on Timeline, 125–126
   moving mask shape to, 199
   resizing objects between, 143
   shape hints, 185–189
   sound event, 221
   tweening object between, 138
   type of animation between, 127
keywords, 280–281, 288

L

Lasso tool, 20, 24–25
layer outline colors, 86
Layer Properties dialog box, 85
layers, 328
   actions, 77
   adding, 64, 77–78, 195, 198, 203
      objects, 80
      second under mask, 205
   adjusting object layering, 89–90
   animation, 78, 130
   changing content, 131
   contents appearing on Stage, 85

defining, 76
deleting, 64, 81
descriptive names, 197
displaying and hiding, 63
folders for grouping, 64
grouping with masking layer, 196
height, 86
hiding, 82–83
imported sound, 221
last frame not playing, 135
locking, 83–84, 86, 196
    deleting and, 81
    unlocking and, 63, 84
managing from Timeline, 63–64
motion tweening, 138–142
moving into folder, 88
naming, 85
normal view, 84
object outline, 86
organizing
    in folders, 87–88
    and separating different pieces of movie, 76
outline color, 86
outline view, 84
pencil icon, 80
properties, 85–86
recovering deleted, 81
renaming, 78–79
selecting, 80
shape tweens, 171
sound, 225
symbols, 110
Timeline row, 132
viewing outlines, 84–85
Learn HTML in a Weekend, 4th Edition, 269
Left Channel effect, 227
length property, 298
Less than (<) operator, 291
Less than or equal to (<=) operator, 291
Library
    changing and manipulating symbols, 59
    common, 117, 119
    conflicts, 119
    copying symbols between, 117
    importing sound files, 217–219
    organizing symbols, 116–119
    Properties command, 230
    shared, 118–119
Library panel, 92, 110
    Ctrl+L keyboard shortcut, 110
    imported sound file, 219
    New Folder button, 116
    New Symbol button, 96, 97

newly-imported symbol, 107
    Play button, 219
    resizing, 117
    symbol icon, 114
    Symbol Properties button, 118
License Agreement dialog box, 307
Line tool, 26–27, 161, 168
linear gradients, 40–41
lines, 26–27
    changing color, 43
    erasing, 46
links, 271–272
ListBox component, 330
local variables, 287
locking
    layers, 63, 83–84, 86, 196
    masked layer, 201
    masking layer, 201
looping
    movie clip symbols, 111
    movies, 134
    sounds, 222
loops
    Do[...]while loops, 296
    For[...]in loops, 295
    infinite, 297
    For loops, 294–295
    While loops, 295–296

M

Macintosh
    AIFF (Audio Interchange File Format) files, 217
    system requirements, 306–307
Macromedia Exchange for Flash page, 333
Macromedia Flash MX 2004. See Flash 2004
Macromedia Flash Support Center, 332
Macromedia Product Activation dialog box, 311–312
Macromedia sample files Web site, 333
Macromedia Web site, 17, 305
Mask command, 196, 200, 204, 211
mask layers and motion guides, 207
masked layer, locking, 201
masking layer, 196, 201
masks
    adding, 194–212
    animated over animated content, 207–212
    defining, 194
    drawing, 198, 203
    movie clip symbols, 212
    moving over static content, 197–200
    multiple tweened segments, 203
    scrolling marquee effect, 201–205
    second layer under, 205–207

static over moving content, 201–205
static over static content, 195–196
measurement units, 67
menu bar, 14
menus, 14
methods, 286
Modify, Break Apart command, 182, 184
Modify, Document command, 66
Modify, Layer command, 85
Modify, Shape, Add Shape Hint command, 186
morphing. *See* shape tweening
motion guide layer, 64
motion guides
    animating objects along, 159–164
    attaching tweened object to, 145
    direction up from, 145
    mask layers, 207
    registration point, 109
    snapping anchor point to, 161–162
motion tweening, 138, 329
    animating objects along motion guides, 159–164
    applying
        effects, 143–153
        transform settings, 149–153
    layers, 138–142
    objects entering and leaving Stage, 141–142
    rate of change, 144
    resizing object in, 145–147
    rotating objects, 147–148
motion tweens, 164–168
    changing colors, 154
    first keyframe, 172
.MOV format, 240–241
movie clip symbols, 93, 95
    adding behaviors, 96
    creation of, 101–102
    looping, 111
    masks, 212
    naming, 101
    previewing, 111–112
    symbol-editing mode, 101
    synchronizing frame rate, 145
    won't play, 135
movie clips, 95–96, 98, 329
movie elements, 71
Movie Explorer panel, 68–71
Movie Explorer Settings dialog box, 70–71
movies
    ActionScript debugging, 247
    ActionScript version, 245
    adding
        content and keyframes, 129–131
        folder for grouping layers, 64
        layers, 77–78

masks, 194–212
sounds, 220–224
text, 36–38
animation creation, 128
audio streams, 248
background color, 54, 65, 67
blank document, 54–55
changing
    frame rate, 205
    properties, 65–67
choosing scenes, 59
closing, 56–57
components or objects, 71
compressing bitmap images, 248
compression, 247
controlling flow, 15
creation of, 54–56
cumulative number of bytes, 267
default size, 54, 67
deleting layers, 64, 81
disabling trace debugging, 247
downloading, 245
editing, 61
elements of, 68–71
fitting
    into available space, 58
    entire contents of Stage into, 67
Flash Player version, 66, 245–246
fonts, 268
fps (frames per second), 61
frame numbers, 267
frame rate, 54, 67
frames, 60, 125
height or width, 66
hiding layers, 82–83
inserting layer, 64
labels, 126
locking layers, 83–84
looping, 134
maximum size for printed page, 67
measurement units, 67
motion guide layer, 64
number of bytes in frame, 267
optimizing for Flash Player 6, 248
organizing, 71–73
organizing and separating pieces, 76
overriding sound settings, 249
passwords, 248
previewing, 111, 134–135, 143
    movie clip symbols, 111–112
properties, 15
protecting from import, 246
publishing, 240–266

removing all shape hints, 189
resizing, 65
saving, 56–57
scenes, 71, 267–268
scripting, 15
searching for items, 70
size of, 266–268
size report, 246
sound, 216–217
sound events, 249
symbols, 268
time to selected frame, 61
unlocking layers, 84
vital information about, 59–64
MP3 compression, 232
MP3 (Motion Picture Experts Group, level 3) files, 216
multiple languages, 5
multiple objects, selecting, 20, 24–25
multiple platforms, 6
MyVar variable, 293

N

NASA Web site, 5
navigation requirements, 9
New Document dialog box, 54–56
New from Template dialog box, 56
New Symbol (Ctrl+F8) (⌘+F8) keyboard shortcut, 96
non-interactive movie, 241
Normal layer, 86
normal view, 84
Not equal to (!=) operator, 291
Number function, 287
numbers, 286
NumToSquare variable, 299, 302

O

object-oriented programming languages, 277
objects, 286
    adding to layers, 80
    adjusting layering, 89–90
    animating along motion guide, 159–164
    changing scaling and proportions, 38–39
    converting
        to component parts, 173–174
        on Stage to symbol, 108–109
    defining, 286, 290
    deleting, 49
    displaying properties, 20
    editing, 38–47
    ending point for animation, 140
    entering and leaving Stage, 141–142
    erasing entire, 47

methods, 286
moving, 39, 49
path to, 71
properties, 15, 20, 281, 286
repositioning, 22–24
reshaping, 22–24
resizing, 39
    between keyframes, 143
    in motion tweening, 145–147
rotating, 39
    with motion tweening, 147–148
selecting, 20–22
shape tweens, 170–173
skewing, 39
templates, 71
viewing outlines of, 64
on handler, 301
onion skin markers, 62
Onion Skin mode, 62–63
Onion Skin Outlines, 209
onion skinning, 61, 209
opening tags, 269
operations, shortcuts for common, 16–17
ordered dithering, 255
outline view, 64, 84
outlines, 29
    changing color, 43
    erasing entire, 47
    objects, 64
Oval tool, 29–30, 195
ovals, drawing, 29–30
overlapping sounds, 220

P

<P> tag, 271
Page Setup dialog box, 67
Paint Bucket tool, 44–45, 45
painting, 42
panels, 16–19, 316, 328–329
paragraph blocks, 271
paragraphs, formatting, 38
parameters, 280
passwords, 248
paths, animating objects along, 159–164
.PDF format, 105
pen strokes, changing color, 43
Pen tool, 27–29, 161, 168, 195, 317
Pencil tool, 33–34, 160–161, 168, 195
pi constant, 285
pictures, 124
    See also graphics
    static, 197

PNG files, 257–260
.PNG format, 240–241
polygons, drawing, 31–33
PolyStar tool, 31–33
PostScript
    disabling, 315
    formats, 105
preferences
    ActionScript, 319
    Clipboard, 317–318
    editing, 317
    general, 315–317
    setting, 314–320
    warnings, 318
Preferences dialog box, 314
    ActionScript 2.0 Settings button, 319
    ActionScript tab, 319
    Bitmaps area, 318
    Clipboard Preferences tab, 317–318
    Color depth text box, 318
    Disable panel docking checkbox, 316
    Disable PostScript checkbox, 315
    Disable timeline docking checkbox, 316
    Drawing settings area, 317
    Editing options area, 319
    Editing preferences tab, 317
    Font mapping default drop-down list, 316
    FreeHand text area, 318
    General preferences tab, 315–317
    Gradients area, 318
    Highlight color area, 316
    On Launch area, 316
    Maintain text as blocks checkbox, 318
    Names anchor on Scene checkbox, 316
    Open/Import script, 319
    Panel options area, 316
    Pen tool options, 317
    Printing options area, 315
    Quality settings for drop-down list, 318
    Reset to Defaults button, 319
    Resolution text box, 318
    Save/Export script, 319
    Selection options area, 315
    Shift select option, 315
    Show pen preview checkbox, 317
    Show Precise cursors checkbox, 317
    Show solid points checkbox, 317
    Show tooltips option, 315
    Size limit text box, 318
    Span based selection checkbox, 316
    Syntax coloring option, 319
    Text area, 319
    Timeline options area, 316

Undo levels text box, 315
    Use layer color checkbox, 316
    Use this color checkbox, 316
    Vertical text options, 317
    Warnings tab, 318
Preferences (Ctrl+U (⌘+U)) keyboard shortcut, 314
Premier Press Web site, 271
Preview Movie (F12) keyboard shortcut, 163
previewing
    exported file, 265–266
    movie clip symbols, 111–112
    movies, 111, 134–135, 143
    sound, 229
    tints, 157
printing options, 315
programming
    building blocks, 285–296
    concepts, 279
programming languages
    functions, 276
    rules, 280
    syntax, 279
properties, 15, 286
    commas between, 290
    documents, 20
    frames, 126–127
    layers, 85–86
    movies, 65–67
    objects, 20, 281
Properties command, 85, 230
Property Inspector, 15, 65, 328–329
    Advanced color property, 158
    Alias text button, 37
    Alpha Amount text box, 158
    Alter Character position, 37
    Auto choice option, 148
    Auto Kern checkbox, 37
    Auto option, 144
    Background color box, 65
    CCW option, 144, 148
    changing frame rate, 205
    Character Spacing box, 37
    Color drop-down list, 155, 156
    Color Mixer, 44
    Color settings, 154–159
    Color transform settings, 166
    Custom button, 26
    CW option, 144, 148
    document properties, 20
    Ease drop-down list, 144, 149, 173
    Edit button, 227
    Edit Envelope dialog box, 227–229
    editing symbol instances, 112–113

Effect drop-down list, 222, 227
Event option, 222, 226
expand/collapse the information area, 127
file name for movie document, 65
Fill color, 34, 44
Flash Player version, 66
Font drop-down list, 37
Font Size box or drop-down list, 37
Format button, 38
Frame Label text box, 126
frame rate, 66
Input Text command, 299
Instance Name text box, 301
Label Type, 127
Loop option, 222
Motion option, 140
None option, 144
Number of times to loop text box, 222
Options button, 32
Orient to Path checkbox, 145, 162–163
properties assigned to object, 20
Repeat option, 222
RGB option, 157
Rotate drop-down menu, 144, 148
Rotation Count text box, 144, 148
Scale checkbox, 143, 146
settings
    available for tools, 19
    for formatting text, 37–38
Settings button, 158
Shape option, 172, 175, 178, 183, 208
Show border around text option, 299
Size button, 66
Smoothing settings, 34
Snap option, 145, 161
Sound drop-down list, 221, 225
sound effects, 227
Sound Loop drop-down list, 222
Stage or movie size, 65
Start option, 224
Stop option, 224
Stream option, 224
Stroke color button, 26, 43
Stroke height box or slider, 26
Stroke style pop-up menu, 26
Sync drop-down list, 145, 222, 224, 226
Text (fill) color box, 37
Text Type drop-down list, 299
Text Type text box to Dynamic Text option, 300
Tint Amount box, 157
Tint color property, 156
Tint Selector box, 157
Tween drop-down list, 127, 140, 172, 175, 178, 183, 208

URL Link box, 38
Var text box, 299, 300
W and H values, 39
warning icon, 176
proportions, changing, 38–39
Publish Settings
    (Ctrl+Shift+F12 (⌘+Shift+F12)) keyboard shortcut, 242
Publish Settings dialog box, 231, 242, 264
    8-bit bit depth, 258
    24-bit bit depth, 258
    24-bit with Alpha, 258
    ActionScript Version option, 245
    Adaptive palette, 256, 259
    Alpha drop-down menu, 261
    Alpha option, 255
    Alpha Transparent option, 261
    Animated option, 254
    Audio event option, 231, 249
    Audio stream option, 231, 248
    Auto option, 261
    Bit Depth drop-down list, 258
    Cancel button, 242
    Compress movie checkbox, 247
    Controller drop-down list, 262
    Copy option, 261
    custom palettes, 256, 259
    Debugging Permitted checkbox, 247
    Default option, 252
    Default (Show All) option, 252
    Device font option, 251
    Diffusion option, 255, 259
    Dimensions drop-down list, 250
    Dimensions options, 253, 257, 261
    Display menu option, 251
    Dither area, 259
    Dither drop-down list, 255, 258
    Dither solids option, 255, 258
    Exact Fit option, 252
    File option, 263
    Filter Options drop-down list, 260
    Flash alignment drop-down menu, 252
    Flash for Pocket PC 2003 option, 249
    Flash Only option, 249
    Flash Only template, 246
    Flash tab, 231, 244–249, 263, 266
    Flatten option, 263
    Formats tab, 242–244
    Generate size report checkbox, 246, 266
    GIF tab, 253–256
    Height and Width options, 257
    High setting, 233
    HTML Alignment drop-down menu, 252
    HTML checkbox, 249

HTML tab, 233, 246, 249–253
Info button, 250
Interlace option, 254, 258
JPEG quality slider, 248
JPEG tab, 256–257
Layer drop-down list, 262
Load Order option, 245
Loop Continuously option, 254
Loop option, 251, 262
Match Movie checkbox, 250, 257
Max Colors drop-down list, 256, 260
No Border option, 252
No Scale option, 252
None option, 259
Omit trace actions checkbox, 247
Opaque option, 255
Opaque Windowless option, 251
Optimize colors option, 254, 258
Optimize for Flash Player 6 r 65 checkbox, 248
Options area, 254–255, 258
Ordered dithering option, 259
Override sound settings checkbox, 232, 249
Palette icon, 260
Palette Type drop-down list, 256, 258, 259
Password text box, 248
Paused at start option, 251, 263
Percent option, 250
Pixels option, 250
Play Every Frame option, 263
Playback area, 250–251, 253–254, 262–263
PNG tab, 257–260
Progressive checkbox, 257
Protect from import checkbox, 246
Publish button, 242
Quality drop-down list, 233, 251
Quality slider, 257
QuickTime option, 249
QuickTime tab, 261–263
Remove gradients option, 255, 258
Repeat option, 254
Scale drop-down menu, 252
Select Publish Destination icon, 244
Set button, 231, 248, 249
Show warning messages option, 253
Smooth option, 255, 258
Static option, 254
Template drop-down list, 246, 249
Transparent drop-down list, 255
Transparent option, 255
Transparent Windowless option, 252
Type column, 242
Use Default Names option, 244
Use QuickTime compression checkbox, 262
Version option, 245

Web 216 palette, 259
Web Snap Adaptive palette, 256, 259
Width and Height options, 250
Window Mode option, 251
Window option, 251
publishing .fla file, 56
publishing movies
    Flash movies, 244–249
    formats, 240–241, 243–244
    GIF files, 253–256
    Helper files, 241
    HTML files, 249–253
    interactive movie, 241
    JPEG files, 256–257
    naming files, 244
    non-interactive movie, 241
    options, 241–263
    PNG files, 257–260
    QuickTime, 261–263
    static picture, 241
PushButton component, 330

Q
QuickTime files, 217, 261–263
QuickTime player, 234
QuickTime player or browser plug-in, 261

R
radial gradients, 40–41
RadioButton component, 330
Raw compression, 232
Readme file, 311
recently used files, opening, 16
Rectangle Settings dialog box, 31
Rectangle tool, 30–31, 161, 168, 195
rectangles, 30–31
redoing actions, 49
registration point, 109
regular view, 64
Remove All Hints command, 189
Remove Hint command, 189
repositioning objects, 22–24
requirements, 8–9
reshaping objects, 22–24
resizing
    motion tweening, 145–147
    object between keyframes, 143
    objects, 39
    tweened object, 145–147
resources, 332–333
ResultDisplay variable, 300, 302
review stage, 10–11
Right Channel effect, 227

rotating
    object with motion tween, 147–148
    objects, 39
    tweened objects, 144, 150
runtime sharing, 118

S

sampling sound, 216
Save As dialog box, 56–57
Save (Ctrl+S (⌘+S)) keyboard shortcut, 57
saving
    button symbols, 104
    graphic symbols, 100
    movies, 56–57
scale, changing, 38–39
Scene panel, 72–73
scenes, 71–73, 268
    choosing, 59
    information about, 68
scope, 287
scripting, 6, 15
scripts
    adding items, 284
    associating with elements, 280
    automatically indenting code, 319
    Classpaths, 319
    color-coded formatting, 284
    finding coding errors, 284
    finding strings, 284
    font and size, 319
    frame number, 282
    layer name, 282
    listing, 284
    pinning active script, 282
    pop-up code hint, 284
    replacing strings, 284
    syntax color, 319
    target paths, 284
ScrollBar component, 330
scrolling
    marquee effect, 201–205
    Stage contents, 47
ScrollPane component, 330
section headers, 271
Select All (Ctrl+A (⌘+A)) keyboard shortcut, 21
Select Publish Destination dialog box, 244
selecting
    all objects on Stage, 21
    frames, 60
    irregular areas, 24–25
    layers, 80
    objects, 20–22
    options, 315

    parts of multiple objects, 24–25
    symbol instances, 155
Selection tool, 20–22, 40, 42, 108, 153, 155, 161, 166, 168, 179, 182, 184
selection tools, 20–25
set variable statement, 289
Setup Status dialog box, 310
shape hints, 185–189, 330
shape tweening, 170, 329
    beginning keyframe, 171–172
    complex shapes, 173–177
    creation of, 170–173
    layers, 171
    shape hints, 185–189
    shapes to characters, 177–180
    text, 177–185
    Timeline Effects, 189–191
    tweening words or phrases, 180–184
shapes, 29, 177–180
shared libraries, 118–119
shared symbols, identifying, 118
size report, 266–268
skewing
    objects, 39
    tweened objects, 151
sound effects, 220, 227
sound events, 220–223, 249
sound files, 216–217
    compressing, 231
    cutting silence from, 233
    importing, 216–220
    large, 230
    playing, 219
Sound Properties dialog box, 230–231, 233
Sound Recorder, 216
Sound Settings dialog box, 231–233
sounds, 216
    adding
        to button state, 225–226
        to movie, 220–224
    anchors, 229
    changing
        frame play rate, 234
        volume, 229
    channels, 228
    choppy playback, 233–234
    compression, 229–233
    customizing, 226–229
    Down state, 225
    effects, 222
    frames, 127
    layers, 225
    looping, 222

modifying, 226–229
overlapping, 220
previewing, 229
sampling, 216
sound events, 220–222
starting point for playback, 220
streaming, 223–224
time in seconds, or frames, 228
troubleshooting, 233–234
volume level, 228
Speech compression, 232
spell checking, 50–52
Square function, 276, 298
squares, 30–31
SRC attribute, 272
Stage, 15, 328
  adding symbols to, 109–110
  built-in tools, 58
  changing view, 47
  controlling object overlapping, 89–90
  converting object to symbol, 108–109
  displaying and hiding layer contents, 85
  drawing objects on, 25–35
  editing objects, 38–47
  fitting contents into movie, 67
  hiding content, 194
  managing, 58–59
  objects entering and leaving, 141–142
  preset zoom percentages, 58
  previewing movie, 134–135
  reducing clutter, 82
  resizing, 65
  returning to, 59
  scrolling contents, 47
  selecting
    all objects, 21
    irregular areas or parts of multiple objects, 24–25
  Show All option, 58
  Show Frame option, 58
  showing all objects on, 58
  symbol instance, 114
  text box, 201
  tools for graphic content creation, 15
  Zoom tool, 58
  zooming, 47, 58–59
Star 1 movie clip symbol, 96
Start Copying Files dialog box, 310
Start Page, 16–17
startup options, 316
statements, 280
states, 94
#Static label, 241
static masks
  adding interest with shapes, 204

over moving content, 201–205
  over static content, 195
static pictures, 197, 241
static symbols, 94
static text, 36–38, 300
stopAllSounds command, 224
straight lines, 29
straight-line segments, 26–27
streaming sound, 223–224, 230, 248
Strict Equality (===) operator, 291
String function, 287
strings, 286
Stroke style dialog box, 26
strokes, 26, 48
Student object, 290
Submit button, 94
Subselection tool, 20, 22–24
substitute fonts, 322
.swf format, 56, 240–241
switch statement, 293
switches, 292–293
switching
  between documents, 14
  between scenes, 72
  stroke and fill colors, 48
Symbol definitions, 71
Symbol Editor, 59
symbol instances, 164
  editing, 112–114
  resizing and reshaping, 110
  selecting, 155
  tweening with color settings, 154–159
Symbol Properties dialog box, 118
symbol-editing mode, 97
  button symbols, 102–103
  graphic symbols, 100
  movie clip symbols, 101
  symbols, 115
symbols, 92, 268, 329
  ActionScript, 98
  adding to Stage, 109–110
  anchors, 109
  buttons, 93–95
  changing and manipulating, 59
  common libraries, 117
  converting
    existing graphics to, 105
    on Stage objects to, 108–109
  copying between libraries, 117
  creation of, 96–97
  editing, 112, 114–116
  font, 93
  frames, 110
  graphic, 93–94

identifying shared, 118
importing graphics as, 105–107
including behavior, 92
increasing playback speed, 92
instances of, 92, 109
layers, 110
movie clip, 93, 95–96
naming, 97–98, 108
organizing, 116
reducing movie file size, 92
registration point, 109
reusing, 92
runtime sharing, 118
static, 92, 94
symbol-editing mode, 115
tweening, 176–177
synchronizing frame rate, 145
syntax, 279

T

tags, 269
templates
   document creation from, 55–56
   HTML files, 249
   objects, 71
Test strict inequality (!==) operator, 291
testing Web sites, 10
text, 15
   adding, 36–38
   aliasing, 37
   as blocks, 318
   color, 37
   converting to graphics, 182
   dynamic, 36–38
   finding and replacing, 52
   fonts, 37
   hyperlinks, 38
   input, 36–38
   kerning, 37
   morphing shapes into individual letters, 177–180
   paragraphs, 38
   shape tweens, 177–185
   sizing, 37
   spell checking, 50–52
   static, 36–38
   style, 37
   tweening words or phrases, 180–184
   vertical options, 317
Text, Check Spelling command, 51
text boxes, 201, 300
Text Expand layer, 76
text files, naming, 98
Text menu, 50

Text tool, 36–38, 129, 179, 181, 184
TextField.StyleSheet class, 271
Timeline, 15, 59, 328
   Add Layer button, 205
   Add Motion Guide button, 64, 160
   Always Show Markers button, 62
   Anchor Onion option, 62
   Back to Stage button, 104
   Center Frame button, 61
   centering on frame, 61
   collapsing layers in folder, 88
   complete tween, 173
   Create Motion Tween command, 202, 210
   current frame, 61
   Delete Layer button, 64, 81
   Ease option, 167
   Edit Multiple Frames button, 62
   Edit Scene button, 72
   elapsed time, 61
   frame rate, 61
   frames composing movie, 60
   identifying frames and keyframes, 125–126
   incomplete tween, 172–173
   Insert Keyframe option, 104
   Insert Layer button, 64, 77, 195, 198, 203, 221, 225, 237
   Insert Layer Folder button, 64, 87
   inserting frames, 132
   labels for frames, 126
   Lock/Unlock All Layers button, 63, 83, 84
   managing layers, 63–64
   markers, 61
   Mask command, 200, 204, 211
   Modify Onion Markers button, 62
   Motion option, 142
   Onion 2 option, 62
   Onion 5 option, 63
   Onion All option, 63
   Onion Skin button, 61, 203
   Onion Skin Outline button, 62, 203
   options, 316
   Orient to Path checkbox, 167
   Over frame, 104
   redisplaying layers, 88
   Rotate option, 167
   Rotation Count option, 167
   selecting frames, 60
   Show All Layers as Outlines button, 64, 85
   Show/Hide All Layers button, 63, 83
   Show/Hide All Layers (eye) button, 82
   Snap checkbox, 167
   starting and ending streaming sound, 223
   Tween drop-down menu, 142
   unused frames, 60
   wave form for inserted sound, 221

Timeline Effect tween, 190
Timeline Effects, 190–191
Timeline variables, 287
Tint color property, 155
tints, 157–158
<TITLE> tag, 270
toolbars, displaying and hiding, 14
tools
    colors, 48
    for creating graphic content on Stage, 15
    drawing, 25–35
    editing, 38–47
    Enlarge button, 47
    Reduce button, 47
    selection, 20–25
    settings available for, 19
Tools panel, 15
    adding or changing tools, 320–321
    Black and White button, 48
    brush modes, 35
    Brush Shape option, 35
    Brush Size option, 35
    Brush tool, 34
    customizing, 320–322
    drawing mode button, 33
    drawing tools, 25–35
    Eraser tool, 45–46
    Eyedropper tool, 44–45
    Faucet button, 47
    Fill Color box, 48
    Free Transform tool, 38–39
    graphic symbols, 94
    Ink Bottle tool, 43
    Ink mode, 33
    Lasso tool, 20, 24–25
    Line tool, 26–27
    Magic Wand button, 24
    Magic Wand Properties button, 24
    No Color button, 48
    Oval tool, 29–30
    Paint Behind brush mode, 35
    Paint Bucket tool, 44
    Paint Fill brush mode, 35
    Paint Inside brush mode, 35
    Paint Normal brush mode, 35
    Paint Selection brush mode, 35
    Pen tool, 27–29
    Pencil tool, 33–34
    Polygon Mode button, 24
    PolyStar tool, 31–33
    Rectangle tool, 30–31
    removing tools, 321
    Rotate and Skew button, 39

Round Rectangle Radius button, 31
Scale button, 39
Scale mode, 39
Selection tool, 20–25
Smooth mode, 33
Straighten mode, 33
Stroke Color box, 48
Subselection tool, 20, 22–24
Swap Color button, 48
Text tool, 36–38, 299
Transform Fill tool, 39–40
view tools, 47
Tools Settings dialog box, 32
Trace() command, 247
Transform Fill tool, 39–40
Transform (Ctrl+T (⌘+T)) keyboard shortcut, 149, 152
Transform panel
    applying transform settings, 149–153
    close button, 153
    Constrain checkbox, 150
    Copy button, 152
    Height text box, 149
    Rotate button, 150
    Rotation Angle text box, 150
    Skew Horizontally text box, 151
    Skew option, 151
    Skew Vertically text box, 151
    Width text box, 149
transparency and tweened objects, 158
troubleshooting
    animation, 135–136
    sound, 233–234
tweened objects, 138
    attaching to motion guide, 145
    constraining, 150
    entering or leaving Stage, 161
    height, 149
    number of rotations, 144
    resizing, 145–147, 166
    rotating, 144, 150
    rotating with motion tweening, 147–148
    skewing, 151
    transparency, 158
    width, 149
tweening, 138
    converting text to graphics, 182
    subtle or gradual, 181
    symbol instances with color settings, 154–159
    symbols, 176–177
    words or phrases, 180–184
.txt text file, 266

U

Undo (Ctrl-Z (⌘-Z)) keyboard shortcut, 49
undoing
    actions, 49
    levels of, 315
unlocking layers, 63, 84
unused frames, 60
unwanted animation, 136
Update Preview, 191
upgrading Flash Player, 245
URL (Uniform Resource Locator), 38
user interactivity, 241

V

var statement, 288
variables, 285–290
    arrays, 297–298
    declaring, 288
    desired value for, 289
    global, 287
    local, 287
    methods, 286
    naming, 288
    numbers, 286
    objects, 286
    properties, 286
    scope, 287
    strings, 286
    Timeline, 287
    types, 286–287
    usage, 287–290
vertical text options, 317
video, 5
Video Import wizard, 235–236
view tools, 47
Virtual-fx.net Web site, 333

W

warnings, 318
WAV (wave) files, 217
Web browsers
    Apple QuickTime player or plug-in, 241
    Flash plug-in, 241
    title bar, 270
Web sites
    decision-makers' expectations in general look and feel, 8
    development process, 6–11
    formal and informal, 8
    purpose of, 8
    testing, 10
Web Snap Adaptive palette, 256
welcome dialog box, 307

While loops, 295–296
WIDTH attribute, 272
Window, Design Panels, Color Mixer command, 41, 42
Window, Design Panels, Scene command, 72
Window, Design Panels, Transform command, 149, 152
Window, Development Panels, Actions command, 282
Window, Development Panels, Behaviors command, 277
Window, Library command, 92, 110, 219
Window, Other Panels. Common Libraries, Buttons command, 300
Window, Other Panels, Common Libraries command, 117, 119
Window, Other Panels, History command, 50
Window, Other Panels, Movie Explorer command, 68
Window, Panel Sets, Default Layout command, 19
Window, Toolbars command, 14
Window menu, choosing panels, 19
Windows
    installing Flash MX 2004, 307–312
    QuickTime player, 234
    Sound Recorder, 216
    system requirements, 306
    WAV (wave) files, 217
workspace, 14–17, 19, 328

Z

zig-zag line or shape, 29
Zoom tool, 47, 58–59
zooming
    custom percentages, 59
    in and out, 47
    preset percentages, 58
    Stage, 47, 58–59